THE
PLEASURE
GAP

THE PLEASURE GAP

AMERICAN WOMEN & THE UNFINISHED SEXUAL REVOLUTION

KATHERINE ROWLAND

SEAL
PRESS
New York

Seal Press
Hachette Book Group
1290 Avenue of the Americas, New York, NY 10104
www.sealpress.com
@sealpress

Printed in the United States of America

First Edition: February 2020

Published by Seal Press, an imprint of Perseus Books, LLC, a subsidiary of Hachette Book Group, Inc. The Seal Press name and logo is a trademark of the Hachette Book Group.

The Hachette Speakers Bureau provides a wide range of authors for speaking events. To find out more, go to www.hachettespeakersbureau.com or call (866) 376-6591.

The publisher is not responsible for websites (or their content) that are not owned by the publisher.

Print book interior design by Amy Quinn

Library of Congress Cataloging-in-Publication Data
Names: Rowland, Katherine, author.
Title: The pleasure gap : American women and the unfinished sexual revolution / Katherine Rowland.
Description: First edition. | New York : Seal Press, [2020] | Includes bibliographical references and index
Identifiers: LCCN 2019032150 | ISBN 9781580058360 (hardcover) | ISBN 9781580058346 (ebook)
Subjects: LCSH: Women—Sexual behavior—United States. | Libido. | Sex—United States.
Classification: LCC HQ29 .R69 2020 | DDC 306.7082—dc23
LC record available at https://lccn.loc.gov/2019032150

ISBNs: 978-1-58005-836-0 (hardcover); 978-1-58005-950-3 (ebook)
LSC-C

10 9 8 7 6 5 4 3 2 1

To Alma

CONTENTS

The world experienced . . . comes at all
times with our body as its center.

—*William James, "The Experience of Activity," 1905*

A NOTE ON HOW I WROTE THIS BOOK

THIS BOOK REPRESENTS a years-long reporting effort involving interviews and roundtable discussions with roughly 120 women as well as with dozens of scientists, researchers, advocates, and sexual health practitioners. I connected with the women whose stories inform the heart of this project through a number of channels. For many it was via a snowball method, that is, I approached friends and acquaintances, who in turn pointed me to their friends and acquaintances, and so on. While this yielded an overwhelming response, I additionally found informants at the various workshops, classes, meetups, and conferences I attended as part of my research. I reached out to some women directly through social media, largely because of what I saw in their existing digital presence. Lastly, I was introduced to a handful of women by various sexuality professionals.

Given the highly sensitive nature of the subject—sexuality, pleasure, and desire—I have altered the women's names and identifying details. No one presented here is a composite character—everyone is her own unique person. However, I have chosen at times to edit quotations for clarity as well as to eliminate some idiosyncrasies of speech. In some instances, women selected their own pseudonyms, but in most cases I used a first or middle name, or assigned a name based on an individual's general demographic background.

Although I spoke with women of all sexual orientations, this book focuses most closely on the experiences of women who have sex with men, because that was where (in step with the existing research) I identified the locus of sexual distress, the target market for solutions, and the largest appetite for sexual recovery. While older research has suggested that queer women are not as libidinous as their heterosexual counterparts, more recent scholarship has brought such tired assumptions to pasture. Compared to straight women, queer women report having fewer sexual problems and more frequent orgasms, as well as being more easily aroused and more sexually assertive.[1] A 2018 review of the evidence states: "Despite ample accounts of 'lesbian bed death' in the literature, recent empirical, theoretical, and clinical work disputes such death as either a myth propagated by the patriarchal male-centered norms of sexuality or a dated cohort effect that is not relevant in the current sociocultural climate for younger generations of lesbians."[2]

None of which is to say that sexual health and its expression are unproblematic for queer women. Rather, it seems that, at least in terms of pleasure and satisfaction, queer women may have some advantage. Based on my conversations, I would speculate that this has something to do with the fact that by coming out they have done some fundamental work on understanding their own desires, whereas for heterosexual women that is not necessarily the case. In addition, queer women are not as mired in the logic that sex means penetrative intercourse, a concept that, as I'll discuss, is remarkably ill-suited to female pleasure. All the same, I acknowledge that one does not need to be straight or to have sex with men in order to be affected by the cultural privileging of male sexuality and function. As one queer woman told me, "Just because I don't have sex with men doesn't mean the patriarchy doesn't end up in my bedroom."

While this book engages with scientific subjects, I have steered away from weighing in on some of the biological factors that shape female sexuality, namely, the enormous influence of hormones, reproduction, menopause, pain, depression, and chronic illness. These are hugely important topics that indelibly shape arousal, desire, and pleasure, but given their complexity, they are discussed here as points of reference rather than as dedicated topics in their own right. Many excellent books have been written on these issues, and my interest here lies in how day-to-day experiences of contemporary womanhood shape how we feel in our bodies.

At times I write in the first-person plural. Such statements of *we* and *us* are meant neither to be presumptive nor to exclude readers—including male readers—but rather to reflect the fact that the writing of this book, at this particular moment in history, was a politicizing exercise. Sex is so much greater than an act of intimacy.

People have often asked me whether my own sex life benefited from writing this book. The answer is both yes and no. I absolutely learned to value my own pleasure more than I had previously and to rethink how I inhabit and express my sexuality. But it was a more somber education than I had anticipated. In the four and a half years between first researching desire and handing in this manuscript, I birthed my son, lost my father, birthed my daughter, and lost my younger brother. My revelations about sexuality were therefore bound in serial reconstitutions of my own identity. Given that pleasure is not the opposite of pain, but rather the receptiveness to feeling, I hope that these experiences enrich rather than impoverish my words.

PART 1

SEXUALITY IN THE CROSSHAIRS OF CULTURE

1 THE PLEASURE GAP

Tomorrow sex will be good again.

—*Michel Foucault,* The History of Sexuality, *vol. 1, 1978*

IN THE LOBBY of Building 31 at the Food and Drug Administration's White Oak Campus, a display case houses a small but terrifying exhibit of recalled or otherwise perilous medical inventions. As I passed by, the iconic shape of the Dalkon Shield snagged my attention. An oblong disk ringed with spikes, in appearance it has been compared to a stingray or a crab, but it has also been described as an instrument of torture, which, it turns out, is precisely what it was. Marketed in the early 1970s as a "superior" intrauterine device—the Cadillac of IUDs for a new birth-control-savvy generation, the shield resulted in the deaths of more than twenty women and rendered at least thirteen thousand women sterile or infertile. By the mid-1980s, some two hundred thousand women claimed to have been injured by its use.[1]

This totem to regulatory caution lingered in mind as I made my way into the FDA's Great Room for the day's proceedings. Although in the past the agency had weighed in on women's access to quality contraception, that particular week in the fall of 2014 it was considering another matter: women's access to quality sex. Several hundred experts, activists, pharmaceutical reps, and lobbyists had gathered to make—and contest—the case that female sexual dysfunction represented an unmet medical need.

Shortly after I entered, a woman who called herself Vicky took the stage and delivered an emotional testimony. Thirty-nine, a mother of four, she said she used to enjoy her sex life with her husband. "Our friends would even make comments about how we couldn't keep our hands off each other." But out of the blue, her desire vanished. It became *nonexistent*. She turned to specialists, but in vain, and tests revealed no ready answers. Her symptoms worsened; she found herself avoiding even "simple hugs and kisses." Matters came to a head during a child-free escape to Mexico. "In the past when we had taken vacations together we barely left the room," she said. "My mom always joked, 'don't get pregnant' when we left. But unfortunately my symptoms stayed the same. In a beautiful place with the man I love, my body was like a shell with nothing inside."[2]

As the conference continued, a steady parade of women came on stage to explain how their libidos had been whittled down to a fraction of their former size.[3] For some it was a gradual diminishment. For others it was "like a switch that went off." One woman lamented, "I don't even think about sex." Others spoke of how intimacy had become more a form of duty than a source of delight. "I am able to grit through it," said one. Another: "I might not even want to have sex but if he wants sex and I give it to him then, yes, I was a good wife today." One woman, who had spent over $35,000 on thirty specialists for treatments that included pudendal nerve injections, painkillers, and muscle relaxants, said her diminished interest affected far more than her sex life. In addition to the pain, it caused depression and low self-confidence and undermined her relationships with friends and family. One after another, the women described the anguish provoked by their dimmed desire: anxiety at the mere thought of sex, heartache over their inability to enjoy what they once heartily did, shame and embarrassment about something so essential having gone awry, disconnection from their bodies, and injury to their relationships.

The loss of female libido is a relatively recent addition to the annals of human suffering, one made possible by modern revelations about human health and sexuality. Authorities in the nineteenth century belabored women's *frigid* temperament, at times insisting that their coldness reflected a natural antipathy toward sex; however, by the mid-twentieth century, frigidity had been recast as a form of pathology. Healthy women were expected to be receptive to intercourse, so long as it took place within the proper social bounds of heterosexual marriage, and within these strictures they were supposed to enjoy their sexuality. But somewhere along the way, in the midst of the sexual revolution, women's liberation, and the Stonewall riots, something changed. Otherwise healthy women began to report that they were losing their appetite for sex—or at least for the kind of sex that was expected of them. Suddenly, it seemed that desire, once believed to be the steady propeller of erotic life, was becoming vulnerable. In 1980, a new diagnosis appeared in the *Diagnostic and Statistical Manual of Mental Disorders* (DSM) the so-called bible of psychiatry: inhibited sexual desire. Within a matter of years, it was the most prevalent sexual complaint of women in America.

Whether in the hands of poets or physicians, sexual desire has been defined in various ways, from the wondrously ethereal to the ploddingly mechanical. For the purposes of this book I have thought of it in terms of hybrid longings: to be sexual with oneself or another person; to experience pleasure; to experience connection; to become the object of another's hunger; to express one's own passions; to gain access to one's interior self. Today, experts estimate that roughly one-quarter to one-half of American women experience low desire and other sexual concerns, including diminished arousal, difficulty reaching orgasm, and the presence of sexual pain.[4]

However, pinpointing the number of women who struggle with these issues is tricky, because the statistics shift markedly depending on how you approach the subject. How, for instance, are we to understand what is high or low, normal or unhealthy, in realms as subjective, mysterious, and thoroughly unquantifiable as human sensuality and sexuality? What is the baseline for comparison, and to what extent should we regard the documented differences between male and female sexuality as artifacts of the given age, as opposed to a realistic capture of essential distinctions? What, moreover, are we to make of the fact that women so often have sex for reasons other than the simmer of lust? Some interpret such reasons as evidence of a lack of underlying motivation—that women have a lower drive—while to others, they chiefly reflect the social circumstances of intimacy. And when we find that experiences differ across peoples, times, and places, that passions wax and wane, and that bodies can rise in thrall or turn insensate, should we look to biology as the arbiter of Eros? Or are our most intimate sensations inextricably bound up in the web of people, pressures, and ideas that surround us? Barraged as we are by sex-saturated messages

that either neutralize or ogle at our marvelous diversity, do we hold
ourselves hostage to harmful fictions that cannot accommodate the
fluctuations that occur naturally over time? Or perhaps the only valid
measure is the most elemental yearning: our desire for desire, wherein
pleasure is our birthright and satisfaction our due.

▼▲▼▲▼

From the vantage point of just a half-century ago, the sexual world we
occupy today would scarcely be imaginable. We have benefited from
a sustained momentum toward liberalization and equality whose impact has rippled across our laws, our institutions, our relationships, and
our imaginations. But as Michel Foucault argued in the late 1970s, it is
impossible to simply liberate sexuality as though springing an animal
from its cage. Sexuality is not a stable thing, but rather a tapestry that
we continually unravel and reweave. To agitate for liberation—as we
have, and as I believe we should—begs the question of what our social
churnings have accomplished against the next horizon line visible from
today's standpoint.

    In this book I take as my starting premise that the sexual revolu-
tion is unfinished. By that I do not mean to imply that nothing was
gained through the sexual convulsions of the 1960s and the women's
and LGBTQ movements that followed. Far from it. Today, in many
ways, we enjoy an unprecedented level of sexual freedom. We are now
engaged in a remarkably vocal debate over the meaning of both sexual
difference and gender equality. It practically smacks of the caveman to
assert male domination over women or to claim that heterosexuality
is the more correct identity. Though we're struggling to make sense of
what parity really means, and what it looks like in practice, as historian
Jeffrey Weeks has put it, "the real achievement is that inequality has lost
all its moral justification."[5] In place of the presumed, and at times socially enforced, ideal of monogamous heterosexuality within marriage,
today's world is home to multiple forms of sexual identity alongside
countless opportunities for exploring eroticism in both public and private life. The idea that women should be exclusively available to their
husbands has been steadily eroded and paved over by a new culture
that, for better or worse, encourages women to flaunt their sensuality
and revel in sex as a source of casual recreation. Rape is condemned

as the crime that it is, rather than dismissed as a social lapse, and the country's leading pundits are weighing in on the true meaning of consent while also reckoning with the implications of its all-too-frequent absence. We're also in the midst of what British sociologist Anthony Giddens has called a "transformation of intimacy."[6] Our very rationales for romance, partnership, and sexual expression have changed dramatically. Instead of seeking partners for security and companionship, we have, in the words of one set of researchers, portaged our unions to the peaks of "Mount Maslow."[7] We expect our intimate partners to aid in our quest for self-realization.

To the passing glance, it would seem that we, as a culture, are more sexually liberal than ever. Compared to the early 1970s, today's Americans are more accepting of premarital sex, adolescent sex, and same-sex activities.[8] Rates of casual sex have increased, and married people are having more sex outside of marriage—or at least admitting to it more—as well as placing a greater premium on the quality of sex within marriage. Individuals report having sex earlier on in new relationships, as well as engaging in a wider range of sexual acts.[9] Survey data suggest that a quarter of women gave oral sex in their last encounter (though only 10 percent were on the receiving end), and that one-third of sexually active millennial women have anal sex "at least some of the time."[10] (For comparison, data from the 1990s showed only about one-fifth of women reporting that they had ever had anal sex, with less than one-tenth having done so in the past year.) We're also increasingly using sex as a way to communicate with one another. These days, we widely share our sexual stories—of our first times, of coming out, of surviving abuse, of learning how to orgasm—as a way to mark our place in the world and describe this time in history.[11] Technology is further broadcasting and transforming our sexual behaviors. In addition to sexting and lobbing explicit content between personal devices, individuals are creating mammoth amounts of noncommercial porn—apparently to the delight of consumers, who watch it with discernible commitment.[12] A slew of dating apps facilitate no-strings hookups, homing in on available bodies in the vicinity—there are so many out there that third-party sites now rank them for you.

And the media, of course, both responds to and reinforces these trends. Never before has the popular culture been so inundated with allusions to sex, representations of it, and promises to help achieve pleasure. Our daily lives are positively saturated with depictions of sex that are casual in their abundance and yet increasingly explicit in their content. It's no longer a mere truism that *sex sells*, in media-speak. Instead, in our multiplatform screen-time-all-the-time existence, there is a swampy blur of advertorial, personal confessional, and elevated raunch, which all the while preserves the omnipresence of the female body as the fetishized stand-in for what she is meant to sell.[13] Perfume ads allude to semen dappling bare skin. Designer campaigns pair denim with scenes of date rape. In advertising for their "BK Super Seven Incher," Burger King couldn't resist posing a pert-mouthed blond gaping at an oncoming meat-filled sandwich. Primetime TV shows, which skew increasingly explicit, muse on the benefits of masturbation, the ethics of blow jobs on first dates, and the erotic potential of the "micropenis."[14] In response, entrepreneurs have eagerly swarmed to meet our new demands. Gwyneth Paltrow's Goop website advertises 24k gold–finished vibrators alongside alpaca sweaters and fine-line-eliminating balms. Subscription services aim to teach women how to orgasm via online instruction. And a bumper crop of millennial-oriented websites garner clicks by running features on *my first time fisting* and tell-all accounts of polyamory. *Teen Vogue* published a guide to anal sex.

However, for most indications of progressive momentum, we confront caveat upon caveat. I would argue that many achievements of the revolution remain only partially realized, while some have been so thoroughly repurposed by our neoliberal climate as to be barely recognizable. Though American women today now have roughly equal access to education and health care, our status lags behind men where it concerns wealth, material security, physical safety, and health outcomes, including—critically—our sexual health. And these differences reach their most extreme levels for low-income women and women of color, for whom promises of wellness and prosperity often fall flat. Despite overperforming in higher education—women are in the majority among undergraduate students, and since 2009 have outnumbered men in earning doctorates—we still take home the lesser share of the payroll.[15] Although the division of household labor is more democratic than ever, women still assume the brunt of domestic and emotional labor—and are expected to do so. Sexual violence, in spite of its increasing public visibility, remains stubbornly endemic. Meanwhile, women are disproportionately plagued by eating disorders, poor body image, low self-esteem, and mental health conditions. Indeed, women are diagnosed with post-traumatic stress disorder (PTSD) at more than twice the rate of men—and that includes men who have seen armed combat.[16] Although women have new license to roam, they still contend with near-constant objectification—coming not only from the outside world, but also, and more disconcertingly, from themselves. Even as we celebrate women's agency and autonomy, the "male in the head" can persist in undermining our embodied sense of power, begging the question of who benefits from our more visible sexuality and attendant expectations for nonstop lust.[17] Some commentators have gone so far as to argue that the terms of sexual liberalization have subverted women's interests.[18] Whereas once the culture circumscribed female behavior by insisting on propriety, it now casts women as hypersexualized creatures of desire.

These tensions are playing out in America's unique fashion, in which the public gorges on explicitness while finger-wagging a censorious morality. Even as we have grown accustomed to seeing nude or near-nude figures stalk across screens and billboards, Americans remain reluctant to engage in frank discussion about the basics of anatomy. We may be comfortable with raunch, but we are uneasy in the face of simple reproduction. Over the past two decades, the US government has spent more than $2 billion on sex-stigmatizing abstinence promotion programs.[19] In 2011, it is estimated that nearly half the nation's 6.1 million pregnancies were unintended.[20] As recently as 2012, Michigan state representative Lisa Brown was barred from the statehouse floor for using the word "vagina" in a speech.

However, it is in women's bodies and in their relationship to pleasure that this unfinished business is most apparent. In simple terms: our libidinous cultural moment may not actually be all that pleasurable, because a giant share of women are not satisfied with their sexual lives. Between low desire, absent pleasure, genital pain, guilt, shame, quiet self-loathing, and viewing sex in terms of labor rather than lust, it would seem that we have increased sexual quantity without improving sexual *quality*. The revolutions of decades past have stopped short of the bedroom door, and women's feelings in their own skin have not kept

pace with our supposedly liberal climate. Our social and political empowerment has yet to encompass our complete humanity—that being
full access to our erotic selfhood and its unencumbered expression.

This state of affairs becomes even more troubling when you look at
how women compare to men on many of these issues. To be certain,
men shoulder their share of sexual difficulties and dissatisfactions.
While female libido tends to be underappreciated, as a culture we over-
emphasize male sexual appetite and denigrate men's needs for intimacy
and nurturance.[21] Nonetheless, whether in terms of sexual dysfunction rates, sexual anxiety, or sexual pain, women appear to be having
a harder time in their intimate lives. Compared to men, they report
less satisfaction during their last sexual encounter and less satisfaction
over their lifetimes. Regardless of sexual orientation, women are having fewer orgasms *and* placing less importance on the value of their orgasms compared to those of their partners. They also don't appear to be
taking delight in the recent additions to America's standard repertoire:
despite historic highs in the number of women having anal sex, for example, a significant proportion report not actually liking it. Strikingly,
the same is also true of vaginal sex, which, in a recent survey of orgasmic frequency was a poor predictor of heterosexual women's pleasure.[22]

For the past several years, the subject of the orgasm gap has received
much attention. The commentating world is troubled by the fact that
men more reliably reach orgasm during sex. The *gap* here is freighted.
It implies, as it is intended, to show an injustice that is social in origin rather than a naturally occurring difference. As a result, there are
abundant calls for pleasure parity and orgasm equity. There is a nice
ring to that, and in its dutiful way, the popular media has trotted out
a number of ready fixes. For women it's all about finding that missing climax—stress less, focus more, Kegel like crazy, exercise, medi-
tate, embrace your inner goddess, excise your old repressive baggage,
become a wild adventurer, be at once selfish and altruistic. For men, it's
about tricks to get her there: like a boss doling out a raise, it's the guy's
job to furnish pleasure, frequently in parsimonious fashion—e.g., *Bring
your lady to boil quicker than a pan of pasta.*[23]

The way we've framed the problem—she gets less of *that*—is, I
think, but a piece of the larger problem of treating female sexuality, including orgasm, as fundamentally elusive and difficult. It's an approach

that shrouds female sexuality in mystery and yet does not take into account the constellation of pressures and actual inequities that contour the way we experience our bodies and the world. Female pleasure likely will remain elusive and difficult so long as we—as a culture and as erotic individuals—approach sex as a linear experience that forecloses on the wider universe of eroticism.

CANARIES IN THE COAL MINE

Even as the evidence piles up that women are sexually dissatisfied, the experts are splintered over why. The subtext at the FDA meeting was the agency's upcoming regulatory review of flibanserin, a failed antidepressant that an upstart drug developer, Sprout Pharmaceuticals, was trying to advance as a treatment for women with hypoactive sexual desire disorder, or chronic low sexual interest. Sprout and the researchers who trialed the product framed desire as a matter of neurochemical balance. If women's libidos had tanked, the brain was to blame. Flibanserin is thought to work by decreasing serotonin and increasing dopamine, altering the neurotransmitters believed to inhibit and ignite desire, respectively. But this idea—like the drug—is highly controversial, as we'll see later on.

A host of social scientists, by contrast, maintain that desire is a subjective experience, resistant to measurement and contingent on social, emotional, and contextual factors. To the degree that a woman feels her libido is lacking, it could be due to stress, anxiety, a history of trauma, poor body image, relationship problems, or just plain monogamy. Low libido might cause women distress, this group maintains, but it isn't necessarily a disorder and may be a cultural creation, evidence of a media-fueled expectation that women constantly yearn to hop into bed, as well as the pharmaceutical industry's rush to pathologize—and profit from—a condition that's variable and natural. Leonore Tiefer, a psychologist affiliated with New York University and an outspoken critic of the medicalization of women's sexuality, said at the FDA meeting: "There is no 'normal' that you lost."

Much is at stake over how we choose to interpret the evidence. Whether we frame women as disordered patients warranting a pharmaceutical fix, as choice rich consumers shopping for their own brand of bliss, or as capable individuals endowed with the social and political capital to learn the rhythms of their own bodies, any approach we take will have far-reaching implications.

No small number of experts, either today or through the ages, have looked at female sexuality and concluded that women are not as libidinous, or desirous, or pleasure-seeking, as men—that they are *innately* less sexual and therefore less interested in sex. I take umbrage with this view in the chapters that follow. Guided by my conversations with women, I believe that persistent sexual dissatisfaction is a sign that many women do not feel free to enjoy their sexuality, or know how to do so, and that they therefore engage in sexual activities that are not necessarily inclusive of their pleasure. Our society might speak to and defend the equality of the sexes, yet still this one arena has been parceled out as a domain of accepted imbalance. In reporting for this book I have alternated between astonishment and heartache in hearing women—many of whom are successful, if not downright powerful in other aspects of their lives—describe how they assume a second-class position in their sexual interactions. While in their day-to-day identities women may wield authority, garner respect, and exhibit self-possession, in their sexual lives they become demure, self-deprecating, numb to sensation, and dismissive of their own pleasure, even as they carefully tend to that of their partners.

There are clearly instances when low desire and its sister maladies—among them tepid arousal and general sexual aversion—are in themselves medical conditions. And there have been excellent books written on the subject of hormones, mood, illness, and anatomy.[24] My interest, however, is in looking beyond biology. That women struggle in near epidemic numbers to inhabit their own bodies speaks to the extent to which we continue to feel objectified, sexualized, stressed, scared, judged, undervalued, and hemmed in. In this regard, pleasure and desire may be like canaries in the coal mine, showing us that the world is neither as equal, nor as safe, nor as liberal as we claim it to be. It is in our intimacy, this most sensitive gauge of how comfortable we feel in our own skins, that we apprehend the truth of circumstance.

The pleasure gap is not just a matter of how men and women compare. It refers as well to the separations that so often exist within ourselves: between mind and body, or behavior and emotion, or between our external actions and our internal feelings. In the words of sex educator Emily Nagoski, "pleasure is the measure," and we could stand to learn, or relearn, how to listen to the wisdom of our bodies. Feeling is the crucial guide: it instructs us on where and how to find safety, it puts us in touch with physical arousal, and it illuminates our desires. Even if sex is often a partnered activity, pleasure originates from within. Tuning in to these authentic cues brings us to the third dimension of the pleasure gap: the gulf between the sex we think we should be having and the sex we actually desire. I'm not talking about the *mind-blowing* blather we see all the time in the media, but states of eroticism and connection that exist on the high end of experience. It would behoove us all, to reference the Canadian psychologist and sexologist Peggy Kleinplatz, to learn from the great lovers: the ordinary people who enjoy "wonderful, memorable sex." The sex these everyday women and men are having may not even look like sex in our common, and often narrow, understanding of it, but it reflects who they are and what they want, and as such represents the rich and wildly diverse potential of our sexual selves.[25]

▼▲▼▲▼

The same fall that I went to the FDA meeting, my husband and I paid about $200 to a company called OneTaste to learn the basics of Orgasmic Meditation, or OM (*ohm*), as its adherents call it. On a Saturday, we slid into a bright Manhattan loft to the svelte bared legs and lipsticked smiles of our weekend's hosts. Alongside a few dozen fellow participants, we sat in folding chairs and listened to OneTaste employees recount all the wonderful changes unleashed in their lives as a result of this practice. They now enjoyed deeper sleep and clearer complexions as well as greater social confidence and cognitive acuity. And, of course, more fulfilling sex. We in the audience, when surveyed as to why we wanted to learn this "miraculous technique," offered that we yearned to feel more, go deeper, overcome pain, reach climax, resolve depression, rescue relationships, and experience ecstasy. "All was possible," we were assured. "Just watch." One of the beautiful lipsticked women shimmied out of her short black dress and climbed onto a massage table at the front of the room. An equally beautiful male *colleague* helped her spread her thighs and comfortably position her butterflied knees before donning a latex glove and scooping up a dab of OneTaste's proprietary lube. We watched as he, remaining fully clothed, touched his index finger to the upper left quadrant of her clitoris and, moving in the most concentrated way, stroked up-down, up-down, up-down for the next fifteen minutes.

Nicole Daedone, the San Francisco resident who started OneTaste, gave a TEDx talk in 2011 that has since been watched more than 1.7 million times. In it, she says the clients who enter her office are chanting "the Western woman's mantra": "I work too hard, I eat too much, I diet too much, I drink too much, I shop too much, I give too much, and still there's this sense of hunger that I can't touch." Daedone says we suffer a "pleasure deficit disorder" in this country, and its only cure is orgasm—specifically, the sort of orgasm realized by OneTaste's brand of ritualized fondling. Daedone refers to this as "slow sex," a goalless approach to generating pleasure. In a 2013 speech at South by Southwest, she called female orgasm "the regenerative human technology."

OneTaste, which as of the fall of 2018 had ceased all in-person classes, tends to stir up a lot of controversy, and I am not interested here in parsing whether or how it served its high-paying clients (or if it is a cult-like multilevel marketing debt trap pitching itself as an erotic wellness company).[26] Plenty of others have peered into its inner workings and observed OM as a piece of America's sexual patchwork.[27] I see OneTaste, with its thousands of enrollees, as yet another example of how sexual pleasure is entering mainstream consciousness—and mainstream consumer markets.

It is not just media that impresses our tender sexual beings. It is, perhaps more so, modernity—specifically, the neoliberal moment in which we are continually reappraising and remaking ourselves. A hallmark of this era is the vaunting of the choice-driven individual whose great imperative is to exercise agency. Where it concerns sexuality, this can get problematic. On the one hand, it is easy to celebrate sexual self-determination: of course we should exercise our fundamental freedoms of identity and expression. But on the other, we've entered a minefield of new pressures to appear and act free and empowered, and these pressures to perform are out of sync with—and exacerbate—our internal disquiet. The outward display of boldness, sexiness, the eager libertine, may have little relation to the anxiety, self-censorship, and pleasure neglect contained within. And so, women set to work to fix themselves. Much like we have been pushed to obsess over our outward appearances, we are now similarly urged to make over our sexuality, to root around our very psyches in order to dislodge our inhibitions, overcome our histories, and wrest ourselves from personal legacies of trauma.

Given this landscape, it's important to consider the feedback loop between women's self-perceptions and the market that caters to them. The increasing visibility of gratified libidos beckons us on the one hand to delight in more. But on the other, it provides little other than a gesture of rebuke: elevated expectations for great sex and supercharged partnerships contribute to the widespread sense of sexual inadequacy, dysfunction, and dissatisfaction. It might seem like the woeful testimony onstage at the FDA exists in a universe quite apart from the explicit displays of the OneTaste workshop. But I view them as tributaries of the same river: they both attest to lacuna in our sexual progress and our aggrieved conviction that, in major and disruptive ways, we are lacking.

Between 2014, when I began this project, and 2019, when I completed it, I spoke to roughly 120 women about how they experience their sexuality. Focusing primarily on their desire and pleasure, we talked about how they learned about sex, their first intimate encounters, how they experience intimacy inside and outside of their relationships, and what they wanted from their erotic lives. Many of these discussions focused on women's experiences of pain, frustration, and loss. In the first half of the book, I delve into some of the sources of constraint that they identified, namely, the cultural messaging that can quash women's pleasure and self-knowledge, the endemic nature of trauma and its lasting resonance in mind and body, and the challenges of sustaining desire in long-term partnerships. Against this mapping of sexual problems, in the second part of the book I explore pathways of sexual discovery, recovery, and healing. Given the overgrowth of the solutions market, I was also interested in women's experiences as consumers and what it is to navigate an uncharted terrain of promise.

Each path, whether sexual medicine or sex coaching, self-help or bodywork, has its own view of the issues and how they should be addressed and so provides its own narratives about the *nature* of female sexuality and what women should reasonably strive for or reconcile themselves to. While the medical view, for example, tends to focus on restoring sexual function, the fast-growing field of sex coaching encourages radical self-discovery and reaching for the moon and stars. As a result, the avenue a woman chooses can greatly shape her process of reclamation, leading some to angle toward "good enough sex" and others to aspire to progressive states of ecstasy. The approaches I write about here reflect two main strands of research: what the women I talked to had pursued in the name of health and sexual enhancement, and what I saw as having a prominent position in the market. It might seem awkward to some readers to encounter pharmacology alongside genital touch, but this is the crowded field women venture into when they look for resources to aid them in their libido and sexual relationships.

Just as sexuality is not a single thing, as I mentioned above, to seek liberation means something different for every person. I have come to think of desire as the interplay of body, mind, soul, and setting. That makes it our most subjective, most personal form of communication. As such, I do not offer pat solutions—although I do try to indicate, as I chart some of the varied routes to bliss, where here there be dragons and here there lies hope. However, were I to endeavor an answer to how one crosses the pleasure gap and moves from a numbed-out, curtailed, or disembodied reality to discover new planes of sensuality, I would return to this fundamental subjectivity. For all that the world insists on the proper shape and magnitude of our desire, we alone speak its language. And so it makes sense that it would be viewed as mysterious or mute to its legion observers. They lack fluency in what is uniquely our own. The health of our sexuality does not depend on mastering *this* trick, or adopting *that* communicative style, or altering the structure of our relationships in a particular way. These tools can help, but they're hardly contingent. Rather, seducing our own pleasure, encouraging it to bloom, is a matter of turning down the volume of the outside noise and looking with reverence within, so we can begin to apprehend the language of our own selves.

2 WHAT'S ALL THE FUSS ABOUT?

The male orgasm is more of a-rose-is-a-rose-is-a-rose sort of thing. Now a thing of beauty, it is a joy forever, but still a rose. The female goes all the way from poppies to orchids.
—*William Masters,* Psychology Today, *July 1969*

AFTER I LEFT the FDA meeting on female sexual dysfunction, I recalled Sigmund Freud's well-worn question: "What does a woman want?" The participants onstage had spoken, at times quite movingly, about their loss of sexual longing. They pined for "the old me," or "the woman my husband married not too long ago."[1] One explained, "It is horrible to have someone you love want you, make love to you, and wish that they would stop." Their desire for desire was clear. But the participants and professionals alike at the meeting were more circumspect when it came to elaborating on what it is that women want from sex. Did they want only to rekindle intimacy with their partners, to delight in, or at least dread less, their monogamous bonds, or did they chafe from something lacking in sex itself? Desire, as we know, is a state of yearning, an appetite, a craving. But to speak of desire without reference to its object is like talking about hunger without mention of food.

So, what *do* women want? The question stirs intense debate because female sexuality shoulders an immense weight. It's where experts have long looked for clues about human nature and for proof of immutable differences between men and women, which we continue to chronicle and quantify obsessively. The chief distinction, we're told, is that women are less sexual than men. As one prominent researcher, Roy

Baumeister, put it: "Men think about sex more often than women, desire sex more often, desire more partners, like more different sex acts, masturbate more often, sacrifice more resources and take more chances for sex, initiate sex more often, refuse it less often, desire it earlier in the relationship, and rate their own sexual desires as stronger than women's."[2]

The drumbeat message is that gendered motivations for sex are fundamental, coded in our very genes. Men are hardwired to sow their seed, and pleasure is their reward for furthering the species. As a result, they crave variety and frequency. Biology's mandate for women, by contrast, is to secure resources for the long and vulnerable haul of pregnancy and childrearing. In consequence, female drive is not motivated by passion so much as by a search for security. The modern-day translation is: men want to get naked, but women, at their core, just really want to nest. Look at gay men, goes the cocktail-hour provocation. Stripped of worrying about paternity and courtship and resource allocation, they are like Ur beings, the purest distillate of male lust. They do it all the time and with an array of partners; an encounter curries no more meaning than buying a cup of coffee. And then there's lesbian bed death. Case closed. Male eagerness and female reticence, we're simply built this way.

Unlike men, who presumably have sex because they like getting off, we're further told that women don't really need physical pleasure to be satisfied. Our gratification is of a different order: we're chiefly on the make for closeness, kindness, support, and, of course, babies. We have sex not because we are filled with sexual desire, but because we see hovering beyond sex the affective and material ends that truly drive us. After all, the joke goes, women need a reason, while men just need a place.

As luck would have it, researchers from the University of Texas set out to enumerate our aims. When clinical psychologist Cindy Meston and evolutionary psychologist David Buss published their findings in 2009, they identified 237 reasons why women do it.[3] They suggested that the lustful male versus loving female split is more folklore than fact, with motives like "It feels good" ranking among women's top three in documents. And yet, they argued, women are *complex*, and their sexual interactions often have little to do with craving physicality or release. Their reasons also include bonding, boredom, migraine relief, mate poaching, ego boosting, wanting to be degraded, raising social status, economic leverage, a sense of duty, dodging a fight, and having been coerced, assaulted, or drugged.

For all the ways that our culture strips women of their physical desire, it in turn exaggerates male appetite, so much so that it is often at the cost of men's need for emotional meaning and connection. If there were a simple formula for male sexuality, it might look like this: desire + activity = orgasm. This overgeneralizes the matter, but even science scarcely stops to question the assumption. While researchers have cataloged the form, frequency, and verity of women's orgasms— clitoral, vaginal, G-spot, faked—no typology exists for male pleasure. There is simply the all-important and yet literally unremarkable orgasm. Imagine how laughable it would seem if the media reported on new studies solving the *mystery of male arousal* or the *enduring enigma of ejaculate*. But these are precisely the sorts of questions that gall those who professionally ponder female sexuality. The media chorus responds accordingly.

"Scientists Have Finally Worked Out Why Women Have Orgasms— And It's All Thanks to Monkeys," *The Independent* declared.[4] At the *New York Times*: "Scientists Ponder an Evolutionary Mystery: The Female Orgasm," and *Newsweek* asked, "Has the Mystery of the Female Orgasm Been Solved?"[5] An NBC feature led with "Unraveling the Mystery of Female Desire," while the BBC had probed "the Enduring Enigma" of the same, though it conceded that "we still have no idea how desire works or what triggers it in the first place."[6] CNN simply asserted, "Women's Desire for Sex Is Complicated."[7]

Indeed, we hear that women are *complicated* ad nauseam in popular media contrasting them with men, whose desire for sex and pleasure is seen as simpler and more straightforward. An equation for women would run something like this: (possible but not required) desire + activity = indeterminate outcome. Female pleasure is neither sufficient nor necessary.

And yet, if we listen to women's voices, we encounter odes to their own ecstasy. Literature brims with women's descriptions of orgasm as a source of joy, along with pleasure as a font of wisdom and empowerment. There is nonfiction by lusty ladies crusading for their thrill, and a crop of memoirs that recount the triumphs of erotic awakening. Newer scientific research, too, has begun to challenge the legacy of difference. Recent studies have underscored the centrality of female pleasure, demonstrating that orgasm is the single most important predictor of women's sexual satisfaction.[8] The data further show that orgasm gains in importance as a woman learns to fine-tune her response to arousal. The more pleasure a woman experiences, the more she values her own bliss. Others have argued that the dissimilarities between men and women that we've come to take as truth are not as great as we thought. There may in fact be more variability within the groups—whether among women or among men—than there is between them. More telling is that difference tends to shrink in proportion to equality—as when women exercise more social clout, or in contexts where female pleasure is the norm—and to disappear when the sex is good. Among those who have "optimal" sexual experiences, stereotypes dissolve. Men and women, regardless of age, orientation, or kinkiness, then uniformly describe great sex in terms both "male" and "female": that is, in ways that include intimacy, communication, exploration, and orgasm.[9]

Thus, this question *What is female satisfaction?*, and how we answer it, is crucial. It drives to the heart of the sex wars and the different forces we ascribe to male and female *nature*. It informs what we think of as right and just and healthy. A world in which female sexuality is cast mainly in terms of emotional security, altruism, connectedness, and reproduction looks very different from one described chiefly by embodiment, empowerment, and entitlement to pleasure.

THE CLITORIS, UNICORNS, AND OTHER MATTERS OF DEBATE

Thanks to the pill and other miracles of modern contraception, we're on easy terms with separating recreation from procreation, adding to the ease with which we debate the relevance of women's pleasure. But for the better part of known history, female fertility and female delight went hand in hand. Historian Thomas Laqueur has maintained that for the ancients, Eros was inseparable from generation: "Apart from pleasure nothing in mortal kind comes into existence."[10] The Greeks believed that male and female bodies were essentially the same but inverted. Because climax was necessary for men, it must have been necessary for women, too. The vaginal canal was the penis flipped inside the body, the ovaries were testes, the uterus the scrotum, and eggs, like sperm, were released as orgasmic ejaculate. The Greeks also likely gave us the word for clitoris. Though its precise origins have been lost to time, some etymologists propose it stems from *kleitorìs*, meaning "little hill." Others have suggested this diminutive relates to the Greek word *kleìs* for "key," as in the key to open what was shut or sheathed. Yet other sources reference the verb *kleitoriázō*, meaning "to touch" or "tickle"—or to be inclined toward pleasure—which is another way to characterize desire.

So long as arousal was central to reproduction, the clitoris—and its ministrations—were seen as having a vital role to play in maintaining the species. A popular Renaissance-era midwifery text described the clitoris as the organ that "makes women lustful and take delight in copulation." In its absence, they "would have no desire, nor delight, nor would they ever conceive."[11] Other early anatomists were leery of the clitoris, deriding it as "an instrument of venery," or sexual indulgence, and "the devil's teat."[12] Jacques Duval wrote in 1612: "In French it is called temptation, the spur to sexual pleasure, the female rod and the scorner of men: and women who will admit their lewdness call it their [great joy]."[13] Charles Estienne, credited with the first anatomy of the clitoris in 1545, referred to it as woman's "shameful member." Fortunately, his contemporary Renaldus Columbus claimed in parallel to have discovered "a beautiful thing, made with so much art, gratified with such great utility."[14] He did not use the word "clitoris," but he wrote: "S'il m'est permis de donner des noms aux choses que j'ai découvertes, je les appellerai *amor Veneris* ou *dulcedo*" (If I may give names to the things I discovered, I will call them the love or sweetness of Venus).[15]

However, and to our lasting detriment, the importance of female gratification began to topple in the eighteenth century. The sort of conception advice dispensed by the doctor tending to the Empress of Hapsburg—"I am of the opinion that the vulva of Your Most Sacred Majesty should be titillated for some time before intercourse"—was no longer deemed sound.[16] Within a century, a new doctrine of female passionlessness blanketed Western culture. Suddenly, in the words of British physician William Acton, the majority of women became "not much troubled by sexual feeling of any kind."[17] Why the fall from grace? Progress in anatomical studies had revealed that orgasm was apparently not required to release female seed. Ovulation was an automatic function: no outside assistance was needed to ferry ova for fertilization. This information, mind you, came from animal studies. One particularly sadistic German researcher, Theodor von Bischoff, allowed his bitch to mate and then killed her to prove that spontaneous ovulation was wholly independent of coitus.

Laqueur speculated in 1990 that this seismic shift in thinking was not solely attributable to emerging canine models. Rather, it reflected a cultural realignment based on firmer and more punitive social divisions. A "new biology" emerged centered on fundamental differences between the sexes and a "tortured questioning of the very existence of women's sexual pleasure."[18] As the Victorians spun a new cultural world around the ideal of virtuous wives and nurturing mothers, they shunted the female libido into the hinterlands.

But *why* the clitoris? What need have women for this pesky gadfly of Venus? The question vexes still. Despite Freud's rumblings that the clitoris was the plaything of infants and neurotics—healthy women enjoyed mature vaginal orgasms—we now know that only a small minority of women, perhaps as few as 8 to 15 percent, can climax from otherwise unassisted penetration.[19] So great was the distance between intercourse and pleasure in the eyes of sex researcher Shere Hite that in 1976 she deemed the thrusting penis to be "more like a Rube Goldberg scheme than a reliable way to orgasm."[20]

Women in the decades following Freud held themselves hostage to the notion that they were sexually inept or broken for "failing" to orgasm from "proper" (i.e., penetrative) sex. But today, after countless permutations of erasure and ignorance, we are finally starting to appreciate, or re-appreciate, that the clitoris and orgasm are practically synonymous. In fact, the pangs commonly described as vaginal orgasm may have nothing to do with the vagina, but rather owe to the anatomy of the clitoris, whose true expansiveness was virtually unknown until just twenty years ago.

When Helen O'Connell trained in urology in Australia in the late 1980s, she observed that there were all manner of protocols for sparing sexual function in men undergoing surgery for prostate cancer. Doctors took special care to avoid harm to particular nerves and blood vessels. However, they exercised no equivalent cautions for women undergoing pelvic surgeries. The available textbooks contained scant information on the blood supply or nerves of the clitoris, so preserving women's sexual function was largely a matter of guesswork. O'Connell began conducting her own anatomical research, dissecting cadavers and mapping her findings into what she came to call the "clitoral complex." When she compared her discoveries to the medical literature, she confronted a catalog of gross inadequacies. Her research, which she published in 1998, showed that the clitoris extends deep into the body. No "little hill," it is more like a mountain whose peak we've long mistaken for its entirety.[21]

Be it a mountain or a butterfly—as others have described its winged crura—its responsiveness can be fickle, and women report a tremendous range in orgasmic ability, frequency, and consistency. While some women, perhaps as much as 10 percent of the population, do not have orgasms (and therefore are considered *anorgasmic*, or *preorgasmic*, for a more optimistic spin), 15 percent appear to be multi-orgasmic. Some climax easily from penetrative sex, while for others penetration appears to be strikingly ill-suited to their pleasure. Likewise the G-spot: to some essential, to others its very existence hangs in doubt. Some women report orgasms from stimulating their ears or nipples. Some say they can "think off." Women with spinal cord injury have described extreme sensitivity on the skin near the injury site that, when stimulated the right way, produces an orgasmic feeling perceived in the genitals.[22]

But for this incredible range, women appear to be deriving less pleasure from sex than men and more frequently claim to be unsatisfied. Studies show that among heterosexual partners, more than 90 percent of men say they usually orgasm, compared to only 50 to 70 percent of women.[23] Other scorecards indicate that women who have sex with men have about one orgasm for every three of their mates', leading experts to flock to the so-called orgasm gap.[24] Like its wage-based corollary, the term is meant to summon feelings of injustice and deprivation. It suggests that orgasms are a resource that should be—but

are *not*—equitably distributed. This conversation is overdue. It flags
our right to pleasure. And yet it veers off point by implying that female
sexuality should look like male sexuality, with its linear progression
to a finite end. We hear too often that female pleasure is mysterious,
or that the clitoris is difficult to locate, harder still to operate. We hear
about the mundane ballast that so readily tanks women's moods. Like
a finely calibrated instrument, the smallest slip—a dirty dish, a ragged
nail, a thoughtless observation—and it swerves out of tune. We tend,
above all, to implicate women's bodies as too tricky, slow, or susceptible, rather than aiming to improve the kind and quality of the sex that
leaves so many underwhelmed.

It's instructive, therefore, to look at which women are having orgasms and how. Women who sleep with women, for instance, tend to
experience a lot more pleasure than women who only sleep with men,
with research suggesting that they climax more than 80 percent of the
time during partnered sex.[25] One compelling study looked at the likelihood of orgasm among roughly fifteen thousand heterosexual college
students by hookup and relationship status.[26] Among first-time hookups, the orgasm gap reflected the national average: the men had three,
on average, for every one of the women's. But the likelihood of orgasm
among the women increased over repeat encounters. Moreover, when
sexual interactions entailed more than penetration, the women's orgasms increased dramatically. Among couples who engaged in a combination of intercourse, oral sex, and self-pleasuring, women's orgasms
became nearly universal.

We know further that female orgasm tends to favor age, assertive-
ness, and patience. If sex consists of merely a hasty prelude followed by
three to thirteen minutes of penetration (the range considered "adequate" to "desirable" by sex therapists[27]), it's little wonder that women
aren't fulfilled. But orgasm also rewards practice: not only can women
learn to stimulate themselves and receive pleasure, they can also become versed in different pathways of arousal. Learning to masturbate
or to orgasm with a partner becomes more automatic with experience,
as the woman's brain registers new sensations as pleasing. As she engages with new bodies, smells, sounds, and tastes, her brain expands
its repertoire of excitement, increasing her access to pleasure over time.
Writing of this process, neuroscientist James Pfaus and colleagues

observed that a woman's erotic body map "is not etched in stone, but rather is an ongoing process of experience, discovery, and construction which depends on her brain's ability to create optimality between the habits of what she expects and an openness to new experiences."[28] In other words, pleasure is learned and can increase over time.

Orgasm also appears largely indifferent to demographics, though there is some evidence that more education is associated with greater pleasure, and poverty, as we know, drags down health across the board. Time and place also seem to make a difference. Women may have been more orgasmic in the past, when orgasm was considered a more straightforward result of intercourse (or even a necessity). Anthropologists have observed that in cultures that expect women to enjoy sex as much as men do, women have regular orgasms, whereas cultures that question the propriety of female pleasure are home to greater orgasmic difficulties.[29] If the climate doesn't cloak pleasure in mystery, it may lie within easier reach. Baumeister has argued that women are more susceptible to culture than men are. They have, in his words, greater "erotic plasticity."[30] While this term, I think, runs the risk of conveying male sexuality as the steady, stable, natural standard against a female libido defined by the passing winds, it does suggest that the zeitgeist makes landfall in the body and affects sensation on the most intimate level.

THE PURPOSE OF PLEASURE

This inherent range in pleasure muddies efforts to ascribe a particular raison d'être to the female orgasm. How can it serve a singular purpose when it is such a variable phenomenon? David Buss, an evolutionary psychologist, wrote, "Women's sexual orgasm has puzzled, frightened, delighted, disturbed, and mystified men for centuries."[31] Donald Symons, an evolutionary anthropologist who was among the first to wade into this theoretical arena, suggested it is the very uncertainty of women's pleasure that seeds fascination. "Unlike the unicorn, which is specially interesting precisely because it does not exist . . . and the male orgasm, which exists in monotonous regularity . . . the female orgasm definitely exists and yet inspires interest, debate, polemics, ideology,

technical manuals, and scientific and popular literature solely because
it is often so absent."[32] Some researchers, whom we'll meet in the chapters that follow, have devoted themselves to making sense of this array
of experiences with the female orgasm. However, many strains of science have been less concerned with enhancing women's pleasure than
with asking why it exists at all. The question is not why some women
don't orgasm, it's why others do.

Evolutionary researchers have swarmed to this problem. Even if
orgasm is not necessary for conception, surely it must boost fertility.
Maybe orgasm is an inducement to copulation for otherwise sexually
reluctant females, or a way for females to *manipulate* sperm. Maybe its
contractions are designed to gratify the thrusting male. Perhaps waves of
pleasure compelled our predawn sisters to lie still, thereby giving sperm
the easiest glide path to the womb—though the author of this theory
also furnished the idea that female breasts are essentially extra alluring buttocks loaded on the front. Or maybe orgasm is a test of fitness,
and giving pleasure is the calling card of a decent guy. Whichever mate
can provide the best ride is the one selected for paternity. Enduringly
popular is the so-called upsuck hypothesis, which paints the uterus as a
Hoover vacuum. While studies have since shown that women's orgasms
tend to be expulsive rather than retentive, this one continues to hang
on. More recently, we hear of the possible role of oxytocin, which, when
released by orgasm, then may affect the motility of the uterus and fallo-
pian tubes along with inducing warm interpersonal feelings.[33]

Philosopher Elisabeth Lloyd has been studying these theories for
decades and roundly dismisses the majority of them as bad science.[34]
These ideas matter, she told me, because the stories we spin around our
deep history inform how we think of ourselves today and the values we
assign to female sexuality. In her book *The Case of the Female Orgasm:
Bias in the Science of Evolution*, she challenges the link between female
orgasm and fertility. Orgasm, she argues, does not help genetically superior sperm best the competition; nor does it exist to maintain the
sacred pair-bond. Rather, it is a "fantastic bonus."

Lloyd sides with Donald Symons and paleontologist Stephen J.
Gould, who proposed that female orgasm is an exquisite accident of
natural selection. In a 1993 paper coyly titled "Male Nipples and Clitoral Ripples," Gould hypothesized that the clitoris, much like the useless

male teat, is a vestige of fetal development, when the same nerves and tissues are laid down for both sexes.[35] Symons believes that female genitals have been "designed" to confer pleasure to their owner, but nonetheless orgasm is unnecessary to the fitness of the species. It's simply a byproduct of the male ability to have orgasms.

Psychologist David Barash thinks the byproduct hypothesis is incorrect and runs the risk of presenting women's orgasms as mere "evolutionary hitchhikers" while "crediting male orgasm as the Real McCoy." Female orgasm is "downright Technicolor compared to its relatively feeble male counterpart," he wrote. Rather than existing as an insignificant addendum to male pleasure, he noted, female orgasm was carefully honed by evolution.[36]

The feminist evolutionary biologist Sarah Blaffer Hrdy is also unconvinced.[37] Speaking to the *New York Times* in 2005, she said orgasm in women may have been an adaptive trait in our primate forebears, but that we separated from these common ancestors about seven million years ago. "Perhaps the reason orgasm is so erratic is that it's phasing out. . . . Our descendants on the starships may well wonder what all the fuss was about."[38]

Hrdy has committed her long career to giving common caricatures of femininity a run for their money. She holds that, along with warlike Amazons and wholly selfless nurturers, the sexually passive woman who is devoted exclusively to kin is pure conjecture. Mother nature favored females who were sexually assertive, who were competitive with other females, and who swayed male behavior to their own advantage. Their interest in status rivaled their interest in childrearing. It's a primate ideal that reads in parallel to the have-it-all working mothers of the 1980s, which is when Hrdy began publishing these particular ideas.[39] She looks to other branches of the phylogenetic tree and notes that a great deal of the sex taking place has nothing to do with reproduction. In some species, females copulate during nonfertile windows; other estrous females mate more often and with more partners than would be necessary for a single pregnancy. Our primate legacy, she argues, is not found in female reserve, but in sexual appetite. Lust is our true inheritance.

Hrdy offers that the clitoris is not a vestigial penis, but a vestigial clitoris, whose sole purpose was transmitting pleasure.[40] Our female ancestors, far from settling down with a single, sturdy provider, used sex in much the same way as our monkey cousins: with abundance. "Prolonged solicitations involving multiple partners" was a valuable form of social currency, helping to establish relationships, obscure issues of paternity, ease group tensions, and garner resources.[41] And the clitoris, the nervy but oddly inefficient bundle found throughout the primate world, may have induced this serial behavior, encouraging an "active, promiscuous sexuality." The inimitable journalist Natalie Angier furthers this line of thinking: an efficient pleasure organ would not have compelled our ancestors to rove as they did, scratching the itch and keeping the peace at the same time. And this same reasoning may explain one of the most pronounced differences between male and female pleasure: while men are reliably quick to fire, the clitoris can be obdurate—and yet, with sustained attention, capable of rising again and again to ariatic heights.

Personally, I am enamored of Angier's take on the why. If the clitoris is capricious and out of sync with male response, it is for a reason: the clitoris is a woman's spur to take charge of her own sexuality. "It can vote with its behavior, working best when you treat it right, faltering when it's abused or misunderstood," she wrote. "In truth, the clitoris operates at peak performance when a woman feels athunder with life and strength, when she is bellowing on top, figuratively if not literally."[42]

MEASURING SENSATION

To speak of an orgasm gap presumes that women and men know what's at stake in order to make a tally. Okay, for men, there's pretty clear feedback. But for women? How do they know for sure *this is it*? What if the sensation they call orgasm is merely a foothill obscuring the summit?

Neuroscientist Nicole Prause spends a lot of time in service of answering this question. Her work investigates some of the major omissions in sexual health research, including the benefits of pleasure. Does it assuage stress, enhance emotional fluency, improve sleep, relieve depression? The implications are potentially huge: Could doctors one day recommend masturbation instead of melatonin, or prescribe a vibrator instead of an SSRI? Fair questions, but ones, as her own career arc attests, that are hard to ask in our conservative funding climate. Prause says that sex research tends to reinforce a mind-body split: researchers set up camp either in psychology or in physiology. She, however, aims to look at what's taking place in the brain alongside activity downstream.

It's late winter, but you'd hardly know it for the strength of the sun on the Pacific coastline, and I'm visiting Prause's sex biotech lab. This label, *lab*, is a generous one. The rented unit near Santa Monica's Third Street Promenade is without gloss or high-tech trappings. It is more of a walk-in closet blessed with a window, attached to another windowed closet. A sea-foam-green wall stands across from a nest of computer monitors, larval with wires, where Prause's attention trains on the dancing colored lines of an electroencephalogram (EEG) feed. She seems unfazed by day slipping into night. "See you Monday!" her assistant says, the clock past seven on a Friday. When Prause corrects— "Sunday!"—the assistant's face betrays a twitch. Unenthused, she leaves by the unmarked door and exits through the lobby, where Prause's name appears nowhere in the mounted directory. "I don't think anyone has figured out what we're up to here yet," she says, an important consideration when your work involves porn and genital stimulation.

Prause has every reason to be cautious. Her wide body of work frequently courts harassment; trolls love to dig into her claims. For years she kept the legal team at the University of California, Los Angeles busy—that is, until she was strong-armed into giving up her position as the director of the university's Sexual Psychophysiology and Affective Neuroscience Laboratory. Prause suspects that there are health benefits to orgasm and wanted to conduct a pilot study using orgasm as part of a depression intervention. However, the federal ethics reviewers at her university challenged the significance of using sexuality research that was so explicitly sexual. After a seven-month review, UCLA's ethics board told her to remove the orgasm component of the study, thus rendering it pointless. Undeterred, Prause left academia to set up her own sex biotech company, Liberos, in 2015. The startup's motto is "The freedom to desire." However, given Prause's rocky founder's story, it could just as well be "The freedom to study desire."

If science is political, sexual science is a minefield. Both the questions asked and the methods used are subject to a level of scrutiny rarely matched in other research fields, and often by people with no expertise in the matter. The general public doesn't bat an eyelash over funding yet another study on the leukocyte-common antigen of rats, but gets in a tizzy that hard-earned tax dollars might support something so base as understanding human mating. In years past, members of Congress have gone so far as to legally block studies of human sexuality, calling them unethical.[43] Of her own work, Prause told me, "I've gotten NIH [National Institutes of Health] reviews back on grant proposals, and they've literally said, this study is immoral." She adds that male researchers have turned down collaborative projects on the grounds that their wives don't approve of using sexual images or videos. This climate of funding constraints, moral scrutiny, and personal hazard directly affects what we know and don't know about the body's intimate functions, particularly when it comes to women.

In the 1950s, Alfred Kinsey and his team of researchers proposed that an objective indicator of orgasm in women was "the abrupt cessation of the oft times strenuous movements and extreme tension of the previous sexual activity and the peace of the resulting state." William Masters and Virginia Johnson similarly described it as "a sensation of suspension or stoppage." By the end of the twentieth century, there were no less than twenty-six definitions of women's orgasm circulating in the literature. By way of compromise, in 2003, the World Health Organization's Women's Orgasm Committee offered: "An orgasm in the human female is a variable, transient peak sensation of intense pleasure, creating an altered state of consciousness, usually accompanied by involuntary rhythmic contractions of the pelvic striated circumvaginal musculature, often with concomitant uterine and anal contractions and myotonia that resolves the sexually-induced vasocongestion (sometimes only partially), usually with an induction of well-being and contentment."[44]

Count it as progress to have a comprehensive classification in place. But what good does it offer to the woman who has never experienced an orgasm? How does she know it's actually happened? To women who regularly climax, this question might seem like a no-brainer: it's *obvious*. But for those with little or no prior experience, the standard self-report item (or standard bedroom repartee)—*Did you come: Yes/ No?*—may be of little value. Barry Komisaruk, a pioneer in conducting functional magnetic resonance imaging (fMRI) studies of the brain on pleasure, has instructed subjects to press a button at the point of climax. But again, how can you be sure?

To do away with these uncertainties, Prause deploys an array of measures. An EEG headset measures brain activity, a finger device assesses skin conductance, the genitals are fitted with a tiny temperature-reading electrode—a thermistor—and a pneumatic, 3D-printed device inserted in the butt measures the air displaced by orgasm contractions. (Masters and Johnson proved to the world that a signature of orgasm is rhythmic spasms at 0.8-second intervals.)

Participants are then taken through a set of tasks. First, they view porn to see if they can successfully self-regulate, increasing or tamping down arousal as instructed. Then there is a motivation game in which each correct response earns the participants a few seconds of vibrator stimulation. Finally, participants self-stimulate to orgasm and press a button at the point of climax, if they can attain it.

Prause has just started publishing the results, but one finding stands out. Half of the women in the study reported that they had an orgasm, but there was no evidence for it. They pressed the button but had not actually climaxed. Prause tells me that at first she was thrown by the results. "We didn't know that was going to happen. Maybe a woman or two, but it was like half of our freaking sample." They triple-checked their instruments and considered whether something might be amiss in their methodology, but eventually they were convinced of their results. "This is real: a lot of women think they are having orgasms when they're not." Despite her initial shock, Prause says she's not ultimately that surprised. Women are taught that orgasm is a pleasurable release of tension, and that's about it. Outside of porn, it's rare to encounter women in ecstasy. Even as the culture grows more comfortable with talking about our sexual acts, we are less forthcoming about our sexual sensations.

Prause and I were eating lunch at a trendy spot as she elaborated on her findings. The collective murmurings of the well-heeled crowd sounded like a roar, and I had to lean close to hear her above the din. "I don't think they're faking it," she told me. "We make clear that the most important thing is honesty, we don't need you to orgasm for your data to be useful. So my guess is that women literally do not know what an orgasm is because there is no way for them to learn it." Prause's study involved a small number of women, so one can't generalize her findings to the population. Nonetheless, the proportion of false positives—half the sample—gives serious pause, especially since it dovetails with what we know women learn, or rather don't learn, about their own bodies (read: all those dismal surveys showing that a quarter of female college students can't locate the clitoris on an anatomical rendering). I wondered, as I looked around the room of trimmed and plucked and tanned women, aloft on slender footwear like so many delicate statues, whether we have learned to mismeasure our own baselines. Are we reading the songs of our bodies to a tempo that's not our own?

▼▲▼▲▼

Maybe all this talk of biology's inscrutable aims misses the point. We can't dwell on nature and leave nurture aside. If women are less sexual, less interested in sex, and less orgasmic than men, it's likely they have learned to police their own eroticism. It may not be the case, for instance, that women are more monogamous, but rather that they pay a greater social price for promiscuity and so have fewer partners. By extension, it is not necessarily a truism that women are less desirous of sex; perhaps they have simply been taught from girlhood onward to be wary of their own physicality. When journalist Daniel Bergner set out to answer Freud's freighted question, *What do women want?*, he concluded that "women's desire—its inherent range and innate power—is an underestimated and constrained force."[45] Culture keeps a firm grip on female sexuality, and were it possible to wrest it free, women would be nakedly libidinous.

I think this is an important perspective, but that it does not go far enough. We have not only inherited a broad ambivalence toward the meaning, importance, and worth of female sexuality, but we have internalized a distorted vision of Eros that regards female pleasure as the second fiddle to the main (male) act. Taught from the start to equate sex with male orgasm, women, consciously or not, cede pleasure to their partners. Raised to the illogic of the double standard, we learn to filter our desire: sculpting raw passion into acceptable shapes, ever vigilant to how we're perceived. The anthropologist Carole Vance described this process as an ongoing dance between pleasure and danger.

Women's sexual reserve is not *natural*, she argued back in 1984; rather, it is a sign of "thoroughgoing damage." The effects of gender inequality are not only manifest in overt instances of brutality, but also appear in the internalized containment of women's impulses, "poisoning desire at its very root with self-doubt and anxiety."[46]

Vance's musings from more than three decades ago may sound dire: we drink in the message that pleasure is men's due and women's accidental aside. And yet her words remind us that this is a social problem, not a biological fact. And there, I believe, lies cause for hope. It's far harder to rewire biology than it is to alter belief. If sex is a web of meanings, we can spin new threads. Pleasure and its value can be learned, and once learned, are not readily relinquished.

3 LEARNING (NOT) TO LUST

When one is pretending the entire body revolts.
—*Anaïs Nin*, Winter of Artifice, *1939*

It's also a good idea to spend some time thinking about why
you were pretending. Maybe you were afraid of bruising his
ego, or perhaps you worried that he'd reject you if you told
him the truth. You could even have felt like you had to live
up to some false ideal of porn. Then, if he asks you point-
blank if you were faking . . . or, if you feel compelled to "fess
up about your 'performance'" . . . you will be able to focus
the discussion on your actions rather than his "action."
Making it about you and shouldering the responsibility
will help prevent him from feeling like a lousy lover.
—Cosmopolitan, *October 20, 2006*

THE KID WHO used to sit in front of Yvette in her marriage and values
class had the unfortunate habit of picking at the acne on the back of
his neck. He ran with the cool set—football, beer, baggy flannel—
and was openly scornful of the abstinence-skewed curriculum that
served as sex ed in their West Texas high school. He talked back to the
teacher and took advantage of the ample opportunities to make comments filled with lewd innuendo. Yvette attended the class in the early
2000s, and in her telling, it sounds more like parody than pedagogy.
The teacher presented misinformation and sometimes patent lies as
truth. Yvette recalls hearing about premarital sex in the same breath

as poverty, prison, addiction, and oozing sores, and was told that one in seven condoms didn't work.[1] But even as a teenager, she knew that faulty contraception was not the reason girls in her school became pregnant. "There was nothing to do," she says of her small Christian town. "There was lots of drinking, we did drugs, and people had sex."

I met Yvette through a chain of acquaintances, and our conversations took place by phone. A white woman, now thirty-one, she currently lives in New Mexico, where she practices law. She tells me that the cool kid was also in the habit of thrusting his index and middle fingers into the faces of his classmates. *Smell that?* He'd gloat, then laugh about whomever he claimed was his conquest. It wasn't lost on Yvette how absurd it was to hear about fornication and brimstone while the kid in front of her kept bragging about finger fucking. Meanwhile, an in-school nursery for the children of students operated down the hall.

She credits her parents, both of whom had college degrees, that a sexual debut came a bit later for her than for most of her peers. Her mom talked with her "about being a woman" and the importance of being safe. As a result, she said, she sensed that her attitude was a little different from that of most of the other students. "I could see through a lot of it," she says in reference to the boredom and bravado that filled daily life. But, she continues, "It was still my world. There were rules and I knew them and you had to play by them if you wanted to get along." She explains that the girls had three options: you could be a good girl and really wait for it—though this would also make you a loser; you could be a bad girl and be open about the fact that you were doing it and didn't care; or you could be a "bad good girl" or a "good bad girl" and do it according to a Byzantine code of deflection, sublimation, and compliance.

There is a narrow band, lined by judgment, of what constitutes acceptable behavior: available but not assertive, interested but not invested, open-minded but discerning, aware of significance but not disposed to taking any of it too seriously. Typically, "you wouldn't call the person after or expect them to treat you different," Yvette recalls. "It was more the opposite, they'd ignore you. They'd go out of their way to act like you were extra inconsequential, unless there was another party and people were drinking and it might happen again."

Yvette says having a boyfriend, as opposed to a string of unattached hookups, also made her an outlier. They had a close connection, but their sexual interactions were rutted with difficulties. Her boyfriend was either quick to orgasm or had trouble staying at full mast. He'd become embarrassed, then mean, and blamed her for his slips in performance. She responded by giving him a lot of oral sex. All the same, he insisted their problems lay with her. She was too tight, or had bad technique, or wasn't moving right, or vocalizing enough. When I ask her how she responded to this criticism, she tells me, "I would apologize. God help me, I would apologize. I thought, he's telling me what to do, so it must be my fault. I genuinely felt bad. That's pretty pathetic now." Yvette says it did not occur to her until recently that they never talked about her body or her pleasure. "He never asked, Did that feel good, are you happy? I'm saying, I'm sorry, I'm sorry, but I don't remember enjoying it, physically. I don't think we even ever talked about that."

Looking back over my conversations with Yvette, two issues stand out. The first, and perhaps most obvious, is the wildly speculative nature of formal sex ed in the United States. In states across the country, teachers have license to opine rather than educate, and belief routinely overtakes positions that should be occupied by fact. This approach is on par with teaching creationism over evolution or presenting climate change as a political conspiracy. But in the case of human sexuality, it distorts reality much closer to home—at the level of the body. Yvette's town strikes me as a metaphor for the greater culture: the more we deny and denigrate sexual behavior, the riskier sexual behavior becomes.

As Jesseca Boyer, a researcher at the Guttmacher Institute, has pointed out, abstinence-based education is associated with *increased* rates of unintended pregnancy and sexually transmitted infections (STIs), and at the same time, it stigmatizes healthy sexual expression. In the United States, the majority of eighteen-year-olds—some 65 percent—have had intercourse, which means that millions of sexually active teens have never received credible information on issues such as contraception, consent, and healthy relationships.[2] Critics further point out that abstinence-based curricula fuel unflinchingly hetero gender stereotypes that cast women as sexually passive while endowing men with hard-to-manage drives and minimal emotion. One expert review went so far as to say that abstinence-only programs "threaten fundamental human rights to health, information, and life."[3]

Sex ed has seen a lot of improvement in recent years, with notable programs—such as Our Whole Lives—including progressive discussion of typically hush topics such as masturbation, pornography, and pleasure. A new generation of sex educators is also now targeting adults in an effort to fill in the many gaps left wide open by school systems. But while the Obama administration prioritized funding for evidence-based and comprehensive sex ed, the social conservatives presently in control of the White House and Congress increasingly require that federal programs promote abstinence. Boyer, quoting the Champion Healthy Kids Act of 2017, noted that the law includes "requirements that 'ensure that the unambiguous and primary emphasis and context . . . is a message to youth that normalizes the optimal health behavior of avoiding nonmarital sexual activity.'"[4] Within the current political climate, regressive groups have seized opportunities to froth up public indignation, claiming that comprehensive programs expose children to abortion rights, promiscuity, and transgender ideology. Their conservative approach, however, too often presents sexuality as shameful, wrong, and best experienced in secret. This system asks young people to build robust sexual lives on debris in place of foundations. It does nothing to alter human behavior or to forestall sexual activity among youth. It succeeds only in swaddling normal desire in ignominy and confusion, which some spend years, if not a lifetime, trying to shuck.

Which takes me to the second point: How do young women learn about pleasure? When I asked this question of Yvette, she responded with a sharp laugh and said it didn't occur to her until she was well into her twenties—and dating the man who would become her husband—that her pleasure mattered. "It wasn't until we were settled down that we could start figuring out how it all works," she said. Other women I talked to had similar answers: personal pleasure scarcely registered as part of their early experiences. These absences are not strictly attributable to inadequate education. Rather, they are striking examples of how women learn a male-centric logic of pleasure from a relatively young age. Call it "The Gaze" or the tentacled reach of patriarchy, women are encouraged to identify as sexual objects rather than to become

independent individuals deserving of their own sensual delight, whatever its form.

Even in more progressive, urban environments where young people
have better access to fact-based information, sexual interactions continue to prop up male pleasure while obscuring female erotic agency.
Christine is a Chinese American woman in her late twenties whom I
met at an adult sex-ed workshop in New York City that I attended as
part of my research for this book. A former women's studies major at
an elite college, today she is studying to be a sex counselor. When I ask
her what she hopes to do with her training, she tells me she wants to
help women overcome the sorry notions about sexuality that many are
saddled with.

"Clitoris? What clitoris? Almost everything we're taught is wrong,"
she says. "There's so much bullshit pervading our lives, social media
especially, everyone is buried in their phones, and we're interacting
with false stories about sexuality." Growing up, Christine played with
Barbie dolls, dressed in pink, and wore floppy hair bows. "My parents
didn't know any better," she says, noting that they weren't conscious of
how "girls are socialized to obsess over how pretty they are and to always think about how other people are looking at them." She casts her
upbringing as a split screen between gender conformity and academic
achievement. In the latter realm, her life was expansive: she was a solid
student, she spent a semester abroad, she enjoyed and was rewarded for
her crackling intellect. But on a social level, her experiences were more
hemmed in. "I was so self-conscious—the smallest thing, a little mistake, it would be nothing but I was mortified."

Christine became sexually active midway through high school. Losing her virginity was "a major disappointment," which was unsurprising, she says, considering that "no one knows what they're doing. You're
equally lost." These early experiences were also painful. One night in
her sophomore year of college, she was hooking up with an on-again,
off-again boyfriend at a party. It was late, the hours thick with alcohol.
He started to penetrate her with his fingers. I ask, "Were you ready?"
She shakes her head and makes a jabbing upward motion. She remembers yelping, to which he said, "Hasn't anyone ever got your G-spot before?" She said no, and to her distress, he continued jamming his digits
inside her vagina.

She tells me that since making the decision to focus her career on sexual health, she's revisited this scene a number of times in her thoughts. Along with the pain and discomfort, she remembers feeling embarrassed, worrying that she was not sophisticated enough, and feeling angry. She also felt unable to express herself, anxious about the experience not being pleasurable, and worried that he would think less of her for not enjoying it. She didn't want to be a *downer*. As a result, that night was the first time she pretended to orgasm: she just wanted to end an unpleasant situation. She had not experienced orgasm during sex before, but she had never felt any particular pressure to act as though she had, either. Most interactions happened so quickly that it didn't seem to really matter. That night set a new precedent that would last for several years. Part of it was the acute pain she had experienced. In later encounters, anticipating hurt, she would tense up, which sadly meant that sex tended to hurt more. Nevertheless, she remained sexually active, even though she didn't always like it. "I got into the habit of faking it," Christine said. "I would start making noises before even realizing I was doing it. Initially I didn't want to feel the pain, so I would fake it to hasten it along. Then it became a bigger thing, like I would default, I would cut myself off." This pattern continued until she became aware that she had started to lose interest in sex—a realization that gradually led her to her current course of study.

Talking to Christine, I wondered at the mechanisms by which we elide our own pleasure or remain mute rather than articulating our discomfort. Christine's story made me want to understand this calculus of silence. Why do we pretend? I believe that part of the reason is that we co-opt an external logic that holds someone else's pleasure as more urgent and more consequential than our own. But still I wonder: Has the greater culture so deflated our self-worth that we will not only tolerate pain, but pretend that pain feels good, rather than cry out, *Desist!*

The possible harms stemming from our hypersexualized culture and the gender polarity that it tends to reinforce are hardly new or novel topics. In the years since 1990, when Naomi Wolf observed that feminine attractiveness had been reinterpreted as sexiness, the culture has surged toward an explicit, at times raunchy, ideal of womanhood.[5] The American Psychological Association even sponsors a Task Force on the Sexualization of Girls. The group's 2007 report cited an array of disturbing indicators of how deeply the mold of femininity presses into childhood: we market thongs for seven-year-olds and toy dolls in leather minis; promote prepubescent dieting and makeup lines for grade schoolers; allow breast augmentation surgery for minors.[6] Unnervingly, what is so disturbing is not just that culture makes leering eyes at girls; it is that girls respond by absorbing the culture's lessons—that they should be pleasing, alluring, and enticing—and they come to sexualize themselves. The consequences are ghastly. They include body dissatisfaction, eating disorders, low self-esteem, depression, anxiety, a range of physical health problems, and even impaired thinking and "fragmented consciousness." The APA authors state that, taken together, these decrements suggest "sexualization practices may function to keep girls 'in their place' as objects of sexual attraction and beauty, significantly limiting their free thinking and movement in the world."

There's reason to believe that this cultural fantasia continues to affect women's sexuality over time, and that early exposures translate into adulthood. The APA report noted that a woman who has been socialized to separate from her inner feelings of arousal and desire may feel less entitled to sexual satisfaction. "She may instead opt to let events unfold based on her partner's wants and interests."

I saw this process at work in some of the women I spoke to for this project. When our discussion spanned both adolescence and adulthood, most of the women drew distinctions between their early sexual encounters and their later experiences. However, through-lines emerged: concern over their appearance, ambivalence toward expressing what they really wanted, and framing sex in terms that prioritize male desire, excitement, and timing—"from boner to wad shot," as *MEL* magazine so eloquently put it.[7] One forty-something woman I met at an empowerment seminar told me her pleasure was routinely second tier. I asked, "Do you consider your own orgasm to be important?" She answered: "Of course, I guess? Sure! It's nice when it happens. But it's not, how do I say this? It's not like the main thing. When my husband can't come, which does happen these days, for whatever reason, then it feels like sex wasn't complete, like we prematurely stopped the show. But whether I orgasm—it's nice, we both enjoy it—is kind of irrelevant. I think I'm more concerned with him." Another woman, in a different context, put it in starker terms: "Let's be real. We can have sex, and if

I come, wonderful, we're all happy. But if I don't come . . . Well?" She shrugs. "But if we're having sex and he's not finishing, then that's another story."

One of the most prominent carryovers I noticed was that many women felt an obligation to smooth the emotional landscape of their relationships. I find my thoughts returning to this tendency, trying to make sense of why it is that a partner, even a casual hookup, ranks first. It appears that in our *she can do it all* culture, women feel like it is their responsibility to manage other people's subjective reality; as for Christine, the woman I met at the New York City workshop, a repulsive violation was recast as an erotic interlude in which she played the grateful recipient to the male's dexterous generosity.

▼▲▼▲▼

In the late 1980s, the psychologist Michelle Fine wrote about what she called the "missing discourse of desire" in America's sexual education.[8] Women are taught to be on guard, ever alert to sexual dangers, but not encouraged to be versed in their own pleasure. They are told in subtle and not-so-subtle ways to view their own desire as suspect; meanwhile, the policies that supposedly protect them from harm often end up placing them in peril. Then, for a book published in 2002, developmental psychologist Deborah Tolman talked extensively with teenage girls about how they viewed their own sexuality. Her research revealed a jarringly bifurcated world in which young women were encouraged to appear sexual, and yet their own erotic nature was undermined. Girls were supposed to make themselves desirable, but their own longings, as the cultural script read, were for emotional closeness and comfort. The end result, Tolman said, was the desexualization of girls' sexuality, wherein erotic impulses were insistently displaced by the desire for relationships.[9] Tolman was refreshingly clear: desire is "important and life sustaining." It informs how we make decisions, influences how we behave in the world, and undergirds entitlement to pleasure. But this was not what the current order looked like, in her assessment. Rather, young women were being assailed with messages about how to primp their sexuality for public consumption, but at the same time society was steadily guiding them away from cultivating and expressing their own wants.[10]

Tolman's observations still hold true. In 2016, journalist Peggy Orenstein interviewed young women about how they were trying to make sense of the shifting sexual mores of our day, and she, too, found that pleasure was commonly missing in women's intimate interactions.[11] While girls have the latitude to be sexual—she argued in fact that hypersexualization is the "water in which girls swim"—they do not necessarily feel entitled to enjoy it.[12] Between popular culture and pornography, Orenstein said, young women learn to *impersonate* rather than embody sexiness. This absence is sustained from the beginning, starting with how we name—or rather, do *not* properly name—female body parts, and shelter young women from the knowledge that sex "can and should feel fabulous."[13] Orenstein likens this practice to a "psychological clitoridectomy." She has found that girls are engaging in a wide array of sexual acts, particularly oral sex (giving, but not receiving), which they frequently write off as no big deal, or as the new *third base*. On the one hand, oral sex serves as a strategy to foreclose on having to go all the way, as in having penetrative sex. On the other, it helps buttress expectations for male satisfaction, as read by the female. Hookups follow an "unspoken sequence," one of Orenstein's subjects explained. "You make out, then he feels you up, then you give him head, and that's it. I think girls aren't taught to express their wants. We're these docile creatures that just learn to please."

But for all the critical commentary, trends toward objectifying women, sexualizing youth, and appropriating signifiers of gender nonconformity for commercial ends continue unabated, intensifying with the media's increasingly pervasive reach. There is no reprieve from the messaging that collectively communicates this: we are sexualized at all times. "We live in a world *suffused and saturated with representations of intimate relationships*" (emphasis in original), observed activist academic Meg-John Barker and colleagues.[14] And these messages convey not just how we should appear or behave but also how we are supposed to gauge the merit of our own psyches and desires. As we lie in bed or commute to work, lost in the blur of endless feeds, these mediated ideas accrue significance. The more we interface with them—supposed standards for performance, pleasure, even meaning—the more real they become. And what's often on display are ideals that remind me of the impossible *good bad girl* or *bad good girl* of Yvette's telling: today we are supposed to enjoy sex, and if we don't, the fault surely lies with us. And so it is our very selves, rather than the circumstances of bad sex, that we are supposed to change.

THE POLITICS OF FAKING IT

In a classic *Seinfeld* episode, "The Mango," George and Jerry are in their usual seats at the diner, riffing on how very hard it is to understand women "below the equator." Just dive in and hope for the best, advises Jerry. "It's a haaazy mystery." When Elaine joins them, the subject turns to *faking it*, and she lets it be known that that's just what she did back when she and Jerry were dating. Jerry is indignant, then crestfallen, while Elaine crows over the mastery of her performance.

> JERRY: You faked it?
> ELAINE: I faked it.
> JERRY: That whole thing, the whole production, it was all an act?
> ELAINE: Not bad huh?
> JERRY: What about the breathing, the panting, the moaning, the screaming?
> ELAINE: Fake, fake, fake, fake.
> JERRY: I'm stunned, I'm shocked! How many times did you do this?
> ELAINE: Uuuhm, all the time.

This episode ran way back in 1993, a full quarter-century ago, but the subtext remains relevant. The faking problem is not framed as Elaine's lack of climax—that she doesn't get off when she and Jerry had sex—but as a slight to *his* esteem. Her orgasm is important, chiefly, to his masculinity.

Catapult to the present, and research shows that female orgasm is still framed as a masculine achievement.[15] We interpret her orgasm as a measure of his fulsome maleness, rather than as a barometer of her comfort or delight. When she fakes it, he is the wounded party: her pretending becomes *his* loss.

Psychologist Sara McClelland at the University of Michigan has found that young women often measure their own fulfillment by the yardstick of their mates' pleasure.[16] She argued that satisfaction is entangled in cultural values and in one's individual sense of entitlement to pleasure, something she calls "Intimate Justice."[17] The absence of orgasm, she concluded, is not an individual phenomenon, but a social experience formed by power, gender, and belief.[18] For a woman who does not feel deserving of pleasure, it is her partner's orgasm that becomes the crucial outcome. Other researchers have published similar findings: that women frame their own pleasure in relation to male prowess, worrying that their absent orgasm will diminish their partners' masculinity and enjoyment.[19]

The subject of faking it came up regularly with the women I spoke with for this book. It was typically presented in matter-of-fact terms, as though the behavior were so common as to be beyond comment. There's some truth to that. One sex therapist told me, as an aside, that she believes there are more fake orgasms than real ones. The hard data tend to support this view. According to one well-trafficked 2010 report, 80 percent of heterosexual women fake orgasm during vaginal intercourse about half of the time, and another 25 percent fake orgasm almost all of the time.[20] (To the Seinfeld slant above, when CBS News reported on this study, the headline opened with "Ouch": there was no editorializing on shabby male technique; all the focus was on the bruising consequences of women's inauthentic "moaning and groaning."[21]) *Cosmopolitan*'s 2015 survey of more than two thousand women between the ages of eighteen and forty found that only 57 percent of the women reliably orgasmed during sex; 67 percent faked orgasm, with roughly equal numbers doing so to end an interaction and to make their partners feel good. Though, again, there was little attention to the idea that faking it is somehow problematic for women. (To wit, *Cosmo* ran a spread asking women to confess to their "most Oscar-worthy" performances of pretending.[22])

A number of the women I spoke with expressed nuanced motives for faking it. A few, for instance, said it was a way to get themselves more excited; their own noises and more urgent movements were arousing. As one woman put it, "If I'm not feeling that excited, acting like I am can help me get into the mood. I turn myself on." For others, faking it was a way to wrap things up if they were bored, or sore, or hankering for sleep, or if they knew that their own pleasure was not likely to appear. A few told me they thought that seeming to have an orgasm would make them more attractive to whomever they were having sex with. One woman shared that she routinely faked pleasure with new partners: she wanted them to "think it's perfect. . . . It improves the chances that things might work out." She added, "I want them to know I'm cool, I'm *that* kind of girl."

But overwhelmingly, faking it was linked to caretaking. Women took it upon themselves to preserve their partners from feeling as though they had failed to deliver. "He's just so sad if it doesn't happen," is how one woman put it, while others shared variations on wanting to protect men from feeling *bad* about themselves. Another said, "It's easier than making it into a thing. Guys are real touchy. I can take care of myself if I need to." One woman declared, "Men need to believe it's all gone the way it should." When I asked her to elaborate, she explained, "I think who they are, as men, is tied up in it. It's ultimately about their ego."

These patterns were striking to me for a number of reasons. Even though women tended to view their pleasure as their own responsibility—for instance, by masturbating, communicating around their sexual preferences, or opting for certain positions—they still subscribed to the notion that men should be furnishing their orgasms. And yet, if men did not do this, women blamed themselves, while at the same time working to make sure their partners never knew. They assumed responsibility for managing the emotional outcome of the sexual interaction, even if that meant temporarily subordinating their disappointments, pain, or disinterest.

Most women viewed faking it as fairly benign. And for the most part, I did too. That is, until the subject cropped up over and over again, and I found myself preoccupied with an odd contradiction: as we act out ecstasy, we devalue our actual sensations. On the one hand, this performance is an ode to the importance of female pleasure, the expectation that it should be present. But on the other, it strips women of the physical and psychological experience of pleasure. Spectacle bullies sensation aside.

▼▲▼▲▼

Have we always done this? Why is this strange behavior so widespread?

Some observers point straight to Freud, who once, in a direct nod to colonialism, called female sexuality a "dark continent." His authoritative wisdom held that mature pleasure should center on the reproductive tract (vaginal orgasm properly obtained from penetration). Women were *supposed* to derive gratification in this one way, and yet, as we now well know, most did not.

Did women and men back then take his words to heart? The record is spotty. What we do know is that a number of marriage tracts in the early part of the twentieth century emphasized simultaneous orgasm as a sort of holy grail of matrimony: the man's penetrative thrusting should result in the couple's shared ecstasy.[23] The idea perfectly united the esteemed trifecta: marital copulation, reproductive possibility, and male sexual response. One of the most popular texts of the day, *Ideal Marriage: Its Physiology and Technique*, by Dutch doctor Theodor H. van de Velde, described the standard route of pleasure: "In the normal and perfect coitus, mutual orgasm must be almost simultaneous; the usual procedure is that the man's ejaculation begins and sets the woman's acme of sensation in train at once." The book, which was first published in the United States in 1930 and reprinted dozens of times through the 1960s, also cast a new wife as inherently frigid—she "is as a rule, more or less completely 'cold' or indifferent to and in sexual intercourse." It was up to her husband to initiate her into the joys of coupling, "a real psychic panacea" that would ultimately "ripen" her adult character.

Mary Stopes, the British author of the popular 1918 book *Married Love: A New Contribution to the Solution of Sex Difficulties*, brought more depth to the matter. Women were not in a state of erotic slumber pre-marriage, she maintained. Rather, the Victorian twilight had dimmed erotic instincts for men and women alike.[24] Stopes, who was the youngest person ever to become a doctor of science in Britain, wrote *Married Love* while in the midst of divorcing her first husband; she looked to science to stake out how she thought marriage should actually work. For her, female orgasm was expressive of a vital life force; it was a creative energy. And yet the "mists and shadowy darkness" of modern erotic ignorance had produced deep and injurious disappointments. For women, the ho-hum sex of married life was a "slow corrosive wound that eats into her very being." Men, while falling short of their true sexual potential, got the better deal. Husbands, she wrote, "content with their own satisfaction, little know the pent-up aching, or even resentment, which may eat into a wife's heart, and ultimately may affect her whole health."

Stopes was writing at a time when marriage was coming under new scrutiny. Contemporaneous reformers were looking to shore up the institution, to make it more attractive to young people and buttress it as a mainstay of social structure from the pressures of liberalism (think flappers, venereal disease, dating, contraception, working women, and *just*-visible homosexuality). As we'll see in Chapter 5, marriage was increasingly framed as a companionate relationship, founded on love and reaffirmed through intimacy. Like van de Velde, Stopes believed sexual reciprocity was a natural ideal. The "perfectly adjusted" couple "reaches the crisis of nerves and muscular reactions" together. "This mutual orgasm is extremely important," she wrote. However, she abruptly qualified that claim: "70 or 80 per cent of our married women (in the middle classes) are deprived of the full orgasm through the excessive speed of the husband's reactions."

Although these early texts devoted considerable attention to the importance of foreplay (Stopes wrote that the husband "*must woo* [his wife] *before every separate act of coitus*" [emphasis in original]), the underlying message was that penetrative sex was the centerpiece of bedroom life. One could surmise that women, who were repeatedly sold the line that *this* was the apex of nuptial intimacy, faced strong pressures to hew close to script. It might have seemed less risky to fake it than to possibly seem abnormal or unhealthy. Consider also the 1953 book *The Sexually Adequate Woman*, by psychiatrist Frank S. Caprio. Caprio offered that a woman who was "incapable" of having an orgasm from coitus and preferred clitoral stimulation might be "regarded as suffering from frigidity and require[ing] psychiatric assistance."[25]

The midcentury investigations of Alfred Kinsey and his research team challenged these ideas. Based on nearly six thousand sexual histories, *Sexual Behavior in the Human Female*, published in 1953, documented the enormous gap between societal assumptions and the actual sex practices of (white) American women.[26] The text offered what were then revelations about women's masturbation practices, premarital and extramarital sexual activities, and orgasm, including their penchant for clitoral stimulation. The backlash to the publication was swift and intense—it included a congressional investigation into his financial backing and the termination of his funding from the Rockefeller Foundation. At the time, however, Kinsey believed his work was not just a contribution to science, but a service to marriage itself. According to his findings, at least three-quarters of divorces were related in part to problems of "sexual adjustment"; accurate, as opposed to folkloric, information could rescue couples from the "irritating" and "humdrum routines" of coupledom. And to Kinsey, part of the trouble was the insistence on vaginal orgasm, which he said was a reflection of men's faith in the importance of their own genitalia.

But for all their revelations, Kinsey's findings, and later those of Masters and Johnson, did not manage to dislodge long-held notions about the ideal female orgasm: that it should be vaginal, synchronized, and proffered by her mate. The view was so entrenched that feminists eventually struck out against it. Anne Koedt's radical pamphlet *The Myth of the Vaginal Orgasm* met readers in 1970 with bold declarations. "Women have thus been defined sexually in terms of what pleases men," Koedt wrote. She argued that so long as vaginal orgasm was upheld as the standard, women would be blamed—and would blame themselves—for failing to achieve it, even though it was a rarity. Trying to fix the "problem" of vaginal orgasm led women down a fruitless path of anxiety: "Not even in her one role allowed in a male society—the role of a woman—is she successful. She is put on the defensive, with phony data as evidence that she'd better try to be even more feminine, think more feminine, and reject her envy of men. That is, shuffle even harder, baby."[27]

The 1970s reverberated with the message that women should take charge of their own pleasure. Impromptu educational forums taught masturbation; women's groups encouraged their members to foreground their own desires and proclivities. Straightforward information on the mechanics did much to dispense with mystery and shame. So why, today, does it feel as if we've backslid?[28] Orgasm has become all but synonymous with sexual health. Countless resources promise tricks and tools for *getting* there, or detail the exotic poses you should try this year—or this week, for the ambitious. Depictions of women's pleasure are visible to an unprecedented degree. And yet, faking it is commonplace. A strange ellipsis is at work here. We encounter female pleasure more, but what we tend to see or hear or read about is a burlesque of heterosexuality: man climbs aboard woman, and she's delirious moments later; man pins woman to tree or wall or doorframe, and a single thrust induces rapture.

For all the comedy of such scenes, they still prop up normative expectations that women not only orgasm during intercourse but have orgasms that match a certain look and sound. Along these lines, plenty of writers have underscored the influence of pornography in modern sexual choreography, arguing that it is reshaping intimacy and sexuality.[29] There is compelling evidence that the near-ubiquitous engagement with porn, especially among young people, feeds into sex acts and expectations. But this still does not explain the emotional component of pretended orgasm: the burden to enact combustive pleasure for someone else.

Perhaps one of the biggest drivers today behind this behavior is the imperative of personal development and transformation. If women are not orgasmic or desirous of sex, the problem is rarely framed as the man's jackrabbit timing or failure to enchant her clitoris. No, the problem is presented as a failure of Self, and so women are encouraged to treat their own minds and bodies as improvement projects. Meg-John Barker captured this perfectly. The ideal woman, she said, is one "who has banished repression, overcome taboos, dealt with any 'issues,' and become a properly adventurous neoliberal lover."[30]

Backstage to women's bedroom theatrics is the leering figure of self-appraisal, feeding relentless lines of judgment: you take too long, you're hard to please, the folds and curves of your own body should leave you trembling with shame. Among the women I talked to, some were excruciatingly aware of their own pretending. More than one described compensating for her low desire by acting over the top. "It's especially when I don't want to that I give him the full fantasy," one shared, in reference to playing the part of a "hungry, prancing tease." While inside she didn't feel at all inclined, she would "make like I'm so into it, that I can't help myself and have to furiously ride him, then *whoops* he finishes, and we're done."

In reviewing sexual advice as doled out by *Glamour* magazine, British sociologist Rosalind Gill observed that women are encouraged to superintend all aspects of intimacy. They are urged not just to take responsibility for communication, excitement, beauty, passion, and relationship longevity, but also to attend to the *genuineness* of male satisfaction. "Is he *really* happy in bed?" prodded one article, which pointed out that even if a man was dissatisfied, he would keep on having sex. The resulting message, said Gill, was that women were to both sleuth and service in the name of keeping *his* boredom at bay: "Women are called on to monitor their self-presentation, to break down every element of social interaction, and to learn techniques such as mirroring, co-reacting and strategic touch, not to mention learning to calculate precisely the right proportion of eye contact that is necessary."[31]

Gill argued that modern advice weighs in on the very nature of the soul, calling on women both to act a certain part and to remodel their interiority. What is most insidious about these messages is that women are not cast as passive or weak, but encouraged to adopt a facade of booming confidence. Liberal ideals—the skein of freedom—become another facet of the trap.

Looking at how popular magazines portray "great sex," a pair of Canadian researchers similarly detailed how the media plays up women's mandate to delight. Analyzing portrayals of "great sex" in glossies, they found an emphasis on variety—"Place a glazed doughnut around your man's member, then gently nibble the pastry and lick the icing . . . as well as his manhood"; performance—"What men are secretly jonesin' for is an occasional wild, animalistic boot-knocking session"; and self-monitoring—"Stop compartmentalizing and try thinking about sex more often." There are frequent encouragements to introduce new spices—"He'll love it when you . . ." However, for all their tips and tricks, there is no mention of how or why the foregoing would appeal to women, beyond helping them ratchet up their partners' thrills.[32]

I see a remarkable distance between the commentary of Marie Stopes and that of *Marie Claire* and other dispensaries of sexual know-how. To the former, women suffered from overexcited partners, the rash of Quick Draw McGraws and coarse lovers, while to the latter, women bear the blame for faking it and must learn to love sex, to surveil and circumscribe their own attitudes, and to reinvent themselves. Moreover, women are pressed to take responsibility for heating things up: try anal, role-play, watch porn, read erotica, audition different sturdy surfaces. And with each suggestion, the exhortation is to enjoy, and if not, at least play the part of bon vivant. *Push yourself to do something new.* If you're not loving it, it's because you're prude, under-confident, weighed down by the past. Try *30 thrusts in each position.*

Does the imperative to enjoy outweigh the fact that you do not? It seems perverse that the emphasis on good times does not result in more pleasure. I will look more closely at the subject of self-help later in this book. For now, I want to underscore that women are expected to reach orgasm by doing a lot of work on themselves, and that they are also supposed to keep their partners in a state of blissful ignorance (literally) about their truncated or absent pleasure. It is rather marvelous, on the one hand, that we have been released from the presumed frigidity of yore. But "cold indifference" to sex has been replaced by a new mandate: to become the pleasure-hungry creatures of our mediated dreams. If the paradigm in decades past was *good girls don't,* we could say that these days, *good girls do*—that is, they crave, pursue, and relish sex—and that women hold themselves to that standard. But in the absence of changing the circumstances in which women do enjoy sex, circumstances that make them feel safe, secure, deserving, happy, stimulated, and free, authentic and consistent pleasure, for many, will likely remain out of reach.

4 WHAT THE BODY REMEMBERS

> Far too often secrecy prevails, and the story of the traumatic event surfaces not as a verbal narrative but as a symptom.
>   —*Judith Herman,* Trauma and Recovery, *2015*

> It's as if the body's response to the original trauma has just been waiting.
>   —*Staci Haines,* Healing Sex, *2007*

AFTER SHE WAS assaulted, Noelle walked home to the one-bedroom apartment she shared with her boyfriend in urban Texas. It was getting late, and the streets were mostly empty. Maybe people saw her stumbling, piecing together the ripped skirt with her hands, but if they did no one spoke to her. She let herself into the ground floor unit and sat on the sofa, wondering what she would do, what she might say when her boyfriend eventually came home. At some point, she rose and edged over to a vanity laid with a shallow sink. She stood there for what felt like a long time, looking at her swelling face in the light that buzzed above the mirror. She can't remember where the impulse originated, but at some point, she reached down and took off one of her red leather sandals, weighing it in her hand, before bashing the heavy sole against her already puffy eye. It hurt. But she smashed again, this time with greater force. Then again and again, in a rhythm of breath-contact, breath-contact until the skin around her eye ballooned in protest, and she stood squinting at the reflection of her unfathomable face.

Gradually, she returned to her perch on the couch and never spoke of this isolated episode of self-harm until nearly twenty years later, when she confided it to her husband. Later she would throw the skirt away. It had been a gift from her mother from the summer before. But now the seam was ripped nearly right to the waistband, and the cloth had to be surveyed for evidence. The police administered a rape kit, collecting samples, scraping the undersides of her fingernails. Victims often scratch at their attackers. But Noelle had frozen, and for years afterward she would think her own limbs had betrayed her. She wishes she could travel back in time to embrace that wounded young woman and relieve her of self-blame.

When her boyfriend returned home much later in the night, he said something to the effect of having always known this would happen. *This* being the violent rape that Noelle described to him: a casual conversation gone horribly awry. Her boyfriend's comment, an off-the-cuff remark, has sat with her through these years, even as the rest of the night flickers in and out of view. It was like his words were charged with truth, like the attack was some terrible prophecy made good. Maybe, she thought in darker moments, *I had it coming.*

They'd fought over her sexuality. Over where the bounds of her freedom ran up against the limits of his tolerance. He'd get drunk and charge her with all manner of misdeeds, only to forget about them when he was sober. *This must be what you really think of me*, she'd think. When he criticized her sexual history or her appearance, she'd bow her head and concede. She routinely canceled plans with friends he did not like, and more than once, she returned new clothes that failed to pass his muster. Later, when he punched a divot in the wall beside her face, she was the one to apologize. A few weeks after the attack, sliding into a depression that would claim the next two years, Noelle remembers feeling skittish and distracted as her boyfriend drove their car along the highway. Her mind felt fuzzy, like random tufts clinging to a carding brush. She felt an overwhelming urge to fling herself from the moving car. She expressed this to her boyfriend and he power-locked the doors. It would take more than a decade for Noelle to feel safe in her body, and longer still for her to enjoy her own sexuality.

▼▲▼▲▼

Variations on Noelle's experience of rape play out every minute and
a half in present-day America. Roughly 36 times per hour, or 315,000
times a year. Far from a postcard view of secure boundaries forged of
trust, population-level surveys reveal a national portrait of commonplace brutality. Upward of 20 percent of Americans are sexually molested as children. One in five women are subjected to rape or attempted
rape in their lifetime, and as many as a third of intimate partners have
engaged in violent physical contact, with the numbers rising precipi-
tously on both counts for women of color.[1] One in six women have been
stalked at some point in their lives. Nearly half of all murdered women
are killed by their current or former partners. There are almost endless
permutations to these mind-boggling figures.[2] And these forms of violence, whether they exist as lived experience or as perceived threats,
can leave lasting marks on our sexual selves, affecting desire, pleasure,
fertility, and our ability to feel secure within our own skin.

Yet, for all their enormity, these statistics have been oddly mute, at
least until #MeToo brought them (back) to national attention. They
represent a sustained crisis in our midst, but one that as a society we
have consistently chosen to place on the lower ranks of funding, research, and public policy. We make it hard, if not dangerous, for women
to report abuse, and harder still for them to bring their assailants to
justice. In a 2019 cover story for *The Atlantic*, Barbara Bradley Hagerty
reported on the thousands of untested rape kits that have accumulated
in police warehouses across the country, largely because law enforce-
ment officials have been skeptical or dismissive of women's claims of
rape.[3] This is changing as #MeToo, #ChurchToo, and similar testimo-
nials surface the harms resulting from the comingling of masculinity
and privilege. And yet the conversations currently taking place often
remain embroiled in ideas about women's complicity or haplessness,
and have yet to fully contend with the everyday terrors that make womanhood a state of risk.

This response partially reflects our blinkered views on sexuality.
Our hypertitillated conservatism insists on the sanctity of marriage but
shrugs aside domestic violence. It faults women for "falling pregnant,"
in the words of one BBC reporter, while depriving them of choice, and

later depriving children of stable loving homes. It is the same ethos that limits ads using the word *period* while allowing billboards consumed by cleavage and machine guns. The reality of sexual violence and the eroticized imbalance of power that creates and sustains that reality are at odds with the stories we like to tell about fairness, democracy, and gendered equality.

This is not the first time we've had a social reckoning with the universality of coercion and harassment. Every so often, the enormity of the problem gathers like a storm in America's public consciousness and there is a moment of collective indignation, much like we are currently seeing. But we have yet to figure out how to channel outrage in a way that results in meaningful behavioral change. In America, there is a decades-long history of calling out the harms of patriarchy and whiteness and the wildly inequitable way they disperse power across gender, identity, race, class, and history. But collectively, we still stumble in addressing this. Psychiatrist Judith Herman has looked at these uncomfortable subjects and makes the woeful case that we suffer from a sort of "episodic amnesia" in the face of traumatic events. Public attention to an atrocity will flourish, then just as dramatically subside, leaving the matter buried by the clip of time. This is, she argues, because trauma is fundamentally controversial. It is a confrontation with both vulnerability and the "capacity for evil in human nature."[4]

The #MeToo movement has brought this propensity into focus. However, the statistics in current circulation mirror what sociologists unearthed some forty years ago. The question today is why, decades after the first reports on the dire picture of sexual abuse and predation in this country, have the numbers remained obstinately unchanged? Herman suggests that transformation requires more than exhuming social facts. If sexual violence exists in the context of a male-dominant social order, then nothing can truly change so long as that order remains intact.

Our struggle to contend meaningfully with these figures is also a reflection of how we've underestimated the long-term consequences of sexual violence and abuse. Rape is the costliest of *all* crimes, and sexual violence is associated with an increase in unemployment and underemployment, significant losses in wages over a victim's lifetime, and a litany of hidden health-care expenses.[5] Reports on childhood sexual abuse have identified greater incidences of asthma, ulcers, migraines, stomach pain, anorexia, irregular or painful periods, yeast infections, and irritable bowel syndrome, among many other conditions, among survivors compared to the general population. Other evidence suggests that exposure to violence should be considered a chronic disease unto itself. This line of investigation suggests that prolonged exposure to stress hormones released by the body in response to violence disrupts the nervous, immune, and endocrine systems, contributing to other illnesses. Seen from this view, trauma may be the buried culprit behind some of the most prevalent disorders affecting the population, including sexual problems.

However, even as science is beginning to tease out the ways adversity affects our well-being over time, recognition of the *sexual* consequences of sexual violence has been slower to take hold. When Wendy Maltz, a therapist who has worked extensively with victims of sexual abuse, first published her pioneering book *The Healing Sexual Journey* in 1991, she says there was little awareness that sexual violence could resonate over time, disrupting a woman's libido, undermining her self-concept, harming her long-term relationships, and altering the strength, and even the object, of her desires. "People thought sexual abuse often only lasted for the duration of the trauma. They didn't realize it could haunt a person for their whole lives," she told me.

In 1999, sociologist Edward Laumann led a landmark study on the prevalence of sexual dysfunction in the United States.[6] The report furnished some of the most widely cited figures in the field, including the statistic that 43 percent of American women have some form of sexual dysfunction. Toward the very end of the paper, after writing at length on factors like class, education, and marital status, Laumann and his colleagues noted that their results "support the view that sexual traumas induce lasting psychosocial disturbances, which ultimately affect sexual functioning."[7] Maltz believes this finding is key, though majorly overlooked. The universality of sexual violence may go a long way toward explaining why rates of sexual dysfunction appear so high. And yet, she says, we hear little about the sexual effects of sexual abuse.

I was surprised by the extent to which Maltz's observation held true as I delved into this area of research. There is, to be sure, ample literature carefully documenting the sexual ramifications of rape, incest, and intimate violence. This research notes the pervasiveness of desire and arousal problems, a lack of sexual satisfaction, avoidance or fear of sex, and sexual pain among survivors. But there is also a stunning dismissal of these findings among professionals who work with survivors. I found guides for social workers and clinicians that make *zero* mention of how sexual violence can impact sexual function. One 2011 review of forty-three papers details the effects of rape on employment, substance abuse, psychosis, and mental health, but does not even once address sexuality. Even mainstream resources, including the Rape, Abuse & Incest National Network (RAINN), make only fleeting reference to the sexual fallout of abuse, stressing instead related problems with addiction, work relationships, school performance, and increased risk of unintended pregnancy. This focus is out of sync with women's lived experiences and betrays a general reluctance to treat sexual health, especially pleasure and desire, as serious issues that affect women's well-being over the long term. Survivors typically resume work and family life—by all outward appearances, they will return to being "productive" members of society—even if devastating repercussions are playing out in their sexuality.

DISCOVERING TRAUMA

It wasn't that long ago when sexual violence was still considered an unfortunate outlier rather than a crime, and one largely disconnected from the social conditions that make it possible. Although the history of anti-rape activism in the United States extends back to the nineteenth century, most notably with black women protesting the abuses of white men, it was not until the 1970s that sexual violence moved into public view as a political concern. (Let's recall, for instance, that marital rape was not illegal in all fifty states until 1993.*) As a result, victims of sexual violence contended with stigma, shame, and perceptions of their own conscious and unconscious complicity.

---

* Change does not come easily. In response to efforts to make forced sex illegal in the home, Senator Bob Wilson of California infamously asked, in 1979, "If you can't rape your wife, who can you rape?"

The women's movement brought about a major reckoning with the stunning scope of sexual violence. The era's consciousness-raising efforts helped countless women give voice to stories they had harbored in silence. And as these stories came out, the long-held insistence that rape was a rarity became impossible to sustain. As the historian Ruth Rosen puts it, "Between 1965 and 1980, thousands of women participated in an enormous archeological dig, excavating crimes and secrets that used to be called, with a shrug, 'life.'"[8] The dawning recognition of *it's not just me* was fundamental to the coordinated efforts that would come to change laws, social service provisions, and medical practices in the years to follow.

Feminist thinkers produced a flurry of scholarship on sexual violence, implicating the imbalance of power at its root. Susan Griffith's 1971 *Rape: The All-American Crime* made the case that sexual violence is not motivated by lust so much as the desire for domination. Published in 1975, Susan Brownmiller's groundbreaking book *Against Our Will* painstakingly chronicled the frequency of sexual violence across cultures and throughout history, describing rape as a conscious process of intimidation. That same year, Diana Russell's *The Politics of Rape* brought the guarded secret of marital abuse to the public's attention. Investigations into the widespread nature of once taboo subjects, such as incest and domestic battery, followed in a swift cascade.

But it wasn't just the overwhelming evidence that directed the era's outrage toward action. It was that these crimes and their consequences had a new name: *trauma*. The women's movement dovetailed with the fallout from Vietnam, and scores of veterans were returning home with lasting psychological wounds. To some observers at the time, their symptoms seemed to parallel women's reactions to sexual violence. In the early 1970s, Ann Burgess, a psychiatric nurse, and Lynda Holmstrom, a sociologist, interviewed rape victims who came through the emergency room of Boston City Hospital, speaking with ninety-two women and thirty-seven children over the course of a year. They observed a cluster of common responses: victims often felt they had survived a life-threatening event, but that it had left them prone to panic, insomnia, and nightmares, as well as hypersensitivity and numbness. Burgess and Holmstrom were quick to point out that these reactions were similar to those that veterans displayed. Drawing on research describing combat neurosis, they coined the term "rape trauma syndrome," thus granting a name to what Judith Herman later attributed to the "tyranny of private life." She noted that it was finally being "recognized that the most common post-traumatic disorders are those not of men in war but of women in civilian life."[9]

In 1980, a group of combat veterans successfully lobbied the American Psychiatric Association to include post-traumatic stress disorder as a new diagnosis in the DSM. The label was seen as a major step toward validating the enduring nature of psychic pain and removing blame from the individual in torment. Medical labels are more than theoretical concepts: they carry both symbolic and therapeutic importance. On one level, the new diagnosis meant that the public needed to rethink human vulnerability and resilience. Merely surviving a disaster did not ensure that someone could truly live. The past could continue to gnaw away at the survivor's present reality. Moreover, on a practical level, we cannot treat what does not exist, and so the diagnosis carried implications for proper care.

At the time, Bessel van der Kolk was a young psychiatrist who had just left his job at the Boston VA Clinic. Having worked with veterans, he was already sensitive to the presence of trauma in their lives. But when he went on to work at the Massachusetts Mental Health Center, he was especially struck by the number of women he saw who shared stories of molestation and childhood sexual abuse. In his 2014 book, he wrote, "This was puzzling, as the standard textbook of psychiatry at the time stated that incest was extremely rare in the United States, occurring about once in every one million women. Given that there were then about one hundred million women living in the United States, I wondered how forty-seven, almost half of them, had found their way to my office in the basement of the hospital."[10]

Van der Kolk observed that calamities like war are not all "that leaves human lives in ruins." Rape, abuse, and neglect waged quiet but more pernicious forms of devastation. He took issue with some of the mainstream approaches to treating trauma, namely, exposure therapy and cognitive behavioral therapy, or CBT. These methods, he believes, were bound to fail, or even worse, to exacerbate underlying issues, because they focused on the mind at the expense of looking to the body. Trauma, he came to realize, had little to do with cognition. It is stored

within our physical selves, producing extreme states of bodily discon-
nection. He wrote, "The body keeps the score: If the memory of trauma
is encoded in the viscera, in heartbreaking and gut-wrenching emotions, in autoimmune disorders and skeletal/muscular problems, and if
mind/brain/visceral communication is the royal road to emotion regulation, this demands a radical shift in our therapeutic assumptions."[11]
Van der Kolk's perspective mirrors what Maltz and a handful of others know to be true among survivors of sexual violence. Recovery requires healing the body and learning to find safety and joy in one's own
arousal and sensations.

▼▲▼▲▼

Whether treating traumatized veterans, abused children, or victims of
sexual assault, van der Kolk has observed that the traumatic event is
often unmoored from time: it is ongoing. This happens because trauma
does not only linger in the mind as a disturbing memory, but changes
the very structure and function of the brain, leading the body to continue to mount defenses against a threat that no longer exists. When
faced with harm, a structure deep in the brain called the amygdala ini-
tiates our fight-or-flight response and its hormonal cascade. Heart rate
rises, blood flow increases to the brain and limbs, pupils dilate, and
muscles tense. Under normal circumstances, this process concludes
once the threat has passed. But if an individual has not been able to
fight or flee—if, say, she is groped, or forced, or pinned to the ground—
the alarms can continue to sound.

Stephen Porges, a behavioral neuroscientist who has studied involuntary immobilization, has theorized that trauma is associated with
unsuccessful attempts to get away. Some people are overpowered by
their attackers, and others completely shut down and are simply unable
to fight or flee. It is not a volitional response, Porges emphasized: "It's
not a question of why didn't you run, why not fight?"[12]

And yet the popular view is that victims who do not *choose* to resist
yield out of cowardice, weakness, or a sense of resignation. That assumption, though false, forms a common baseline. Take, for instance,
the wildly inappropriate remarks of CNN anchor Don Lemon during
an interview with Joan Tarshis, the fifth woman to accuse actor Bill
Cosby of drugging and assaulting her. Cosby forced Tarshis to perform

oral sex, and on national television, Lemon asked why she didn't bite his penis. "You—you know, there are ways not to perform oral sex if you didn't want to do it," he said.[13]

Some suggest that if trauma represents an incomplete response to a threat, the individual is left in a vulnerable state where she may be easily "reactivated," that is, brought back into the inner chaos of the initial peril. Experts have observed individuals reacting to these stressors in extreme ways. For some, the response is "dissociation," a shutting down of the body so as to avoid pain and suffering, a response that can leave individuals devoid of feeling in the long term. Among van der Kolk's traumatized patients, this sense of numbness pertained to both emotional states and physical sensation. "Sometimes I'd ask [my patients] to close their eyes and tell me what I had put into their outstretched hands," he wrote. "Whether it was a car key, a quarter, or a can opener, they often could not even guess what they were holding—their sensory perceptions simply weren't working."[14]

For others, the response is hypervigilance, a state of keening to possible harm, both real and misperceived, so that it is nearly impossible to establish the sort of deep intimacy that is the mainstay of our mental and social health and sexual satisfaction. Trauma not only undermines a survivor's ability to form secure and trusting relationships but moreover wreaks havoc on her connection with her own body. "It's not surprising that so many trauma survivors are compulsive eaters and drinkers, fear making love, and avoid many social activities," van der Kolk wrote. "Their sensory world is largely off limits."

Our ability to feel or sense the world and our own bodies is fundamental to existence, to our empowerment, and, of course, to our pleasure. Human agency, the sense that one is in control of one's life, starts with *interoception*, which, as we'll explore in Chapter 7, means being conscious of what is taking place inside your own body. But for traumatized individuals, this elemental capacity may be severely blunted. Neuroimaging studies have found a stark contrast between the brains of "normal" individuals and those with chronic PTSD; for the latter, self-sensing sections of the brain appear to have been switched off. Van der Kolk read this finding as evidence that, in an effort to cope with the pain and dread of their trauma, people have "learned to shut down the brain areas that transmit the visceral feelings and emotions that accompany and define terror." He concluded that such people, in trying to keep terrifying sensations at bay, "also deadened their capacity to feel fully alive."[15]

REVISITATIONS

The very nature of trauma, the ways in which it fractures the minds of the afflicted, can make it exceptionally difficult to draw clear connections between what took place in the past and how the brain and body are coping in the present. Observers have grappled with the tricky ways that it can both accentuate and dim memory, sometimes to the point where victims do not even recognize their own trauma as such. Maltz, who is a survivor of sexual violence herself, emphasizes that on an individual level, the process of connecting the dots is rarely straightforward. She says one of the first steps in healing is to recognize that one's current sexual beliefs and behaviors are tied to earlier exposures. "When a survivor, we'll name Tonya, wakes up in the middle of the night and feels like she wants to punch her partner because he has a penis," Maltz explains by way of a hypothetical illustration, "her reaction might be a repercussion from having been molested as a child. It's not that Tonya doesn't like her partner. It's that she's suffering a side effect of what happened to her when she was assaulted by a male perpetrator. She hasn't yet developed positive associations to penises, men, and their sexual arousal responses." Maltz says many survivors don't recognize that their reactions are common corollaries of past sexual abuse.

I encountered this dynamic in a number of women I spoke with. Often, we did not set out to talk about sexual violence, but it gurgled up all the same. For one of my interviewees, an accomplished psychiatrist and mother of three who lives in New York City, it took decades to piece together how a sexual assault in adolescence had resulted in her poor sense of body image, dismissal of her own pleasure, and her ardent need for control and social safety. She shared with me that perhaps her eagerness to marry at a relatively young age had been informed by her lingering sense of risk. If she was married, her logic went, then she would be protected from further harm from men.

Naiylah, an artist based in Washington, DC, tells me that most every woman in her life has experienced some form of sexual violation, and that the experience "ultimately infects the core of their self-worth." She says it is so common that the women in her circle don't necessarily register it as extreme. And yet, the outcome is that "you start losing the boundaries of yourself. There is not a clear yes or no, because something has been stolen." For Naiylah, who was assaulted as a teenager by a group of boys she knew, the experience of sexual violence made her deeply leery of intimacy—a feeling that a decade later she is still struggling to work through. In place of desire, she often finds anxiety or disgust, which make it hard to have romantic relationships, especially with men. But at the same time, she feels like she is missing an important piece of her life. The struggle is compounded, she says, by the values she was raised with, namely, the idea that a "good woman" isn't especially invested in sex or pleasure. Naiylah says she is still learning to regard her body as her own, but is hopeful that one day she'll feel comfortable "really being with someone."

One of the most poignant exchanges I had was with Maria, a humanitarian aid professional who lives on the West Coast. Maria experienced a number of sexual traumas in her adolescence and early adulthood, but eventually her narrative wound its way back to her father. Her parents were separated, but she still spent extended periods under his care as a child. There is a choppy quality to her account, like a slide show clicking through distinct impressions. Sleeping in her father's bed. A passing neighbor alarmed by screams. Hemorrhoids at the age of five, attributable to anal penetration. Later, taking off her clothes at a family gathering and climbing naked into her grandfather's lap, while her family reacted awkwardly, slightly mortified; it was years before it occurred to her that that was not a "normal thing to do."

Maria's most recent and most serious relationship has been with a trans man, who also happens to be a cop. Her account of their relationship struck me as being like a theater in which experiences of trauma, power, and healing play out. In his day-to-day professional life, her partner deals with a wide range of male perpetrators, and he enjoys incorporating elements of these dynamics into their sex life. He also likes her to call him Daddy. Maria wants to please her partner, and yet the thrill she finds in this charged word is tinged with shame and violation, and the request sends her spinning through troubled memories.

In talking with women about their experiences of rape, assault, incest, and intimate violence, I was repeatedly taken by the depth and mystery of trauma. There is the traumatic event and then there is the strength of its resonance, and no one knows why an incident might derail one woman's sense of personhood or sexuality while another is seemingly untouched. For some women I spoke to, the concept of trauma seemed to provide an ample container for a range of feelings and what they perceived as negative behaviors and beliefs. Some viewed their trauma (or traumas) in stark terms of cause and consequence as they surveyed their social and sexual lives over time. But for others who shared their stories with me, trauma was not bound in time. It spilled and sloshed throughout their lives in a seemingly haphazard way. It would go quiet and retreat only to return years later in some altered form.

▼▲▼▲▼

I met Reem through an acquaintance who forwarded her my email. Reem wrote to me to say she wanted to talk about how she was no longer interested in sex with her husband and the trouble that was causing. Recently she'd been feeling nothing. "The middle of my body has been turned off," she said when we first spoke by phone. "Like it's died, like it doesn't exist."

I don't know that Reem would have defined her past experience as trauma, but it tugged mightily on her conscience when we spoke. During high school she worked a floor job at a big-box retailer in a strip mall not far from her house in Northern Virginia. By her own description, Reem has large breasts, and the store-issued shirt was very tight-fitting. When she asked her male supervisor for a larger size, he said, "Why, it's better this way." During some of her afterschool shifts, a man in his mid-twenties, whom I'll call Rob, would come into the store. Rob always seemed to find his way to the parts of the store where Reem was working. He asked her questions about her background, and she told him her parents were from Jordan. He asked whether she believed in God (she said yes) and whether she had a boyfriend (yes again). Over time, he started devising ways to touch her under the guise of being helpful: placing a hand on the small of her back as she reached for an item, brushing an invisible crumb from the front of her shirt. One day, he cornered her in the hallway as she was coming out of the restroom and forcibly kissed her. When she pushed him away, she says, he made a floppy gesture as though to convey, *What? It's no big deal.* He continued to act nonchalant about it when she rushed back to the floor. A few days later, this scene was repeated, but Rob squeezed her breasts and placed her hand on his erection. During a subsequent shift, he came up behind her and whispered in her ear that he had masturbated while thinking about her. Later, he stroked her breast in front of other people in the store, and nobody did anything.

Reem says that her main reaction to all of this was revulsion. But she was also ashamed. Ashamed of his attention, ashamed that she couldn't deflect it. She had no interest in Rob, who was thickset, blond, and ruddy-faced, but after he'd corner her or whisper some graphic obscenity, she'd find herself feeling aroused, and then disgusted by her own arousal. It felt like their interactions were "taking place in an alternate horror universe" where she was not in control of her own body. She began responding to his solicitations—to meet him in the hallway, to wait for him by his car. "It was so confusing. And disgusting. It wasn't rape because I wasn't screaming no, but I wasn't saying yes." When she talks about their relationship she uses the phrases "under a spell" or "like I was drugged." Of their interactions, she says she "put a cover over it" and did not think of it much beyond the immediacy of their time together. She continued with her college applications, kept dating her boyfriend, and still hung out with her friends. She tried to maintain a firm separation between her time with Rob and her normal life. All the same, episodes of "doom" and "ruin" would occasionally overwhelm her. There was no one she could talk to, except for Rob, who would comfort her when she cried by offering crude compliments, like "Coffee is my favorite ice cream flavor," in reference to the color of her skin.

After a period of some months, Rob moved to another state and their interactions abruptly ceased. That fall, Reem went to college, and she quickly became absorbed in new challenges and friendships. Rob would sometimes come to mind, but the memory was too hot to the touch, and she sequestered it away.

For nearly twenty-five years, Rob remained in a banished corner of Reem's mind. But recently, memories of their relationship had started to invade like "fire ants." When I asked Reem why she thought Rob had come back into her thoughts, she launched into a seemingly different story. A year ago, she'd had a complication in pregnancy that had resulted in a miscarriage well into the second trimester. It would have been her third child, a much-desired daughter after having two sons. The experience of losing the fetus was deeply upsetting, both physically and emotionally, and in the period thereafter Reem was often weepy and angry and felt overwhelmed. Her husband wanted to try for another child, but Reem wasn't ready. Still, she felt her husband was pressing her for sex. She wanted space, she wanted time. His persistent efforts to touch and cuddle with her at first annoyed her and then became a sort of agony. She snapped at him, she pushed him away. She avoided doing anything that might excite him. Sometimes she made up excuses to sleep on the couch. And as though out of nowhere, the memory of Rob returned to her. She'd wake up in the middle of the night, panicked. "My thoughts were stuck. It was loss, loss for my baby and then fear, like something bad was about to happen. I could feel it."

▼▲▼▲▼

Given the real and potential hazards to women's minds and bodies that saturate our modern culture and our private lives, it is nearly impossible to avoid interfacing with sexual violence on a regular basis. And these encounters shape the extent to which we are able to feel safe in our bodies and entitled to pleasure. All around us, popular media depicts abuses with an odd mix of sensationalism and nonchalance. At one extreme, the news feasts on atrocity, inviting us to ogle at the most deranged and least suspecting predators, reminding us that we need to be ever on guard, because danger lurks all around. The tendency for the media to focus on the most heinous crimes—gang rape, murder, abduction—runs the risk of minimizing the far more prevalent realities of victimization. Most assailants are known entities; most sexual assaults don't maul the body. Sexual violence is often a theft of dignity that occurs largely out of view, which, by not reporting, by overlooking, the media essentially normalizes. Rather than taking stock of daily crimes and degradations, and hammering away at these points as the public health crisis they represent, we circulate isolated instances of brutality across both the news and our personal social feeds. As a result, we often see sexual violence as a spectacle rather than an endemic so-cial ill that requires our full imagination and commitment to address meaningfully.

These stories also traffic in assumptions about women secretly wanting or deserving it. Variations on *she had it coming* display a re-markable tenacity in both private accounts and public reporting. No-elle, above, literally *beat herself up* after she was attacked. Or consider the *New York Times* coverage of a gang rape in Texas in 2011.[16] Not only does the report reference the fate of the perpetrators before describing the abuse they inflicted ("These boys have to live with this the rest of their lives"), but the editors, who have since apologized, also saw fit to include details implicating the eleven-year-old victim: "They said she dressed older than her age, wearing makeup and fashions more appro-priate to a woman in her 20s. She would hang out with teenage boys at a playground."

At the other extreme, these forms of violence are depicted casually, in the sense of their omnipresence. Across media, and especially in the flaming pot of controversy that is pornography, women are routinely placed in violent—and moreover, sexually violent—scenarios in-tended to arouse. Some studies of the $97 billion industry, whose out-put dwarfs that of Hollywood, suggest that a majority of porn features violence against women in the form of physical harm, domination, or forced sex. Gail Dines, author of *Pornland: How Porn Has Hijacked Our Sexuality*, makes the staggering claim that 88 percent of pornogra-phy contains violence against women. While other reports offer more "modest" figures, critics nonetheless argue that it promotes gendered aggression and the abandonment of empathy. To some this situation begs a return to the age-old question of how fantasy and real life in-tersect: Is the former a low-stakes ground for exploring the taboo, or does it seed desire and come to influence what we do and how we feel? But in porn, unlike an erotic daydream, individuals are consuming ready-made content. The question, then, is whether the pornographic marketplace actually represents consumer predilections or ends up creating and refining taste. Even if watching tiny girls get "destroyed" is not your cup of tea, it acquires real erotic power when it is the im-age accompanying one's orgasm. As noted in the previous chapter, we *learn* to find things sexy, and so one comes to equate pleasure with the

MILF, the sexy stepdaughter, the recalcitrant neighbor, the humiliated employee, etc.

A number of the women I spoke with had no problem with porn, and thought that any troubles it posed were largely theoretical. Some enjoyed it themselves, specifically extolling more feminist or avant-garde varieties, such as the films of Erika Lust. Others were reluctant to weigh in against pornography: to be anti-porn was akin to being anti-liberal, or to identify with a brand of feminism dubbed "sex-negative." Proponents of porn paint it as a matter of free speech, privacy, and the sanctity of consumer choice. Some suggest that the pornographic saturation of everyday culture has coincided with decreased rates of violence against women, and further argue that it contributes to women's sexual (and economic) liberation.[17] But to its detractors, porn represents an unsettling mirror, a debasement of human sensuality, and a form of "cultural violence."[18]

One woman in her early forties told me she feels pressure to be *whatever* about porn. "I choose my battles," she said. However, when she comes across reminders that her husband watches "barely legal" and double-penetration videos of girls who "look like ragdolls," she feels alarmed. "For one thing, these are girls about half my age. But then I think, what about our daughter?" For others, there was a real sense of unease that their partners masturbated to images of violation, whether implicit or explicit. One woman who had been molested by a family member shared that she feels triggered by knowing how common incest-themed porn is: terms like "stepmom," "mom," and "teen" rank among the most searched terms.[19] As researchers and industry insiders observe, pornography consumption is often about a search for extremes. Users habituate to acts that were formerly considered fringe, and so the edge becomes the middle.

In the United States, efforts to regulate or even publicly contend with porn have occurred in a typically misguided fashion. Pornography use has been swept up in quasi-hysteria over its role in "sex addiction," a deeply contested label. Herein, the problem is the beleaguered man who cannot forge meaningful relationships owing to his compulsive onanism; of less concern is the fact that young men and women are being introduced to sex through explicit, frequently unrealistic, and at times violent media. Meanwhile, other countries have begun to view pornography as a facet of gendered risk. In the United Kingdom, government-backed inquiries into sexual harassment, online abuse, and violence have highlighted the ways in which pornography contributes to negative beliefs with very real consequences for the lives of women and girls. Feminist researcher Julia Long believes that pornography functions as a symbolic language that justifies direct and indirect abuse. Ideas originating in porn, she says, do make their way into the mainstream, and cumulatively they relay "that the defining feature of women's bodies is that they are available and violable."[20]

▼▲▼▲▼

We now have an increasingly comprehensive language for talking about the aftermath of violence. In a little more than one hundred years we have moved from thinking about traumatic stress in terms of one person reacting pathologically to a past event to a dynamic response seen as a normal human strategy for coping with pain and suffering. We understand that violations live on in the body. And we realize, moreover, that trauma need not be direct to be experienced; these days, terms like collective, secondary, and vicarious trauma are in circulation. Research is even beginning to dig into how trauma is heritable, altering genetic expression through the generations and transforming an individual's biological disposition to risk and resilience.[21]

But for all the nuance of these conversations, they miss something crucial that I kept picking up on in my conversations with women, which is that contemporary life often *feels* unsafe. As women, we live in constant proximity to risk. Irrespective of whether the women I interviewed had directly contended with some form of abuse, a number of them spoke of feeling sexually numb, shut down, and anesthetized, or conversely, edgy and distractible—feelings that are commonly associated with trauma. Their sensations, or lack thereof, point to how simply being a woman in our hypersexual, hyper-objectifying, casually violent, racist society affects the body in much the same way as an episode of overt abuse. To make sense of why it is that so many women struggle to fully enjoy their own sexuality, we need to be aware of how this landscape of hazard can undermine the strength and integrity of our desire, and we need to return to the body as a source of healing and pleasure. Sexual violence is by definition an assault to our sexuality, and recovery therefore requires that we heal our sexual selves, which includes finding a sense of embodied self-worth and entitlement. Desire wants safety, respect, physical comfort, self-compassion, full body awareness, and, crucially, choice—all qualities that are missing in and affected by sexual trauma. But fortunately, these are qualities that can be learned and met. If women have been wounded, directly or indirectly, in their sexuality, then it is in the realm of their erotic power that recovery is possible.

5 TRADITION AND ITS DISCONTENTS

We drove to the hotel and said goodbye. How
hypocritical to go upstairs with a man you don't want
to fuck, leave the one you do sitting there alone, and
then, in a state of great excitement, fuck the one you
don't want to fuck while pretending he's the one you
do. That's called fidelity. That's called monogamy.
That's called civilization and its discontents.
   —*Erica Jong,* Fear of Flying, *1973*

There is hardly any activity, any enterprise, which is
started with such tremendous hopes and expectations,
and yet, which fails so regularly, as love.
   —*Erich Fromm,* The Art of Loving, *1956*

IN 1979, THE *New York Times* ran a grabbing headline: "Is There Sex
After Marriage?" The article observed that married people were having
less sex than previously assumed, and the reason, it seemed, was that
they simply didn't want to. Low desire was to blame. It quoted a psychiatrist, Harold Lief, who joked about the matter: "A man recovering from
illness is told not to get too excited about sex. 'That's easy,' he says. 'I'll
make love to my wife.'" Carol Botwin, who wrote the article, took pains
to explain the punch line: "Many men feel that making love to the same
woman inevitably becomes boring." However, she declared, "a great reversal has occurred." Suddenly, it was women who were becoming tired

of routine, prompting Botwin to ask, "Is there something in our culture that feeds this inhibition? Or is the destruction of passion built into marriage itself?"[1]

Lief at the time was in the midst of developing a theory of low desire as a psychological condition. In parallel, a sex therapist, Helen Singer Kaplan, was challenging Masters and Johnson's human sexual response cycle. Missing in their model of excitement, plateau, resolution, and orgasm, she claimed, was a desire phase, which was the most important part, as it triggered the rest of the human sexual response. Lief's and Kaplan's observations, developed independently, were incorporated into what soon became a new malady in the third edition of the DSM, published in 1980: inhibited sexual desire. It quickly became the most prevalent sexual complaint among American women and is said to affect some 10 to 55 percent of us, depending on age group.[2]

Kaplan, who considered desire to be a basic human urge, like hunger or thirst, was convinced that low desire was on the rise and laid a share of the blame on what she called "the new hot monogamy."[3] Writing in the mid-1990s, she looked to the 1960s and 1970s as a time when the stakes for engaging in sexual experiments were relatively low. Between access to the pill and a dose of penicillin, there was little to stop the bored or libertine couple from enjoying the occasional dalliance. It was AIDS, she said, that slammed the brief "window of sexual opportunity" shut. Nonetheless, she did not believe that the virus would defeat the sexual revolution. "In my opinion," she wrote, "once having experienced sexual freedom and tasted the joys of 'hot' sex—sexual experiences enhanced by novelty, variety, erotica, fantasy, and variant sexual practices—people will never again content themselves with the lackluster, boring, passionless, mechanical sex that characterized so many marriages in the past."[4]

Kaplan did not foresee the strength of the conservative recoil or how forcefully marriage would be reconfigured as *the* container for sexual fulfillment in the years to come. Women and men alike began to set higher standards for satisfaction, but the proper outlet was still the pair bond, which was meant to be a source of personal growth and erotic gratification. Its success, meanwhile, was increasingly viewed as a result of hard work and commitment. Even as the public culture became more openly sexual, marriage was becoming more insistently romantic, with couples placing a greater premium on monogamy and personal realization. These days we seem to want it all, and as a result we're asking for more and more of a single freighted union. Kaplan's observations beckon a return to Botwin's question. Perhaps more relevant than asking whether the "destruction of passion is built into marriage itself," we should consider how changing expectations for sex in marriage have altered the landscape of desire.

DEAD BEDROOMS AND OTHER HYSTERIAS

Over the past several decades, as women entered the workforce in record numbers, divorce rates spiked and leveled, and new evidence for widespread infidelity slunk into view, this question acquired a churning urgency. Strange bedfellows have gathered here, with anti-divorce crusaders and progressive pleasure enthusiasts all clamoring to improve the state of married sexuality. Far too many of America's partnerships, we're told, are dangerously skimming the borders of sexlessness. The desire for our second half is plummeting, and perhaps the reason is that as we've surged toward ideals of tender complementarity, we've lost the sense of *otherness* on which desire feasts. These trends have researchers polling bedroom acts and the popular presses running wild with tracts like *Red Hot Monogamy*.

And yet, it is a deeply uneasy area of inquiry. Even as the statistics tell us that more than half of marriages end in divorce, Americans appear more invested in the tradition than ever—the wedding industry is currently valued at a whopping $72 billion a year in the United States alone, where the average cost of tying the knot is now over $30,000.[5] And even though marriage rates have declined over the past few decades, with roughly half of adults currently married, compared to over 70 percent in the 1960s, rates of remarriage and cohabitation are on the rise. Some 80 percent of Americans will still likely marry at some point in their lifetimes.[6] As commentators debate whether the institution is bound for obsolescence, the married and would-be married are granting it greater significance. To an unprecedented degree, Americans look to their partners for more than just economic support, reproductive contributions, and friendship: they also want passion, thrill, and existential meaning.

While this emphasis may seem normal in our culture of soul-mate searching, it is actually a relatively new phenomenon in the sweep of human history. Some view the emphasis on romantic passion, paradoxically, as a leading cause of the institution's decline. Stephanie Coontz is a historian of the family based out of the Evergreen State College in Washington state. For millennia, she says, economic security was the sine qua non of marriage, with notions of romance barely registering as a reason for partnership. Marriage was a means of making alliances, allocating resources, divvying up labor, and raising the next generation. It was not until the nineteenth century that love and mutual pleasure came into the picture. The Victorians celebrated the idea of affection between husband and wife. They upheld tenderness in partnership, though at the same time they harbored rigid views of male and female sexuality. In the Victorian imagination, women were notoriously sexless. Good wives complied with the appetites of their husbands in the name of speciation and keeping the peace, while prostitution flourished as a "necessary evil" to protect the domestic sphere from men's more animal tendencies. Only in the twentieth century did married romance become linked to sensual intimacy: mutual pleasure was now seen as the key to strong unions. This emphasis on reciprocity made partnerships more democratic, but with these gains came new stressors, Coontz told me. "New expectations were piled onto marriage—many of which were good. But they occurred in tandem with new pressures, sex among them, as well as diminished expectations for social life outside of marriage."

Today, both women and men have high aspirations for sexual fulfillment in marriage—hopes reinforced by both science and popular media. Desire is not supposed to dim, sex is supposed to only get better with age, and well-matched couples supposedly continue to gaze at one another with unflagging ardor year upon year. We humans are also living far longer, and expectations for steamy sex now carry over into later life in an unprecedented way. The graying of the Baby Boomers has brought with it new challenges for maintaining desire and sexual function into decades once consigned to armchair compatibility. Marty Klein, a sex therapist, told me that "successful aging" means staying in the mood, and yet Boomers are having a hard time reconciling reality with expectations for frisky monogamy through old age. Sold on the idea of an unending honeymoon, women and men alike crash hard against the actuality of long-term partnerships and the balancing act of work, family life, individual development, health, aging, and habituation. Popular neuroscience further condemns us to more modest expectations, as the chemicals that auger attraction are steadily replaced by concoctions better suited for snuggling. Most of the statistics don't look very pretty, with research linking low desire to marriage, infrequent orgasms to heterosexual partnerships, and the gradual cessation of sexual activity to long-term monogamy.

It was long supposed (and remains broadly assumed) that the crash landing is hardest for men. (In 2008 *Psychology Today* blurted out, "An Inconvenient Truth: Sexual Monogamy Kills Male Libido."[7]) The subject of desire discrepancy—a clinical term for *honey I've got a headache*—gets a fair amount of airtime these days. Presumably, the wife is the one with less interest, or at least the public is routinely taken aback by the idea that the man can also lose steam. (The *New York Times* recently considered "When the Cause of a Sexless Relationship Is— Surprise!—the Man."[8]) This differential appetite is often cast in simple and unyielding terms: some people have roaring libidos, while for others it's more of a whimper. This view, while helpful in terms of providing nicer language for it than, say, frigidity, does not necessarily capture the elasticity of lust over time. Women, especially, experience major divots around pregnancy, lactation, and menopause, which can last for years or alter the shape of desire indefinitely. There is also the growing battery of pharmaceutical products to contend with—roughly one in six adult women take libido-dampening antidepressants (twice the number of men prescribed the medication).[9] And overcoming the changed terrain can require careful negotiation. Insofar as desire is a "use it or lose it" urge, it can be hard to muster enthusiasm after prolonged spells of infrequent activity, let alone after extended periods of pain.

But the flailing winds of our attention have begun to settle around the proposition that women, perhaps more than men, chafe against expectations for having sex with the same person year in and year out. Instead of furthering the view that women's libidos start low and thereafter plummet, researchers have begun to ask whether monogamy is the culprit of women's sexual malaise. Perhaps the issue is not that women don't want to have sex, but that they don't want to have sex with their husbands. An infamous cartoon from *The New Yorker* in 2001 captured this possibility nicely. A woman confides to a friend over drinks: "I was on hormone replacement for two years before I realized what I really needed was Steve replacement."[10]

Science is starting to bear this theory out. One recent study of men and women ages eighteen to twenty-five found that for each additional month that the female participants were in a relationship with the same partner, their sexual desire decreased, while men's desire held roughly stable over time.[11] Indiana University researchers Aaron Carroll and Rachel Vreeman reported that women's libidos tend to go down when they stick with one person long term. They noted, "While some would say that this means women have an easier time being monogamous because their sex drive has gone down, sex experts would say this is not the healthy state for these women."[12]

ISOLATED AND OVEREXPOSED

For some women I spoke with, the realities of marriage were a disappointment following their high hopes for partnership. They expressed resentment over major problems and little slights alike, citing divergent views on financial priorities, unequal distribution of household labor, and routine omissions of domestic etiquette. Moreover, they felt bitter about assuming the lion's share of the material and emotional management of the home—whether it was planning meals for the week, figuring out who would watch the kids for the odd night out, or helping a toddler process problems at preschool. These tensions sometimes led to marital spats that cut directly into a couple's sex life, though more commonly they simply simmered.

But perhaps the most frequent story I heard chronicled the dueling hazards of overexposure and isolation. "We're like siblings," is how one woman described her partnership. "It's hard to get excited about the person I see every day." Another said, "We're roommates essentially. We talk at the end of the day, we make food, we watch TV, then we collapse." Another woman put it this way: "We've gone from husband and wife to being business partners running a small company"—the small company being her family.

Many women emphasized a rift between their love for their partners and their lost zeal for sex. A forty-year-old middle school teacher told me: "I come home, there are the kids, it's always this fire drill to get everyone fed, and cleaned and into bed, and then we eat, and it's like, oh it's you *again*. We finally get into bed and it's so obvious he wants to, and I'm like oh my god, you've got to be kidding me. Can't I just have a little space for myself?" A forty-five-year-old executive assistant described feeling erotically neutral toward her husband after more than a decade of marriage. "Early in our relationship I used to think about him. I liked his body. Just the look of his arms in a T-shirt." But now, she said, "He'll be taking a shower while I'm in the bathroom brushing my teeth, and the thought of joining him, or even looking at him, doesn't even cross my mind." A thirty-two-year-old nurse explained that she likes having sex with her husband of two years, "but it's not like I really *want* it." Back when they were dating, she said, "We would have sex every time we saw each other, and it was great. Each time there was this buildup. It was a sweet anticipation." But now, "I see him and it's like *oh that's nice*. I love him, I'm not unhappy, but I think that *grrrr I want you* is never coming back." For another thirty-two-year-old, distance played a big part in her attraction to her husband. They had dated while living in different cities for several years before getting married. "I looked forward to seeing him, planning what we would do, what I would wear." Now that they were married and living together, she said, "It's just different. I still love having sex with him, but it's coming from a different place. I'm not swept up. Sometimes I have to force myself."

The subject of compelling or convincing oneself to have sex came up repeatedly. A number of women described sex as a chore or obligation. "When I'm tired or not feeling into it, I'll do what I can to speed him along," one woman in her thirties told me. "I feel bad for him, I guess. And I know I should even if I don't really want to, so I'll do it and then try to get him to finish." Other women shared experiences of deliberately bypassing their own pleasure or pretending for the sake of getting their husbands off. Speaking of foreplay, one woman shared, "I'll have a big fake orgasm, and then just get him to fuck me. I like making him happy. Sometimes I can let go and get really into it, too, but for the majority of the time, I'm kind of half there."

I did not set out to find women who were sexually (or emotion-ally) discontent in their marriages, and my impression is that a lot of women would not describe themselves as unhappily wed. It was rather that married sexuality, as opposed to sex before, outside of, or in the early stages of partnership, sometimes ranged from pale to lusterless. As themes emerged—of monotony, of complacency, of lost autonomy ("I miss the old me"; "I can't believe I've become this person"; "Ugh, again")—it felt at times like an open secret that nuptial sexuality is sec-ond rate, or at least its own category of Eros. It's a familiar entity, it's often lost its edge, it contains neither heat nor mystery—and maybe it's for these reasons that women frequently described it in terms of la-bor. Popular wisdom holds that men want sex the most, but it is more often women who take it upon themselves to *work* on their sex lives. Even if sexual boredom is the habitual guest of most marriages, women still expressed surprise and sadness that it had shown up in their lives, and so they had taken it upon themselves to *fix the problem*. Whether that meant scheduling date nights, buying nighties, or schooling up on tricks to jumpstart their libidos, it was women who concerned them-selves with sexual frequency. They are, after all, the primary target for the booming spice-it-up market, whose chief message can be distilled in a single phrase: *just do it*.

"You just have to," said Vera, a Latina mother of two in her early forties. "You might not want to, but your marriage needs it." She looked at me with a leveled seriousness as she delivered this information. Vera is a successful media sales professional, who has also long struggled with crippling anxiety, for which she now takes medication. Following the birth of her first child, she said, her anxiety "went off the rails." She decided to quit her former job and to confront what felt like the end of her independence. "Every day felt the same, and I couldn't see a way out." From an active social life, she found herself suddenly at home alone with a squalling babe while her husband, who also works in me-dia, continued on, largely unaffected by this giant change. Vera wor-ried that she would become less appealing to her husband. "*I* thought I was uninteresting. He would come home and could talk about his day, and the people and projects he was working on, and all I had was the baby report. 'I bought new diapers.'" She also had a hard time ad-justing to the ways that pregnancy had altered her body and her desire.

The appearance of stretch marks, "this bloat," and significant hair loss made her self-conscious. "I think what I really needed was to hear, 'You're beautiful, you've been through so much, I love you more than ever, everything will be fine.' But I never got that," she said. Instead, "he blamed me for acting needy, he said he didn't recognize me. He said he missed the *old me*." Vera continued, "My father cheated on my mother. My stepfather cheated on my mother. I just needed to feel like things were solid." She worried that if she did not force herself to be sexual with her husband, he would take his passion somewhere else. "We used to have sex all the time, and after [the baby] was born I didn't even want to be touched." Her disinterest grew less acute with time, but it never returned to its former high. Her husband, in contrast, still had a "really big need for sex." These days, Vera said, they have sex about three times a week, in spite of her exhaustion, in spite of the demands that never respect the boundaries of the working day, in spite of the lust-sapping routine of bath and bedtime for the children. "There is no space for me," she said at one point in our conversation, but she quickly pivoted to declare, again, "You just have to do it. It's like anything else, it's something that has to get done."

I must have made a face when Vera said she had sex three times a week, because she paused and acknowledged, "Yeah, it's a lot." Was that gloating in her tone, was it exertion, or was it sheer relief? At least for the time being, she had brokered sex in exchange for her husband's commitment and steered clear of *dead bedroom* territory. As a nation, we are fixated on the subject of sexual frequency. We love to compare ourselves to the imagined practices of our neighbors, feeling boastful or chagrined, depending on how we size up. But just what are they doing? This is tough information to ferret out. We are notoriously unreliable narrators of our sexual lives: men report having more sex than they really have; women tend to report having less; the average confessional is *once or twice a week*. Nonetheless, we're gnawed by the question "Is it enough?" The media responds with a resounding *no*, and this, we're told, is a big problem. *Time* magazine reports: "Sex and health go hand in hand. Research has linked it to a slimmer waistline, a stronger heart and a lower risk for prostate and breast cancers. It's also a boon for mental health, since sex is associated with lower rates of depression and better mood. But Americans today are having less of it than Americans a decade ago."[13]

A 2017 study by researchers at San Diego State University used sexual frequency data from the General Social Survey, a nationally representative sample of more than twenty thousand adults created and managed by the National Opinion Research Center at the University of Chicago, and found that Americans who were married or living together had sex sixteen fewer times per year in 2010–2014 compared to 2000–2004.[14] ("It's Not Just You," the *New York Times* assured its readers.[15]) This marked a major reversal from previous patterns, said the report's lead author, psychologist Jean Twenge: "In the 1990s, married people had sex more times per year than never-married people, but by the mid-2000s that reversed, with the never-married having more sex." The research indicates that age is closely aligned with how much sex you have: people in their twenties report sex more than eighty times per year; by age forty-five, this figure declines to around once a week; and by sixty-five people average less than twice a month. The main takeaway is that older and married people are having less sex than in generations past. This trend has broad significance. In previous research, Twenge found that the overall happiness of adults over the age of thirty had declined since 2000. She noted, "With less sex and less happiness, it's no wonder that American adults seem deeply dissatisfied these days."

An authority no less illustrious than Dr. Phil has worried aloud that "sexless marriages are an undeniable epidemic."[16] Circulating statistics hold that around 15 to 20 percent of married couples have sex less than ten times per year—the apparent threshold for "sexless." And this is troubling, because healthy couples *should* be having sex about once a week, which experts say is the "optimal" amount (any more does not apparently confer tangible reward).[17] Such routine intimacy brings numerous benefits. Lower sexual frequency, according to an expert published by CNN, has been associated with psychological distress, anxiety, depression, and relationship problems.[18]

This question of frequency is a touchy one. Plenty of women I talked to were content with the quality of their sex lives but were sensitive to the irregularity of the act. One woman in her late thirties told me, "Two weeks will go by and we're like *woah* we should have sex." Or as another said, "We still love sex, don't get me wrong, it's just different. We used to spend the weekend without really leaving the house. Now it's like, okay, it's been a while. We should do this." That women, and men, feel pressure to engage in a certain amount of sex is hardly surprising given the messages that surround us. A 2012 essay in *The Guardian* framed the issue well: "Admit to having shoplifted. Admit to having a bit of a drink problem, or being bankrupt. But living in a sexless marriage? Never. Fidelity, monogamy, still sleeping with the same person after however many years—that is what we are all supposed to value most. To admit to anything else, is to admit to a societal failing so profound, so deep, so . . . almost spiritual, it's beyond the pale."[19]

▼▲▼▲▼

The fixation on sexual quantity—how much, how often—overlooks the crucial matter of sexual quality. All too often, frequency is bandied about as a shorthand for pleasure, but these statistics tell us little about whether women are enjoying the sex they have. The decline of women's sexual interest and satisfaction in marriage may also, and most significantly, be a reflection of the *kind* of sex that married couples tend to engage in. As noted in Chapter 2, penis-in-vagina penetration does not, on its own, have a great track record for conferring female pleasure. Even for newlywed couples, who are thought to still be in the honeymoon phase, men experience orgasm at nearly twice the rate of their female partners.[20] Women report needing other forms of stimulation, either in addition to or separate from penetrative sex, in order to fully enjoy themselves. Societally, we're only just beginning to appreciate what female-centered, or at least female-inclusive, heterosexuality might look like. While foreplay gets a lot more attention these days as a necessary warm-up, it still promotes the idea that caressing or cunnilingus are polite precursors to the *main* penetrative event, which is where time and expectations get piled on. Psychologist and sexologist Peggy Kleinplatz has argued that a lot of low desire simply stems from unfulfilling sex. If sex means perfunctory foreplay and race-to-the-finish-line penetration, she said, "it is hard to imagine why anyone would want it, not to mention why anyone would put up with such uninspired, bland, lackluster, and, indeed, undesirable sex."[21]

All the same, it is incredibly hard to break from the entrenched model that placing a penis in the vagina is the apex of erotic mingling. And it's not just that men are pushing for this as a trusted means of getting off. Women, too, continue to wrestle with the concept that insertive sex is the capstone to intimacy. However, this assumption may be undermining the strength of women's desire, making them less interested in sex with their partners.

A Canadian sexologist, Meredith Chivers, has devoted her career to understanding the variability of female sexuality. The director of the Sexuality and Gender Lab at Queen's University in Ontario, Chivers conducts psychophysiological research to understand *concordance*, that is, the relationship between mind and body when people get turned on. She and her research team outfit study participants with eye-tracking cameras and sensors that measure heart rate as well as genital response before sitting them down in La-Z-Boy recliners and showing them sexually explicit clips.

Her work has unearthed some surprising insights. For heterosexual men, physical and subjective responses to stimuli tend to closely map sexual preference. They find scenes of women, alone or together, and heterosexual couples to be arousing. Queer women also display a more specific response, reacting positively to images of other women. But heterosexual women are all over the place. Physiologically, they react to couples, men, women, even scenes of copulating bonobo apes. But when asked what they find arousing, they report a much narrower band of interest.

The media has been quick to interpret these findings as evidence that women's *real* desire is a base, animalistic, appetitive force that appears small only because culture tries to smother it.[22] Chivers told me, "We continually underestimate women's sexuality," and yet she cautioned against concluding that women's genital reactions are a truer marker of sexual interest than their subjective accounts. One of the pressing questions for her is why heterosexual women display seemingly indiscriminate patterns of arousal while admitting far less readily to being turned on.

One possibility, she offered, is that women are physically rearticulating their own objectification. The depiction of women as sexualized objects saturates Western media, and having marinated in this stew of representations, women may be responding accordingly. However, she noted, the existing data neither proves nor disproves this view. Another theory that she finds compelling is based on the idea that reward patterns our behavior: we desire certain things because we associate them with pleasure. For queer women, sexual intercourse is more consistently associated with orgasm and gratification, and so images of women will activate a clear positive response. But for heterosexual women, there is often no reinforcement of pleasure one way or another. Penetrative sex results in orgasm in only a minority of women, and for some, who equate it with, say, pain or guilt or effort, it may spark outright aversion.

Going back to the context of marriage: if bedroom life revolves around a modest preamble leading up to penile penetration, women may become increasingly uninterested in intimacy, because so far, it has routinely left them underwhelmed, if not sad, angry, or frustrated.

▼▲▼▲▼

Enter the experts. The market for improving marital sex is nothing short of booming these days, with countless titles promising a Lazarus-like resurrection of libido. For the woman in search of solutions to waning passion, there is seemingly no end of resources on how to *revive*, *restore*, *revitalize*, and *rejuvenate* sexual interest and bring desire *back to life*. Even when women boldly proclaim their disinterest—consider titles like *I'd Rather Eat Chocolate*, *I'm Not in the Mood*, and *Okay, So I Don't Have a Headache*—the underlying message is that there are still strategies you can and should employ to get in the mood. But for the abundance of how-to manuals, there is not a lot of variety in terms of the help that is offered. "Work at it," is a frequently touted prescription. Or foster greater emotional connection. Become passionate friends, improve communication. Don't sit around and wait for longing to ignite spontaneously: schedule time for intimacy—and, once again, *work* to make it a priority. Resuscitate the tricks from courtship: try dressing up a bit, do your hair, remember makeup? Flirt like this isn't someone whose dirty socks you wash and fold and who pees with the door open. Project an air of mystery onto a known entity.

One of the most prominent and persistent pearls of wisdom is the old Nike slogan: *just do it*. The biggest proponent of this advice is marriage therapist Michele Weiner-Davis, who says it's unreasonable that the partner with lower desire gets to set the sexual schedule. The *no's* have the veto power, she says; they control the frequency of sex, all the while expecting the deprived partner to stand by faithfully. Her advice is straightforward. Have sex. Even if you're not in the mood, maybe especially if you're not in the mood. Don't belabor excuses, just be a good sport. This message is the centerpiece of her 2003 best seller, *The Sex-Starved Marriage*, which a decade later was condensed into a TEDx talk that has been watched nearly 4.5 million times. It's a message that might well make you squeamish, particularly in the current moment as we reassess the meaning of power and consent. No still means no, Weiner-Davis recently assured a reporter for *The Guardian*. "But it helps to not just say no."[23]

As much as I bristle against this counsel, her thinking aligns with current ideas about the nature of desire. Helen Singer Kaplan viewed desire as a fundamental drive—as essential as hunger or thirst—but more recent theorists say this isn't quite correct. Desire is more likely a register of our sensitivity to stimuli or an awareness of physical sensation that grows in proportion to reward.[24] If we don't feed desire through fantasy, self-pleasuring, or partnered touch, interest in sex can wither. Despite the fact that the idea of a sexual drought is often presented in terms of mounting urgency—the longer you go without, the more you want it—the exact opposite is probably the case, making desire more like a muscle that can become more toned with exercise or atrophy without it. So, back to Weiner-Davis, *just doing it* might be a way to get over the hump.

Moreover, her prescribed hop-aboard-and-start-paddling approach reflects contemporary models for women's sexuality. Between 2001 and 2003, Rosemary Basson, who directs the Sexual Medicine program at the University of British Columbia, elaborated a new model for female sexual response.[25] In her clinical practice, Basson found that women's motivations for sex were not necessarily *sexual*, especially for women in long-term partnerships. Often, they wanted emotional intimacy or simply physical closeness, not necessarily the release of erotic tension. She began drawing circular diagrams to capture this complexity. First came incentives for sex, such as bonding. (Or, as others have theorized, relief of boredom, desire for revenge, mate-poaching, out of duty, for its usefulness as a sleep aid or for headache relief, or any of the other 230-plus reasons that have been identified.[26]) These were followed by sexual triggers—sights, smells, and touch, which produced arousal. And from arousal flowed desire.[27] Women might go into sex from an erotically neutral state but start getting excited midstream, which feeds their motivation for intimacy, and so the cycle continues. Unlike the traditional model, which has spontaneous desire linearly directing sexuality, Basson's circular model hinges on what she terms *responsive desire*. We may not be in the mood for sex, but once we get started we can still have a good time. Plenty have criticized this framework for, among other things, playing up the idea of female sexual passivity. But those criticisms notwithstanding, this view has been integrated into how clinicians and other experts, including Weiner-Davis, conceptualize desire.

Weiner-Davis runs an operation called The Divorce Busting Center, which offers struggling couples strategies for sticking together. A self-confessed marriage "zealot," she believes that divorce is a source of permanent pain and that couples are best served by figuring out how to make it work for the long haul. The context of divorce busting adds an appendage to her message: it becomes something like, "Do it—*or else*." The implicit threat for the sexually disinclined woman is that her partner will get it elsewhere, or worse, will leave.

While some women, like Vera, felt the force of this intimation, I am struck by how anachronistic this message has become. It seems like an artifact of a bygone era, when a wife's sexual availability made her (breadwinning) husband more likely to invest in a new Frigidaire. If he was pleased, it was a win-win all around. But today we have different narratives around the importance of sex in marriage. Running against the logic that sex helps to keep the peace is the notion that intimacy is about personal betterment, and contemporary behavior appears increasingly to favor the latter. Two pockets of data are especially illuminating.

First is the changing landscape of infidelity, in which women are increasingly the ones to get it elsewhere. For decades, research on infidelity demonstrated that men were more inclined to step outside of marriage. The controversy-stoked neuropsychiatrist Louann Brizendine even tells us that the "sexual pursuit area" of the male brain is 2.5 times the size of that of the female brain; never mind that most researchers have never identified said region.[28] Other sciencisms offer that people with more testosterone (i.e., men) are more likely to have affairs. Popular media has tended to report on these differences with a kind of palm-to-face redundancy: of course men cheat—they need to satisfy their soaring sex drives.

But new findings may be laying these weary arguments to rest. Women appear to be engaging in higher levels of extramarital sex than ever before, or at least admitting to it more (though one has to wonder if men in the past were liaising only with single ladies or other men). According to data from the General Social Survey, today's American wives are 40 percent more likely to cheat on their spouses than they were in 1990, while the number of husbands who report infidelity has stayed constant.[29] Researchers from Indiana University, the Kinsey Institute, and the University of Guelph found a slender infidelity divide, with 25 percent of men reporting extramarital sex compared to 19 percent of women.[30] When the data from the General Social Survey is parsed out by age, younger women—between the ages of eighteen and twenty-nine—actually report cheating at higher rates than their male contemporaries (11 percent versus 10 percent). Commentators speculate that this could be due to women's increased economic independence (women "can afford the potential consequences of an affair, with higher incomes and more job prospects," sociologist Pepper Schwartz has said).[31] A 2011 study from researchers in the Netherlands argued that infidelity was a function of greater economic and social power.[32] With improved financial autonomy and social clout, women were as likely to cheat as men. Others have implicated the Internet and dating apps, along with the relative ease with which someone can now hook up with a stranger or reconnect with an old flame.

In recent years it has become almost fashionable to depict women as ill-suited to monogamy. A new generation is challenging the idea that women are inherently less sexual than men, and arguing that women might not be engineered for traditional marriage after all.[33] Christopher Ryan and Cacilda Jethá's gleeful romp through the evidence, *Sex at Dawn*, makes the case that our human ancestors enjoyed an abundance of sex. It was a shared resource for our nomadic forebears, who cared little about knowing exactly whose baby was whose. The authors invoke research indicating that women are simply more malleable or have greater *erotic plasticity* than men—that is, they are able to shift their behaviors in accordance with the changing social tide. That enabled them to weather the changes brought about by the agricultural revolution, which introduced private property and with it fixations on paternity. But while women may be conditioned to like, or at least tolerate, what society expects of them, according to Ryan and Jethá, men tend to tire of the relative monotony of monogamy.

Journalist Daniel Bergner has carried this line of reasoning into the present. In his thoughtful survey of the scientists who are working to address dips in women's libido, he came to the conclusion that culture has been the cruel warden of female nature, exercising such a stern watch that women struggle to decipher their own arousal. As a result, the truth of female sexuality has been misconstrued. The assumption that "female eros is much better made for monogamy than the male libido," he wrote, "is scarcely more than a fairy tale."[34]

Perhaps more telling is the second pocket of data, which focuses on who terminates a partnership. Women have been positively harangued by the message that their supposedly unsatisfied husbands might leave them if they don't make themselves sexually agreeable. But recent research from Stanford sociologist Michael Rosenfeld has found that women initiate divorce 69 percent of the time and that, compared with men, they report lower satisfaction with marriage overall. Among college-educated couples, women initiate divorce in a staggering 90 percent of cases. This is not a wholly new finding; scientists have known for decades that women ask for divorce in higher numbers, leading some to speculate that women are simply more sensitive to relationship issues and are therefore more prone to opt out. But Rosenfeld, in a survey of more than 2,200 adults, also looked at people in nonmarital relationships, from casual flings to long-term partnerships. In these pairs, men and women broke it off in about equal numbers. Rosenfeld concluded that there must be something in particular about marriage that makes it more challenging for women.[35]

One woman who was twenty-three years old in 2009, when Rosenfeld first began the study, reported that her relationship was "good" (a 4 on a scale of 1 to 5). Of her husband, she said, "He is very clever, fun, and sweet. I respect him and feel like we are equals on values, intellect and humor." Four years later the couple got divorced. In 2015, she said, "I used to be a very happy optimistic person and it was like he was slowly starving my soul."[36]

Recent analyses of American attitudes have found that even though most of the population supports the idea of women having careers, a substantial minority of people still believe that women should do more of the childrearing and homemaking than men.[37] Rosenfeld offered, "I think that marriage as an institution has been a little slow to catch up with expectations for gender equality. Wives still take their husbands surnames, and are sometimes pressured to do so. Husbands still expect their wives to do the bulk of the childcare." He said this dissatisfaction reflected what sociologists call "the stalled gender revolution," meaning that even as women's societal roles have evolved, women's position in the family has lagged behind.[38]

EQUALITY AND EROS

The view that marriage feels suffocating to women is not new. Decades ago, writer and activist Betty Friedan documented the enervation of America's wives, and the years since have reaped a plentiful but grim harvest of evidence cataloging how marriage can damage a woman's personal well-being, social satisfaction, and professional ambitions. In the early 1980s, sociologist Jessie Bernard argued that the gap in men's and women's experiences of marriage was so great that it comprised two separate institutions—"his" and "hers" marriages. Bernard argued that "marriage introduced such profound discontinuities into the lives of women as to constitute emotional health hazards."[39] Some of her contemporaries proclaimed that because marriage placed less value on the woman's role and constrained that role more than the man's into the bargain, it increased the risk of mental illness among women.[40] But despite her scathing assessment, Bernard speculated that shifting gender roles and the general drift toward parity would create the "future of marriage," which she envisioned as providing equal benefits to men and women.

Her ideas laid firm foundations for the researchers who would come to consider the problem of marital unhappiness and how to solve it. If marriage is unequal and grants greater advantages to men than to women, then the answer must be to level the playing field. This logic is keenly felt in today's discussions on how to address women's sexual discontent. In a word, get men to take on more of the "second shift."[41] To some observers, this is *the* cause of women's waning passion. A *Newsweek* feature put the matter starkly: women aren't in the mood because they're shouldering the burden of managing the home, and smoldering resentment has mined their lust.

"A lot of women out there are mad," *Newsweek* said. "Working mothers, stay-at-home moms, even women without kids. They're mad that their husband couldn't find the babysitter's home number if his life depended on it. Mad that he would never think to pick up diapers or milk on his way home. Mad that he doesn't have to sing all the verses of 'The Wheels on the Bus' while trying to blow-dry his hair."[42]

Accordingly, a host of advice pipes in that more egalitarian arrangements pave the way to domestic bliss. A Parenting.com poll in January 2008 found that 15 percent of moms were "most turned on by 'chore-play,' i.e., Dad helping with the dishes, laundry, etc."[43] *Playboy* tells its readers that sharing housework "can save your sex life."[44] One study of American husbands even went so far as to quantify just how much more sex the man might enjoy by pitching in around the house (one additional tumble per month), prompting CBS to exclaim: "Men: Want More Sex? Do the Laundry!"[45]

But even as we creep toward more equitable home arrangements, some experts caution that egalitarianism may actually be the undoing of Eros. A wave-making 2013 study in the *American Sociological Review* found that, notwithstanding choreplay wisdom, the more a couple divvies up household tasks, the less sex they have. Men's housework, the authors concluded, does not make their wives more sexually available; rather, "for all the benefits of peer marriage, more egalitarian couples are more likely to have unsatisfactory sex lives and experience a lack of passion due to habituation, and these differences are not explained by a shortage of time."[46] Lori Gottlieb, a couples therapist, considered these results in a cover story for *The New York Times Magazine* with the alarming headline "Does a More Equal Marriage Mean Less Sex?" The very suggestion is enough to make feminism flinch. All the same, Gottlieb underscored how more fluid gender roles at home (defined rather uncreatively as men sharing in "feminine" duties, such as vacuuming) resulted in fewer rounds in the sack than more traditional gendered roles did, where men's responsibilities were confined to men's work, like fixing stuff. Gottlieb reported that she had observed this conundrum in her clinical practice.

"No matter how much sink-scrubbing and grocery-shopping the husband does," she wrote, "no matter how well husband and wife communicate with each other, no matter how sensitive they are to each

other's emotions and work schedules, the wife does not find her husband more sexually exciting, even if she feels both closer to and happier
with him."[47]

Her observations led to an uncomfortable conclusion. Modern partnerships may be more companionable and respectful than they once
were, but these leveled terms lack some essential frisson. Equality might
be a noble social goal, but perhaps human sexuality is not politically
correct. Psychologist Marta Meana suggests it's not. Her work takes issue with the idea that women's desire tends to dim because that is the
natural life course of female sexuality. In one qualitative study of married women she investigated the subject of their waning passion. Going
against the formula that emotional attachment is women's strongest
aphrodisiac, she found that marital closeness and comfort had led to
"efficient but boring sex."[48] Women's sexual desire was undercut by familiarity, the institutionalization of the relationship, and desexualized
roles. It appeared that intimacy itself, while an important precursor for
some, led to diminished desire for others. One woman in her study explained: "You go from being real careful around each other and being
on your best behavior. . . . Then, of course, you start to get comfortable with one another and that changes—your bad habits come out,
your bad moods come out. That takes some of the desire away whereas
when you are dating, it's just so sexual and so amazing and so exciting. . . . Desire dwindles as you become a couple."[49]

Meana has further chipped away at the idea that women pine
for emotional connection and that a good relationship guarantees
good sex. "If safety, comfort, love, and respect were as facilitative to
female sexual desire as some of the relationally focused literature
claims," she said, "then we should not see as many married women
in happy relationships complaining of low desire."[50] Instead, women
want to be wanted—passionately, perhaps with overriding abandon. They may want to be married to a nice and thoughtful peer, but
where it comes to sex, they want to feel raw and unencumbered lust.
One of Meana's graduate students, Evan Fertel, has reviewed this area
of research, noting that these tendencies are evident in women's sexual fantasies—an area long considered to provide unique insight into
women's "nature." Here researchers have repeatedly observed that
women are not daydreaming about cuddling. Rather, they want to be

dominated, overcome, and overwhelmed. Some maintain that being desired is the most common refrain in women's fantasies, and that even when women incorporate a partner's pleasure and arousal in those fantasies, it is chiefly as a measure of how desirable she is. One pair of researchers put it thusly: "The man focuses on the woman's body, whereas the woman focuses on the man's interest in her body."[51]

Meana's research supports what therapist Esther Perel has observed in her clinical practice. It is not intimacy, but distance, that feeds desire. Echoing Stephanie Coontz's observation that marriage has become a search for existential meaning, Perel has maintained that modern couples expect their partnerships to be transcendent—they want their partners to be their best friends (as well as doting co-parents), *and* they want an explosively good sex life.[52] Such expectations, she said, have brought seemingly irreconcilable needs into contact. Men and women look to their spouses for comfort, familiarity, and security, and yet it is mystery, distance, and *otherness* that fan the flames of lasting passion.

▼▲▼▲▼

The contention that women crave domination sat uncomfortably with me for some time. Did it suggest a return to the kind of advice extolled by antiquated marriage manuals: women demonstrate their sexual health by surrendering to men, whose adequacy is defined by their aggression? Like so many women, I have invested a lot in creating a marriage that is based on fundamental equality, and the thought that this might tank my sex life is unsettling, to say the least. Some have interpreted women's longing for erotic domination as an indication that they want to be able to surrender control in at least one aspect of their lives, that is, to relinquish all competing demands so that they can give themselves over to the delights of intimacy. Less happily, other researchers have speculated that women's yen for domination, and even their tendency to enjoy occasional fantasies of rape and coercion, may speak to how uncomfortable they feel in their own longing. By framing sex as something they are forced to do, they bypass the inner voice that tells them sex and their desire for it are wrong. The fantasy allows them to sustain their relative innocence.

But as I spoke with women about what makes for good sex, the meaning of domination started to shift in my head. The second half of this book looks at how women experience satisfaction and considers how they define their own desire, lust, and satiation. A persistent theme was presence. Being fully there, transported, carried away. Enjoyable sex was not a matter of technique or position, it was the sensation of being completely wrapped up in it. One woman told me that she only had orgasms when she felt "absolute presence. He's gazing into my eyes. He's totally on me." Another woman put it in the context of an extra-marital relationship: "I was totally desired, he would devour me. It was like we weren't just having sex. I became my body." For her, there was a brief window when sex eclipsed the workaday, and she could be fully in the moment without thinking about the kids, her job, or the shifting of the domestic sands. A married woman told me that when the sex was *great*, she felt "the electricity of being alive. . . . The boundaries break down." This woman also said that in the context of physically merging, she became more aware of herself and experienced "total sensation, total involvement." These comments suggest that the desire to be dominated does not necessarily mean that women want to be overwhelmed by their partners; rather, they want to be overcome by the sheer force of experience.

PART 2

CLOSING THE GAP

6 IT'S ALL IN YOUR HEAD

We find no advantage in taking a principled stand against pharmaceutical research and treatment for women's sexual complaints. . . . The fact is, we need the whole bag of magic beans. That said, at this moment, we are not sure that any magic bean at all will be forthcoming any time soon.

—*Sandra Leiblum, "Pharmacotherapy for Women," 2005*

To develop drugs to boost libido is like "giving antibiotics to pigs because of the shit they're standing in."

—*Christopher Ryan, personal communication, 2015*

AT THE 2014 FDA meeting on female sexual dysfunction, I met a woman named Julie. I noticed that, unlike most attendees, she was not wearing a badge announcing her professional affiliation. When I asked what had brought her there, she said, "Personal reasons." A white Philadelphian in her early forties, Julie works peripherally in health care and has been following the developments in the women's libido market with interest. A few years earlier, she had noticed her desire for her husband taking a perceptible dip. Her gynecologist assured her this was a near-universal phenomenon, but all the same encouraged her to *do something* to fix it. She and her husband attended couples therapy, which Julie said did wonders for their communication. But it did not do much to incite her lust.

When we met, Julie was using an off-label testosterone cream that has shown mixed results in boosting women's desire and arousal. She

didn't think it was having much of an effect on her, but she was so chagrined by her low libido that she was willing to experiment with just
about anything. A much-planned romantic escape had recently brought
on a confrontation. In the weeks preceding, Julie had squirmed when
her husband had said it didn't much matter where they went, since they
would spend the whole time in bed. He felt excitement; she felt mounting trepidation. And as it turned out, the trip was hardly the erotic interlude her husband had been anticipating. Julie filled their time with
excursions, hikes, and dinners, all the while loving his company but
shrinking from his touch. And when they did, inevitably, end up in
bed, she found herself numbed and disengaged, willing it to be over.
After one particularly disheartening episode, she locked herself in the
bathroom and cried.

Her husband was hardly oblivious, but Julie said, "He was convinced
this was just a phase, that I'd get over it." Julie promised to address the
issue. But even as she gave him assurances of love and lasting affection,
her thoughts snagged on how this was packaged as *her* problem. That
didn't seem quite fair.

The idea that the passions we describe as love might be subject to
forces beyond our control—hormones, age, habituation—is distaste-
ful to her. As it is to many. It doesn't mesh with our most cherished
notions of abiding adoration, our soul-mate myths, the hope that once
you've found *the one*, you are forever fixed in doting partnership. For
Julie, thinking that her fading lust was not a side effect of long-term
monogamy, or a demanding job, or mothering two children, but instead a medical problem that could be solved, was a deeply appealing,
even faith-preserving, way to deal with the situation.

▼▲▼▲▼

For about as long as humans have recorded their time on earth, they've
mulled the vagaries of pleasure and fecundity. And across time and
cultures, the lore of lust-inflaming substances has held a cherished
place. The term *aphrodisiac* comes from the Greek Goddess of Love
herself, Aphrodite, whose arrival from sea to foamy shore atop a scal-
lop shell has fueled our faith in the magical properties of mollusks.
The famed Roman physician Galen prescribed eating oysters as a way
to brighten dimmed desire—though he was also of the mind that
flatulence-inducing foods would bring *wind* to the penis, thus making

it erect.[1] St. Thomas Aquinas held that good old wine and meat should do the trick, while in Asia, the tiger penis, the rhino horn, and the sea cucumber have all been lauded for their potent qualities. Our forebears have tinkered with the ingestion of Bufo toad skin, the Spanish fly, and live beetles.[2] According to one Mayo Clinic neurologist, a poop-like substance called *ambrien* derived from the guts of sperm whales was used in Arab folk medicine to bolster sensual delight. Even humble tubers have been prized for containing special powers. "Let it rain potatoes!" cried the ruffled suitor Falstaff in Shakespeare's *Merry Wives of Windsor*. (In *Troilus and Cressida*, things get even steamier: "How the devil Luxury [lust], with his fat rump and potato finger, tickles these together! Fry, lechery, fry!" says a character described in the Dramatis Personae as a "scurrilous Grecian.") Aphrodite was also supposed to have considered sparrows sacred, leading later Europeans to feast upon bird brains. This practice, the food philosopher Dwight Furrow drily observed, "shows that it doesn't take much to persuade people when the promise of sex is involved."[3]

Today the search for a quick fix for our erotic troubles continues unabated. But instead of scavenging the garden or the forest floor, we've set our sights on modern chemistry to get us in the mood. Men, as we all know, have Viagra and a cabinet of competitors, which, while potent, tend to take a simplistic view of sexuality. Men want to have sex, it's assumed, but physically cannot, and so a feat of hydraulics allows them to consummate the act.[4] But for women, the problem is more, well, problematic: they might be physically capable, but emotionally disinclined. We know that low desire is women's most common sexual complaint. As such it represents a hot market that has multiple labs and drug companies scrambling to find or refine the compound that will move us from disinterest into a "normal" state of lust.

Funnily enough, the contemporary chapter in the quest to help women who *want to want* began at the annual meeting of the American Urological Association in 1983. There, in a bustling Las Vegas conference room, a little-known British neurophysiologist named Giles Brindley took the stage to deliver a talk on "vaso-active therapy for erectile dysfunction." Many of the male doctors in attendance had worn tuxedos, and were accompanied by their wives in eveningwear, in anticipation of a formal dinner to be held later that night. But Brindley wore a zippered jogging suit, deemed "inappropriately casual" by one attendee, who later described the talk as "how (not) to communicate new scientific information."[5]

Clicking through slides depicting various states of flaccidity and tumescence, Brindley credited a compound called *papaverine* for producing robust instances of the latter, and then informed the audience that the images on view were of his own member. Giggles of discomfort echoed through the space, prompting Brindley to announce that he had injected his own *corpora cavernosa* with the substance just twenty minutes prior. Looking "skeptically at his pants," he shook his head with dismay. "Unfortunately, this doesn't display the results clearly enough," he said. He summarily dropped trou, "revealing a long, thin, clearly erect penis," and, pants around his knees, proceeded through the aisles encouraging his colleagues to feel his findings for themselves.[6]

One of the doctors present said the room became extremely noisy, "which was not due to applause, but rather, signs of astonishment, if not panic."[7]

Another recalled women screaming, their arms in the air, as Brindley approached their section of the room with his "erection waggling before him."[8]

Irwin Goldstein, a urologist speaking at the event, was not shocked or panicked, but he certainly recalls the moment. In a 2012 article in the *Journal of Sexual Medicine*, he described it with reference to Aristotle's adage, that "if you would understand anything, observe its beginning and its development." The lecture, he said, was historic, and he felt "lucky enough to 'observe the beginning.'" In any case, the event "changed sexual medicine forever."[9] Goldstein later told a news outlet, "It was an hour that changed the world."[10]

What changed was not just the market for prostaglandin injections, but rather the way that medical research approached sexual problems. If it was possible to inflate the penis like fixing a flat, as Goldstein has described the mechanism, then impotence was not, as had long been supposed, simply a problem that was "all in your head."[11] Sexual function sprouted newly biological roots.

Goldstein and his colleagues went on to study the biochemistry behind erections, and eventually they homed in on a drug called *sildenafil citrate*. Pfizer had originally studied it for high blood pressure and chest pain, but it was a low-priority project with disappointing results; in fact, it was close to being shelved. But during a study of Welsh mine workers, researchers chanced on a critical side effect: a test subject in a discussion group happened to report that he was experiencing more nocturnal erections than usual, at which point the other men in the room "kind of smiled and said, 'So did we.'"[12]

Goldstein became involved in testing the drug and served as the lead author on a 1998 paper in the *New England Journal of Medicine* that introduced Viagra to the world.[13] The FDA approved the medicine in March of that same year, and within weeks more than half the prescriptions—some three hundred thousand in the week of May 8, 1998, alone—were being covered by insurance (compared to a meager one-third of oral contraceptives, which women had been paying for out of pocket for decades). Users described a "miraculous restoration of sexual function," while Goldstein said that the drug had achieved "more or less the dream of humankind from caveman forward."[14] Viagra quickly reached blockbuster territory, and it enjoyed a $32.6 billion run until a generic equivalent came out in 2018.[15] It was such a hot commodity that the CIA even used it to broker influence among tribal elders in Afghanistan.[16]

Looking back on the drug's early days, one doctor recounted, "We used to hand out Viagra like water. . . . [W]e referred to it as Vitamin V."[17] But clinicians also noted a skewed effect. Men were leaping at the chance to banish impotency—rebranded now as erectile dysfunction—but many of their female partners did not respond with equal enthusiasm. The drug, some felt, reduced sexuality to its most crude components, placing the emphasis on getting it up and in without any accompanying attention to the complexities of human feeling—let alone the presence of desire, male or female. Capturing this climate, a 2000 *Saturday Night Live* skit narrated by Christopher Walken featured a number of exasperated wives sarcastically thanking Viagra: it closed with a scene of a woman furtively dumping her husband's little blue pills down the toilet.

THE SEARCH FOR EQUIVALENCE

Goldstein has been at the front lines of efforts to find an equivalent "miracle" for women, and when we first spoke in 2015, he told me he was "frustrated by the lack of comparable treatment options." While

men today have a number of "impressive pharmaceuticals" at their dis-
posal—and as a result are experiencing new levels of mid to later life
potency—doctors too often attempt to placate women with the advice
to eat chocolate, drink wine, or take a bath. "We can't intervene on
one side of a partnership and not the other," Goldstein said.

Just weeks after the little blue pill was approved for sale in 1998, a
group of scientists met to discuss whether the same drug might work for
women. Several of the one hundred or so convened experts were from
drug companies, and they were keenly aware of the implications of dou-
bling the potential market.[18] The landscape of medical consumption
was in the midst of a shift, with patients becoming more active in their
own care decisions. Moreover, just the year before, in 1997, the FDA
had loosened the regulations governing drug-company advertising,
leading to a marketing boom that has continued ever since—alongside
a steady uptick in prescription drug use.[19] In 1990, drug companies
spent a total of $47 million on direct-to-consumer advertising; by 1998,
their budgets had ballooned to $1.2 billion.[20] Industry insiders claim
these promotions improve patient knowledge about treatment options.
However, researchers have widely observed correlations with increased
out-of-pocket spending, higher rates of prescriptions being written for
drugs that are not truly necessary, more off-label drug use, and im-
proper medicalization of natural conditions.[21]

It was clear to the experts in the room that with the right messaging,
big pharma had the public's attention.[22] But in this case, it wasn't clear
what the message might be. Even though doctors understood that female sexual problems were widespread, they didn't know what exactly
Viagra was meant to solve in women. Were arousal and desire linked to
vaginal blood flow? And even if they were, would increasing circulation
to the genitals lead to women wanting more sex?

Goldstein, who at the time ran a urology clinic in Boston, immediately began prescribing Viagra to the wives of his patients, telling the
New York Times in 1998 that female sexual dysfunction was "in essence
a vascular disease."[23] A Pfizer consultant, with whom Goldstein had
coauthored papers on erectile dysfunction, remarked that it was "irra-
tional" to give Viagra to women without waiting for clinical research
to support that path.[24] But Goldstein had already taken up the mantle.
At the time, he also maintained that Viagra could have prophylactic

qualities that could be used to prevent future sexual health problems. "People take aspirin to prevent heart attacks," he told Reuters. "Is Viagra the aspirin of the penis? We think it is."[25]

Pfizer doggedly kept at clinical trials to see if the drug could find a way into women's medicine cabinets. On its surface, the research looked promising. In one early trial, researchers gave six women Viagra and six others a placebo, sat them in front of erotic videos, and used a pelvic probe to measure changes in genital blood flow. The genitals of the women on Viagra were more engorged than those who had been given placebos. But a larger trial that included a questionnaire found that although Viagra seemed to cause greater blood flow, the women experiencing this effect did not feel any more aroused. Pfizer spent years trying to find some well-defined group of women for whom increased pelvic blood flow and desire could be linked. But they couldn't.

In 2004, after eight years of studies involving more than three thousand women, Pfizer abandoned the effort. The problem, researchers claimed, was that men and women had a fundamentally different relationship between arousal and desire. "There's a disconnect in many women between genital changes and mental changes," said Mitra Boolel, who led Pfizer's sex research team. "This disconnect does not exist in men. Men consistently get erections in the presence of naked women and want to have sex. With women, things depend on a myriad of factors." He added that for women, "the brain is the crucial sex organ."[26]

Even with Pfizer out of the running, the search for a female Viagra was in full swing. However, in order to get a drug from bench to bedside, it has to be shown to alleviate a particular condition, and in the case of desire that goal has remained stubbornly elusive. As we've seen, researchers are hard-pressed to say what "normal" desire really is, let alone what aspect of human biology it might relate to, if any at all. Against these uncertainties, investigators were also running up against the confounding question of how one might define successful treatment.

For erectile dysfunction, which is defined as an inability to maintain penile rigidity "sufficient for sexual satisfaction," the end point is fairly obvious.[27] Moreover, the link between healthy function and orgasmic gratification is implicit. But for women, as we've discussed, sex frequently takes place without desire and does not necessarily result in pleasure. In addressing low desire, what then counts as valid symptom relief?

In 2016, the FDA issued draft guidelines for drug developers treating women's low sexual interest.[28] They proposed that an effective drug might work in a number of ways: it could increase arousal and/or desire, boost the number of "sexually satisfying events" a woman has each month, or reduce their sexual distress. While this guidance has done something to clear away the haze, a vigorous debate continues. What, for instance, constitutes a *satisfying* event, and how much of a quantitative boost is needed to count as impact? James Pfaus, a psychologist and neurobiologist at Concordia University in Montreal, has studied a number of sex-enhancing compounds. He told me, "A sexually satisfying event is a real male thing—you have an erection and you put it in a hole somewhere and that's considered sexually satisfying."

The ideas guiding clinical success and its measurement speak volumes about social expectations for female sexuality. It is striking indeed that so much of the therapeutic focus is not on feminine sexual enjoyment so much as on feminine sexual availability, as expressed through heightened interest. By way of comparison, one of the end points for erectile dysfunction drugs is successful entry of the vagina. Approvals of the products for men don't hinge on whether they alleviate distress.

The FDA approved a drug in June 2019, after years of clinical trials, that is, I think, particularly illuminating of cultural mores.* Bremelanotide was originally developed as a sunless tanning agent. During initial testing, however, a researcher "inadvertently self-administered" a double dose of it and experienced an eight-hour-long erection—along with nausea and vomiting.[29] The incident led scientists to consider applications beyond artificial pigment darkening, and they quickly started to investigate them. Bremelanotide binds to receptors in the brain called *melanocortins*, which play a role in several biological functions, including metabolism, pigmentation, and pain regulation. Although the FDA said it was unclear exactly how the drug worked to boost sexual desire,

---

* As of June 2019, the drug has been approved for use in premenopausal women with hypoactive sexual desire disorder and is marketed under the name Vyleesi. It is administered on an as-needed basis by a self-administered shot in the thigh or abdomen.

the theory was that it increased dopamine levels, and thereby allowed women to "process erotic stimulation as rewarding."[30]

A New Jersey–based pharmaceutical company, Palatin Technologies, bought the rights to the compound and formulated it into a subcutaneous injection—that is, through a self-administered shot in the thigh. The company then ran a glossy trial called the Reconnect Study, targeting women "missing" their desire. Though the study declared the drug a success, the results were fairly modest. Participants in the Stage III trial reported an average of just 0.7 more monthly "events."[31] Interestingly, a 2008 study looking at the compound as a treatment for erectile dysfunction measured its efficacy according to average "*weekly* coitus episodes," which suggests a different standard is at play for the male sex-drive market.[32] Nonetheless, Irwin Goldstein said, "It's an awesome drug." He told Fox News San Diego in 2013, "It made women with sexual dysfunction back to normal," and then, in a clearly pre-#MeToo gesture, proceeded to joke with the host that a woman's date could give her a shot to prepare for a fun night ahead.[33]

▼▲▼▲▼

To some, the rush to fix female sexual dysfunction misses the mark entirely: there can be no treatment, because there is no actual condition. The clinical psychologist Leonore Tiefer has for years been a vocal critic of the medicalization of women's sexual health. A seasoned activist as well as a scholar, she told me that low desire, as a diagnosable state, does not exist. That's not to say women aren't grim-faced over their bedroom lives. "Everybody, if not more than everybody, is disappointed in their sex life, for many different reasons," she said over lunch in a lower Manhattan diner. But unlike, say, kidney stones or arterial congestion, desire is an "amorphous concept" that cannot be consistently defined or measured. In Tiefer's view, sex is constituted through a kaleidoscopic set of interpretations; it has no center, no essence, only the meanings people foist upon it. As a result, variations on "female Viagra" are unnecessary. Such a drug would serve corporate profits rather than women's pleasure.[34]

Others have voiced similar concerns that the condition has been manufactured to suit the cure.[35] Barbara Mintzes, who specializes in pharmaceutical policy at the University of British Columbia, told me,

"We've seen wave after wave of different products that attempt to define the problem with women's sexual function. With each one it changes the story about what the problem is." Mintzes and Australian health journalist Ray Moynihan authored the 2010 book *Sex, Lies and Pharmaceuticals*, taking a critical look at global drug companies' attempts to package women's sexual dissatisfaction as disease. They wrote:

> If Pfizer is promoting a drug that enhances blood flow to the genitals, then the condition might best be described as an "insufficiency" of vaginal engorgement. If Proctor & Gamble is pushing a testosterone patch as a cure for women, the sexual disorder is discussed as a "deficiency" of hormones. And if Boehringer has a pill that affects the mind's neurotransmitters, women with low libido may have a "chemical imbalance" in their brains. In a strange way, the disease seems designed to fit the drug.[36]

▼▲▼▲▼

The subtext of the FDA hearing where I met Julie was the upcoming regulatory review of the contested drug flibanserin as a treatment for hypoactive sexual desire disorder (HSDD). Rather than taking aim at blood flow, lubrication, or hormone levels, flibanserin works in women's brains by decreasing serotonin and increasing dopamine, the neurotransmitters believed to affect desire. Stephen Stahl, a psychiatrist who has studied flibanserin at the University of California San Diego School of Medicine, told me that the theory behind HSDD is that "there are circuits that are inhibited, and women can't turn off distracting thoughts and images."[37] Normally, he said, the brain organizes planning over pleasure, but when it gets stuck, pleasure can't flow through. Flibanserin appears to allow women to turn off these intrusions. However, Stahl noted, this is a "speculative theory." Flibanserin is not the first compound to target the mind. A pair of other drugs, Lybrido and Lybridos, developed by Dutch scientists, also tinkers with women's neurochemistry. But flibanserin was the first drug to have traveled so far in the approval process, and that it did so at all is remarkable.

Flibanserin was originally investigated as a treatment for major depression by the German pharmaceutical company Boehringer Ingelheim. The drug turned out to be an ineffective antidepressant, but it appeared to have some sexual side effects. Boehringer quickly pivoted and started running new studies with cute names like Dahlia and Orchid, to see if it had a real effect on libido. When the company submitted a request for FDA approval, the agency rejected the drug ten to one, noting that the "overall response rate . . . is not particularly compelling." The benefits—roughly 0.5 to 1.0 extra sexually satisfying event per month—did not outweigh the risks of dizziness, nausea, fatigue, and potentially dangerous drops in blood pressure, the agency determined. Boehringer made one more unsuccessful bid for approval, then dropped the drug in 2010. In short order it was snatched up by Robert and Cindy Whitehead (now Cindy Eckert), a husband-and-wife team from North Carolina who had just launched Sprout Pharmaceuticals. They resubmitted the drug for FDA approval in 2013, but the agency was again unimpressed by what it deemed modest results. In a further blow, the American Psychiatric Association erased HSDD from its diagnostic manual that same year, as I discuss in the following chapter. The very condition Sprout's drug was meant to treat was no longer recognized in mental health care's guiding text. At this point, drug companies tend to cut their losses and move on, but Sprout opted for a radical tactic that set off a blitz of controversy.

The company helped finance a highly visible campaign called Even the Score, premised on the idea that the FDA's rejection of flibanserin had nothing to do with safety but was instead a case of institutional gender bias. Men have access to a battery of drugs for sexual dysfunction, whereas women have none, the campaign claimed. This was the result of "gender inequality" and "paternalism," Cindy Eckert told me in 2015. It was not a regulatory challenge, it was a feminist issue. But even as she spoke of parity, she was also quick to tell me that the drug was not *too* effective. "Flibanserin doesn't take a woman with HSDD and catapult her sexuality, or make her hypersexual," she told me. Her words conveyed a tone of reassurance, like *don't worry, it won't turn women into men*. (And indeed, the surrounding PR stressed the phrase "modest but meaningful" in its discussion of flibanserin's impact.) The drug's main achievement was not that it increased sexual frequency, but that it reduced the distress associated with low desire—though it is unclear whether this means women were reconciled to being less libidinous, or felt better about having sex in the absence of lust.

Even the Score brought on the former president of the National Council of Women's Organizations, Susan Scanlan, to serve as chair of the campaign. In the late 1990s, Scanlan had been privy to the activist push that had gotten insurance coverage for birth control—a full six months *after* Congress mandated that plans cover Viagra. "With birth control, Congress was forced to recognize that women are sexual beings—before that, it was storks laying eggs," she told me in 2015. "Now, we're fighting for them to understand that women have a right to a sexual life, too." She said that the FDA treated women "like little dears who can't make their own decisions about risks and benefits." There is a well-documented history of women's exclusion from clinical trials—a pattern that Sprout helped perpetuate when it tested the effects of alcohol on the drug, but used a sample consisting almost solely of men. I was taken aback, however, by the extent to which Scanlan made light of the drug's adverse effects. "When compared to male drugs and the dangers they have—sudden death, blindness, penile rupture—the risks posed by flibanserin sound like the Seven Dwarves—sleepy, dopey . . . "

The drug's critics were legion. A scathing letter published in the *Journal of Medical Ethics* accused Sprout of creating a disease just to sell a low libido drug. "There is no scientifically established norm for sexual activity, feelings or desire, and there is no evidence that hypoactive sexual desire disorder is a medical condition," it said.[38] In an editorial in the *Los Angeles Times*, Tiefer and Dutch sexologist Ellen Laan were similarly disparaging, writing, "No diagnostic test has identified any biological cause—brain, hormone, genital blood flow—for most women's sexual problems."[39]

Adriane Fugh-Berman of Georgetown University said the Even the Score campaign co-opted the language of feminism in service of rallying consumer support for a bogus condition. The director of PharmedOut, a research and education project examining the impact of pharmaceutical marketing on prescribing practices, Fugh-Berman has been watching flibanserin for years. "Many conditions, like low desire, are natural facts of life," she told me. "And the best treatment for some might be changing circumstances—like demanding help for work and child care and reducing stress. The idea that there are pills for normal life circumstances does not serve public health."

Controversy aside, the campaigning proved effective, and in June 2015 the drug was approved. Two days after the FDA gave it the go-ahead, the Canadian drug giant Valeant bought the rights for $1 billion, in anticipation of voracious demand.[40]

But the drug proved a massive flop. Sales in 2016 totaled around $10 million, about one-tenth of the projected market.[41] In a typical month following its release, roughly six hundred prescriptions were filled (compared to more than twelve times that for erectile dysfunction drugs). Part of the reason for the dismal performance was the prohibitive cost—$800 per month—and the fact that most insurers balked at coverage. There were also two requirements that turned people off from the idea: women had to take it every day, and they had to abstain from alcohol. Making matters worse, a 2016 review in the *Journal of the American Medical Association* of published and unpublished studies on the efficacy of the drug concluded that the "quality of the evidence was graded as very low."[42] Facing a lawsuit from its investors, Valeant was so eager to drop the drug from its portfolio that the firm gave it back to Sprout for free.[43]

EMPOWERED CONSUMERS?

Having closely followed these events, I was surprised in the fall of 2018 to see the soft glow of a pastel banner above my subway stop in Brooklyn. "Low sex drives, now optional," declared the au courant typeface beside a millennial Asian woman looking glum as she wrapped herself in a protective embrace. Just blocks away, a billboard at the entrance to the other local line gleamed in an equally Instagram-inspired shade. A pale-skinned feminine hand held aloft a single blush-colored pill. "Men have 26 pills to make them hard. It's time we got ours," it said. The campaign was sponsored by a company called Hers, which sells flibanserin online under the trade name Addyi.[44] Hers did not respond to my repeated attempts to ask how women were responding to their ads. However, the campaign struck me as more than just another instance of *talk to your doctor*. Here, the commuting woman was urged to make a judgment about one of the most intimate and subjective parts of her identity—her very desire, which was presented as an entity unmoored from the rest of her life. It is not associated with stress or motherhood or the partner who has yet to lavish attention on her body. It is simply hanging low on a tender balance for which no norm exists.

Despite the media attention it's received (and the brief wallpapering of New York's public transit), the subject of "female Viagra" did not make much of an appearance in my conversations with women. Of the approximately 120 women I spoke with between 2014 and 2019, only 5 had tried or were taking Addyi at the time of our discussions. I came away with a frankly lopsided view. I absolutely concede that these numbers, and women's general impressions, would probably look different had I focused my discussions to coincide with the drug's relaunch; as one recent analysis put it, the new telehealth approach is "likely to produce a lot of positive diagnoses for HSDD."[45] Two of the five women had participated in clinical trials for the drug, and they had been referred to me by Edelman, the PR firm working for the Even the Score campaign, so it was not surprising that they spoke so highly of its effects. They talked freely to me (i.e., we spoke by phone without supervision), but their messages had clearly been workshopped, as they were almost verbatim in stressing the campaign's main talking points along with featuring activist-inflected speech about drug equity.

One of the women, a fifty-three-year-old mother of four from the South, had met her current partner not long after divorcing her husband. By her account, her new man was gorgeous—"he looked like Fabio"—and for the first few years of their partnership they enjoyed each other "like teenagers in heat."

But after a time, she said, something changed. "I started noticing that things just weren't right," she said. "The spark was gone. The desire to do it was just gone." She began avoiding intimacy. "It got to the point where I would suggest a late movie on a Friday, knowing full well that when we got home I would be able to say I was too tired." By then, she said, "I was having sex because I didn't want to lose him, not because I wanted to."

Concerned for her relationship, she looked for help, and eventually she came across a promotional brochure looking for women to participate in the flibanserin trial. Reading over the screening questions—loss of interest in sex, difficulty reaching orgasm, loss of pleasure—she recognized elements of her own experience. She was accepted as a research

subject, and two weeks after starting the daily pill regimen she was visited by a dormant urge and sent her husband a text, "Do you want to
have me for lunch?" She took the pill each night before bed, and the
following months played out with Pantygrams and trips to the Hustler
store. She was skipping dessert to race home to bed. "I was initiating,"
she said. "It took our sex life to a whole new level." She explained that
she was so distraught when the study was over, and she had to return
her unused medications, that she considered claiming that her dog
had eaten them, so that she could hold on to her stash. Not wanting to
give up what she had so recently regained, she sought out other therapies, including an expensive prescription for testosterone. "I grew hair
on my chin, was more acne prone, and could beat [my partner] in an
arm wrestle, but it did not make me want to have sex," she said. "Over
time, things just returned to normal and that made me really sad." This
woman, who was among those to testify at the FDA hearing, said that
she was approached by several therapists telling her they could help
with balancing her expectations. But she told me, "Sex therapy is no
match for this condition."

The second woman that Edelman connected me with shared a similar tale. After decades of a happy and sexually fulfilling marriage, her
libido vanished. Feeling "inadequate," and worried about the health of
her partnership, she consulted with Irwin Goldstein, who enrolled her
in the trial. The results were quick to take hold, leading her to both initiate and agree to sex more often. Her newfound urges were so strong,
she said, they even roused her in the night. But when she was made
to hand over her pills, she returned almost immediately to her former
disinterested state. Her "symptoms came back," is how the PR manager
framed the story for me in a brief that took care to word her experience
in medical terms.

The other emphatically positive review I received was from Sue
Goldstein, a sex educator. Sue serves as the program coordinator at
Goldstein's Center for Sexual Medicine in San Diego, and like her husband, Irwin Goldstein, she is a celebrated figure in the field. She used
words like "transformative" and "life changing" when she told me
about her own experiences with the drug. When we met at her office on
a spring afternoon in 2017, she implied that even after forty-plus years
of marriage, life in the bedroom remained *that* good. She experienced

low desire in her fifties and took testosterone, which she said "took the edge off." But after a while her husband pointed out that it no longer seemed to be working. "You're avoiding sex again," she said, mimicking his voice and wagging her finger. "Flibanserin put me back to where my desire was when I was sexually healthy," she told me. Addyi has only been approved for use in premenopausal women, meaning that Sue was technically using the drug off-label. Nonetheless, she said, it improved her arousal and her orgasms—and she said, without blinking an eye, "Hopefully I'll be on it for the rest of my life."

In all three accounts, I was struck by the way the drug was presented as not just a bedroom aid, but *the* only way to stir libido from dormancy to rousted life. It was not just a solution for low desire, it was Cupid's Arrow in chemical form. However, for the two other women I spoke with, the results were underwhelming.

FERVENT DREAMS AND MODERN CHEMISTRY

After flibanserin hit the market, Julie sought out a doctor who could prescribe the drug. The physician cautioned that it might not be the panacea she was after, but Julie reasoned, "If there is an option available, then I have to try it." The pills were expensive—hundreds of dollars each month—and they were not covered by insurance.[46] Julie said it was nerve-racking to siphon off what would otherwise go to savings. Because Addyi is intended to manage and not cure low desire, the hypothetical patient could go on taking it indefinitely.

Julie was also not sure how to tell if the drug was actually working for her. Did she feel increased desire? Perhaps, but it was hard to tell. She did not find herself visited by fantasies or more inclined to masturbate. The stories she had heard at the FDA meeting—of inspired midlife sexting and lunchtime rendezvous—fell far from the purview of her experience, but not for lack of hopeful trying.

Julie diligently swallowed her evening pill for three weeks before deciding to take the treatment for a spin. Lotion-smoothed, freshly depilated, beneath her top she wore the apricot-colored negligee her husband had bought her—"oh, ages ago"—when the sex was still

good. There was pleasure in anticipation, in the little acts of prepa-
ratory care. She'd read books that promised these observances were
often good enough to push the mind from avoidance to expectation,
that the main thing was to convince yourself. But Julie wanted her
heart to catch, to marvel anew at the dimple to the left of his smile, to
reach unconsciously for his fingers, to drop into the humming under-
current of her body.

"I initiated more," she said of the weeks and months that followed. It
felt good to make the effort and to try to see her husband as the object
of desire she had once found him to be. But it remained an effort, she
explained. "I never stopped having to convince myself to drum up the
energy. So we had a bit more sex, but not necessarily because I desired
more sex."

There is something both tantalizing and sinister in the promise of
a pill, especially one that does not intervene in your enjoyment, but
simply makes you game. I don't mean to imply that Addyi or other
compounds are meant to be coercive—the intended market is women
who want to want—but they lead us down a similarly reductive route
in aiming to address women's disinterest without duly considering its
cause. What does it mean to fabricate desire where none otherwise exists? Is it meant to be a restoration—of what was pure and good and
golden—or is it a summons to perform in step with expectation? Several doctors conceded to me that they're not wowed by Addyi, but they
still thought it was helpful to some women. The physician and sex
therapist Stephen Snyder told me, "Even if nine out of ten women with
psychological desire problems get better with psychological treatment,
there's one that doesn't, and that person may need medication. So the
more tools we have the better."

The kind of desire on offer by Addyi is conservative at best. It more
closely resembles how women are tutored to ask for a raise—*don't be
too pushy, don't get greedy*—than how they are encouraged to pine for
that handbag—*come and get it, you know you want it!* This sort of desire is contained safely within bounds: it's relational, it sustains your
partnership, it quietly accommodates rather than voraciously demands.
Heaven forbid, it's not too strong. I think it's worth pausing at the fact
that the FDA gave the green light to a drug that offers women one

additional romp every one or two months. Could that be all we deserve in enhancing our erotic lives?

For Julie, even that meager improvement wasn't really apparent. Instead, the customary distress over her diminished lust became paired with guilt that she was "throwing money away on something that doesn't work." It added to her sense of having to perform, to prove that she was getting "better," or at least trying to. So she stopped. "I felt kind of dumb," she says, "like I bought into the magic weight-loss pills shown on late-night television and believed that the pounds would magically slide away and leave me looking young and perfect. *That* I know is a fantasy. I had just wanted this to be real."

▼▲▼▲▼

In 2018 an article in the *Archives of Sexual Behavior* surmised that "research has not conclusively demonstrated that biology is among the primary mechanisms involved in inhibiting sexual desire in women."[47] Rather, the authors said, a number of other factors, including body image, relationship satisfaction, sexual subjectivity, and learned values, intervene to shape women's experiences of lust. Even though drugs like flibanserin are marketed in such a way as to suggest that desire dips independently of life circumstances, those involved in drug development are certainly aware of these other influences. The strength of their impact on women's minds and bodies may even be contributing to the challenge of developing effective pharmaceuticals.

James Pfaus, the researcher at Concordia, is one of the most prominent exponents of the so-called "vagina–brain connection." In his lab, he uses rats to see how manipulations of neurochemistry affect sexual behaviors. With his team, he has found that when female rats are treated with opioid-blocking drugs—and thus cannot reap opioid rewards during copulation—they will reject later mating efforts. This finding suggested that bad sex leads to an expectation of more bad sex in the future, leading Pfaus and colleagues to suggest that there is a "critical period" during an individual's early sexual experiences that creates a "love map" of feelings associated with sex.[48] Pfaus has also looked at whether compounds increased female rats' sexual solicitations, and found that when given drugs that activate dopamine they become rabidly sexual. Rats and humans are biologically similar in key ways that make them ideal study proxies. And yet, women don't react with the same abandon to the compounds that send female rats into a libidinal frenzy. Pfaus suspects the reason for this more tepid response is that women's minds are somehow holding them back. "In a way, I think female rats are teaching us something about female desire," Pfaus told me in 2017. "When they have it, it's big, and they are completely in charge of it. There are pharmacological mechanisms that show in an unambiguous way that they want to have sex. But I think we've beaten that out of women in Western culture."

Pfaus's remarks returned to me as I waded through the controversies surrounding flibanserin and critiques of its impact. Rather than chronicling what a drug like flibanserin does, or is supposed to do, I think the question of what it does *not* address is both more interesting and more relevant. Like Viagra, the little pink pill takes aim at sexual capacity. But whereas Viagra renders men able, flibanserin helps make women willing. Neither, however, addresses the major components of satisfaction and true intimacy—physical, emotional, and erotic communion with oneself and one's partners. Like Viagra, flibanserin supports our expectations for command performance. We should love sex, we are told. To be healthy is to be in the mood. And if we're not, we should work at it like a job. But as I'll show in the chapters that follow, health and pleasure go hand in hand, and this connection tends to grow from our vulnerability, our patience, and our genuine self-love.

One might think from the headlines that equal access to pharmacopeia ranks high among women's sexual health concerns. But this was not my takeaway from talking to women who were exploring their sexuality—not even remotely. Indeed, I was struck by the rift between what I saw taking place within the sexual medicine community, with its calibrations of distress and significant events, and women's own reports of surveying different facets of Eros.

With the exception of the few women I spoke to who were ardent proponents of flibanserin, desire and pleasure were never presented as free-floating entities, robust one day, inexplicably extinguished the next. Indeed, almost across the board, women spoke of their sexuality in contextual terms: it changed with time and circumstance, with different partners, different expectations, and different states of self-knowledge. While desire was frequently tinged by a sense of mystery, its retreat was rarely presented in a black box. Overwhelmingly, sexual satisfaction was described in terms of agency: it was comfort with their bodies, self-awareness, and freedom to express and investigate their changing needs. Self-determination was not a matter of free-market access to a pill. Consumer choice is a meager stand-in for personal liberation, and women, as we'll see in the chapters that follow, express desire in grander terms.

7 YOU CAN CHANGE YOUR MIND

Mindfulness is the miracle by which we
master and restore ourselves.

—*Thich Nhat Hanh*, The Miracle of Mindfulness, *1996*

AT THE FIRST session of the group therapy clinic, Lori Brotto passes a
small plate of raisins around the conference table. It is early morning
in British Columbia, on the cusp of fall. The recent rains have let up
and light fills the small room in Vancouver General Hospital, where
each of the eight assembled women, per Brotto's instructions, selects
one wrinkled fruit. "Observe the object," she prompts. "Become aware
of the details on the object's surface, the patches of light and dark, and
the sensation of it lightly resting on the palm. Touch the object with
a finger. Notice the topography. Look at the valleys and peaks." Each
woman dutifully touches her withered charge, lifting it to her nose, her
eyes, as instructed. Each one then rubs her raisin against her lips before
placing it in her mouth and, ever so slowly, chewing and swallowing,
"feeling it in the esophagus."

Brotto directs the Sexual Health Lab at the University of British Columbia. Her work on subjects as varied as asexuality, sexual function in
cancer survivors, and women's arousal has helped position this idyllic
archipelago on the global sexual health map and made Brotto, a psychologist, a leader in the field. Whereas in the United States the scientific study of desire is dominated by the pursuit of a libido-revving cure,
here in Vancouver Brotto has secured both funding and broad support

for her investigations into the ways that pain, stress, and emotion contour women's sexual interest.

Her orientation moves against the tide of much of sex therapy, which
tends to focus on boosting women's excitement. Sexual desire, as research holds, is shaped by two central factors: facilitators and inhibi-
tors, which sex educator Emily Nagoski has likened to gas and brake
pedals in a car.[1] This dual control model has received lopsided attention, with most interventions focused on trying to amplify excitement
through more stimulation, be it from vibrators, pornography, off-label
scripts, or lubricants. Brotto says that instead of throttling the engine,
we should consider releasing the brakes. For the past decade and a half,
she has been exploring how mindfulness can help women overcome
persistent sexual challenges and connect them to their desire. She believes the ancient practice of nonjudgmental awareness holds the key to
the mind-body conundrum; in other words, great sex is mostly a matter of paying attention.

After the women have completed examining their raisins and swallowing them, Brotto asks, "What sensations were you aware of?" The
women mention sweetness, texture, and liking or disliking the raisin.

"How was this experience different from the usual experience of eating a raisin?" One woman, a self-described "raisin hater," says she normally avoids them. Another raisin hater mentions a feeling of disgust so
strong she didn't even want to pick hers up. A third woman offers that
she normally shovels fistfuls into her mouth, without paying attention
to their taste or how they might scatter to the floor.

"So how," Brotto asks, "might this manner of paying attention to
eating the raisin be relevant to sexual interest and arousal?"

In Brotto's program, this innocuous treat shoulders a lot of responsibility. It at once provides an easy introduction to the practice of
mindfulness and beckons the women to have their own moments of
discovery. One of the raisin haters concedes that even though she expected it to be awful, when she just focused on the immediate sensations, it wasn't so terrible. Another woman volunteers that she enjoyed
the lingering sweetness and wanted more. One shares that she was present for each moment and didn't bypass any part just to get it over with.

For the next two months, this group will meet weekly to engage in
mindfulness exercises, attempt to smooth the mottled surface of their

own sexual beliefs, and get a crash course on the latest science of sexual function, attention, and desire. In-session meditation exercises and structured conversations will surface different ways to stay in the present, such as breaking with our autopilot tendencies, realizing that thoughts are not facts, and allowing sensations to take place in the body without expectation, revulsion, or anxiety. The facilitator's manual offers: "A focus on the impermanence of unpleasant sensations can help the practitioner learn to be with unpleasant sensations, rather than attempt to avoid or push them away. This occurs over time with the development of equanimity and non-self."

As I touch my own raisin, I silently consider how its soft folds bear a likeness to the vulva, which, it turns out, will be an object of similar inquiry later on in the program. In the same spirit of nonjudgmental curiosity, the women are encouraged to explore their genitals with a handheld mirror—not with the intent of exciting themselves, but rather to have a hands-on encounter with their own bodies. Brotto says that for many women, this is the first time they've had such an experience, and that it often provokes tears. Women confront the quiet shame with which they've viewed their bodies and all the ways this has intruded on their pleasure. As she tells me this, I think of one woman I spoke to who shared the lengths she would go to in order to ensure that her longtime partner never saw her naked backside. The woman's voice had fluttered between self-conscious mirth and weepy revelation as she described her habit of walking backward to the bathroom after making love.

The women in the conference room have all come of their own volition, recruited by ads on the bus and in bathroom-stall pamphlets, and convinced that the strength of their desire is somehow wrong or lacking. Some are partnered, some are single. One is employed but presently homeless. A young married woman from the Middle East worries that the later exercises involving erotica might be at odds with her religion. At least half of the women in the session I attended have a history of trauma. Their ages range from early twenties to early fifties, and Brotto, who has been running versions of the intervention since 2003, notes the relative youth of this season's participants.

After the session wraps up, Brotto and I talk about how women come into the program with their own ideas about "normal" sexual function and how they compare to the general public, that is, the liberated, lustful denizens of print and screen and fantasy. Older women, she says, who have typically had multiple opportunities to experience their sexual interest rise and fall, oftentimes express wanting to get their desire back, to regain its splendor before kids, or menopause, or the overfamiliarity of partnership dimmed their interest. For some mature women, Brotto adds, desire has never really been present, and they want to explore what they think they've been missing. But how are we to make sense of a very young woman, scarcely out of college, convinced that she is damaged?

"Sexuality is chock-full of myths and misperceptions that contribute to women's feelings of being broken or not working properly," says Brotto. For adolescents and young adults, these myths may be especially powerful, creating an unattainable baseline that women hold themselves to all the same. With Lucia O'Sullivan, a psychologist at the University of New Brunswick, Brotto has tracked the prevalence of sexual dysfunction in young people between the ages of sixteen and twenty-one.[2] To their surprise, they found that sexual problems affected males and females at a similar rate, with roughly 80 percent of sexually active young people experiencing issues like low satisfaction, low desire, or difficulty with maintaining an erection, for males, or having an orgasm, for females. Although their study only followed people for two years, the research suggests that something happens in early adulthood where women continue to experience sexual problems in greater numbers. "We don't know if early experiences set women up on a trajectory for problems in later life," says Brotto. "It seems possible, but we don't have the research."

There are two red flags here. One is that the landscape of youthful sexuality is looking more complicated and less fun than ever, as we saw in Chapter 3. Flying in the face of teen sexual experimentation as a tender but awkward rite of passage, we see young women and men struggling to enjoy their own sexuality. (It's unclear, however, how much of this is new, because of the long-standing taboo against looking at adolescent sex through any lens apart from that of risk.) The other red flag, which is of greater relevance here, is that even if young men and women experience comparable challenges, as they get older it is the women who appear to fare worse. Research by psychiatrist Raymond Rosen focusing on adults in the United States from 2000 suggests that sexual dysfunction affects some 43 percent of women but only 31 percent of men, and that low desire affects about 30 percent of women but only 15 percent of men. Sexual pain also appears to be highly gendered, affecting 10 to 15 percent of women and less than 5 percent of men.[3]

Brotto's work wades into the heart of this apparent discrepancy. A calm and unselfconscious facilitator, she walks to the whiteboard and draws what she calls a *snowball* chart: a series of concentric circles with low desire in the center ringed by guilt, anxiety, avoidance, mood issues, alterations in behavior, and changes in relationships. "Research suggests mindfulness can reduce the suffering associated with low desire," she says. "But I believe mindfulness can help with all of it." She waves a tapered hand across the board.

Her demeanor is warm but efficient, and I get the sense that each piece of her impressively, dizzyingly full life is accorded its own neat compartment. She starts work each day at six in the morning, so that she can finish by three in the afternoon, just in time to manage the active schedule of her three children. Above her desk a printout offering thirteen tips for effective time management is half-obscured by a child's marker drawing mounted on popsicle sticks. When we meet at eight in the morning, her makeup adds a golden hue to her Mediterranean complexion (she's Italian, raised Catholic, with all the sexual baggage that entails). If the spikey heels of her smart bootlets give her feet any grief, she hides it very well. Indeed, the charged spring of her step gives the impression of momentum continually gathering in her form.

Her own supernaturally busy schedule aside, it is Brotto's clinical view that multitasking is the death knell of desire. Women, perhaps mothers in particular, are lauded for their split attention: Cooking dinner while balancing the checkbook. Folding laundry while taking a conference call. Pumping breast milk while grinding through the morning commute. It's doubtful this *I don't know how she does it*–defying capacity actually serves women. Indeed, the evidence suggests that it contributes to our outsized share of stress, anxiety, and depression, plus the generalized feelings of depletion and never being *enough*. Brotto believes this trait really works against women when it comes to sex. Our self-congratulatory multitasking, she says, is ruinous to our erotic health. Rather than tuning into our bodily sensations, we become ensnarled in webs of self-censoring, list-making, and incessant problem-solving. We're caught up in our heads and can't drop into our skin—so much so that a stroke on the genitals might as well be a tap on the elbow.

According to Brotto, a robust experience of desire is about being in the moment. Women in the throes of eroticism are not marching through their *to dos*, or reviewing the day's trials and triumphs. They are both physically and psychologically connected to the immediate; they are, in short, participants in their own sexuality. This may seem like a smack-the-forehead, no-kidding observation—of course our sensual enjoyment demands our full engagement. And yet many women—and men—believe that sex is an automatic function that, left to its own devices, will simply take care of itself. As a result, we wait around for the flames of passion to ignite. We believe that we can just lie back and enjoy the ride—or at least climb aboard and be taken to a pleasing place. But for a large number of women—some 10 to 55 percent, with the exact figure difficult to pinpoint—there is no desire and there is little enjoyment. Brotto believes that is often because they are not really present. Hence the raisin. If you can tune into a piece of desiccated fruit, surely you can awaken to the swan song of your own libido.

▼▲▼▲▼

These days mindfulness makes a regular appearance in the media, in health care, and even in corporate management. Researchers have ascribed innumerable benefits to the practice, including improved mood, heightened focus, sounder sleep, better parenting, deeper compassion, and more expansive creativity. Though the roots of mindfulness reach back several thousand years, its history in American health care extends only a few decades. In 1965, a molecular biologist named Jon Kabat-Zinn, then doing postdoctoral work at the Massachusetts Institute of Technology, attended a lecture by a Zen Buddhist teacher, Philip Kapleau. Moved by what he heard, he started meditating, and eventually he gave up his work in bench science to devote himself to the practice. After having what he described as a "ten second vision" while meditating at a retreat outside of Boston, he believed that mindfulness could spread to hospitals and clinics around the country, transforming the course of care. His basic premise was, "As long as you are breathing, there is more right with you than wrong with you." The idea was not to eliminate pain, but to help people observe it and realize "the pain is not me." His work paved the way for further interventions, including the well-studied mindfulness-based cognitive therapy for people with depression, which has been shown to be at least as effective as antidepressants. Its aim is to help patients view their thoughts as momentary impressions, rather than naked depictions of the world. The popularity of his work helped to broadcast the idea that unpleasant sensations and barbed memories are not in and of themselves the source of suffering. It is rather the stories, anxieties, and sense of stubborn fate we attach to these discomforts that contribute to our anguish.[4]

Brotto began to immerse herself in these ideas as a postdoctoral fellow at the University of Washington. As part of a behavioral therapy program, she trained suicidal patients in mindfulness techniques and found that staying in the "here and now" helped counter feelings of overwhelming despair.[5] Even if the present was challenging, it was the impulse to revisit the past or speculate on what lay ahead that can create dread. Brotto realized that if tuning into the "truth" of the present helped to stave off self-harm, then mindfulness was bound to have broader therapeutic applications.

Meanwhile, in both her research and her clinical practice, Brotto was helping gynecological cancer survivors address their sex-related problems. She observed that many of her patients complained of absent sexual feelings. As one patient put it to her, "My genitals feel dead." And yet, when these women came into the lab, there was no sign of a physical problem. Brotto would show them a series of short erotic films while a vaginal photoplethysmograph recorded their genital blood flow. Despite articulating feelings of sexual indifference, their bodies still showed a strong response to visual stimulation. How was it, Brotto wondered, that women could report no sensation, and yet experience a robust bodily reaction? She speculated that it was an example of mind-body disconnect: changes were taking place beneath the skin that the mind failed to register. If arousal was already there, maybe women just needed to learn to recognize it. Mindfulness, as Brotto emphasizes repeatedly, does not create sensation; rather, it directs one's focus to sensation that already exists. In the case of women, that appears to be a vast pool of undetected arousal.

Brotto's colleague Rosemary Basson, who directs the University of British Columbia's Sexual Medicine program, says distraction is the main thing that prevents women from feeling desire during sex. One might well ask, then, why women are more prone to distraction than men. There are no adequate answers to this question, although Alfred Kinsey saw evidence of it, too: "Cheese crumbs spread before a pair of copulating rats," he noted, "will distract the female, but not the male."[6] Mindfulness is believed to help practitioners defang and disengage from the interior monologue, or *spectatoring*, as Masters and Johnson termed the penchant for negative self-appraisal (*am I close, is this working, do I smell all right*). Without the swarming interference, the practitioner should be better able to perceive the sensations of the present. But is it simply that women are too distracted by the thousand obligations in their lives to enjoy sex, or is something else going on?

DECIPHERING THE NATURE OF DESIRE

So what is desire and why does it dim? For the better part of the past century, this question has been making a slow crossing from the realm of human biology to the wilds of human relationships. To early theorists, such as Havelock Ellis and Sigmund Freud, desire was an innate and powerful drive. "Desire surges from the body," medical historian Edward Shorter wrote in his book on the subject.[7] For Helen Singer Kaplan, sexual desire fuels the rest of intimacy. Healthy men and women have a natural appetite for sex; it is a basic hunger, and desire is like the rumble of the belly reminding them to eat.[8]

For decades, the leading theorists regarded desire in terms of the individual, as though the body might be impervious to its environs. In the 1990s, however, a number of theorists began to question the biological description of desire, labeling it as male-centric. Most concerning was the suspiciously high prevalence of low sexual interest in women. Could it be that one in three women had disorders of desire, as the experts claimed? Or was it the case that the science of libido had no accurate description of women's lived experiences? A vocal group of critics faulted existing models for failing to account for social context. Some went so far as to declare that "sex is not a natural act," but rather a tangled web of meaning, and that designating desire as "low" or "unhealthy" amounted to sexist tyranny.[9]

As we saw in the previous chapter, around the time of Viagra's commercial release in 1998, a major fissure began among experts in sexual health. To one camp, individual biology was the main arbiter of experience, while to the other, it was the social world that forged female Eros. It was also, notably, around this time that views of male and female libido hardened into different, even opposing entities. Male drive ran strong and straightforward. You could set it in motion with a pill. But women were *complex*. There was no simple fix for their lack of lust, because it was seemingly vulnerable to everything.[10] The whole bio-psycho-social universe conspired to undermine their passion. Morals doused water on its embers, media made it shrink with shame, fatigue chased it into retreat, clumsy partners extinguished the pilot light. But more confounding was that women did it anyway. Irrespective of whether they felt inclined, they still agreed to sex. This dawning realization led researchers to ask whether female desire was a more relational force than they had previously realized, one that did not spring from the individual so much as from the dynamic between two (or more) people.

Basson is one of the most ardent proponents of the view that female sexuality is based on receptivity and emotional connection.[11] She believes that the purported rates of low desire (one in three women) speak not to an epidemic of sexual dysfunction, but to a flaw in how we understand desire and define its absence. Based on her clinical observations, Basson has suggested that women's initial motivations for sex are frequently not sexual. Rather, women instigate or agree to sex because they seek closeness, want to demonstrate affection, enjoy sharing a physical experience, or are attempting to increase their own sense of attractiveness, self-worth, and commitment.[12] These nonsexual motives, she argued in 2000, are "often of far more relevance than the women's biological neediness or urge."

The idea that it's typical for women to engage in sex from an erotically neutral state has been a source of relief for some women. Don't beat yourself up for not wanting it; your disinterest is perfectly normal. Many women in long-term, monogamous relationships may approach sex from a place of indifference, but are still capable of feeling desire

and pleasure in response to their partners' overtures. Other sex therapists have stressed the role of emotional intimacy for women. Stephen
Levine read the matter in starkly gendered terms, declaring: "Women
aspire to psychological intimacy as a gateway to sex. Men aspire to sex
as a gateway to intimacy."[13]

But others have been critical of the model. One study, led by Michael Sand, a clinical sexologist who helped lead Boehringer Ingelheim's flibanserin research, surveyed more than 130 registered nurses
to see which model of sexual response (Masters and Johnson, Kaplan,
or Basson) best fit their personal experience. The researchers found
that a roughly equal proportion of women endorsed each, adding
weight to the argument that there may be as much diversity among
women in terms of sexual response as there is between women and
men. But tellingly, the women who resonated most with Basson's
framework were far more likely to report sexual dysfunction, including low desire, as well as lower overall satisfaction with their sexual
lives and emotional relationships.[14] One of the clearest divides in the
data was around women's motivations for sex. For women who identified with Basson's responsive model, most did not have sex because
they were in the mood (i.e., "I want to have sexual feelings, sensations,
excitement, maybe orgasm"). Rather, they had sex because they wanted
to connect with their partners or for other nonsexual reasons, even if
they felt no physical desire. The authors concluded that even though
Basson set out to offer a more representative depiction of women's sexual response than the models that had already grabbed attention in the
scientific community, her model did not describe a pattern of healthy
or satisfying sexuality.

Others have suggested that neither spontaneous nor responsive desire accurately captures women's experiences. Karen Sims, who studied
under psychologist Marta Meana at the University of Nevada, wrote
her dissertation on married women's explanations for why their desire dimmed.[15] The women she interviewed reported losing their lust
as their relationships drifted from excitement into bonds cemented by
obligation and routine. Even as women craved closeness with their husbands, intimacy took its toll, leading Sims and Meana to speculate that
women's desire is a navigation of opposing poles: connectedness, on the
one end, and autonomy, on the other.

The women in the study loved their husbands but were dismissive of their advances. Sims elaborated, "This was not simply a matter of not feeling a sudden urge to have an afternoon roll around in the sheets while the kids napped. It was a dread of the sexual advances and, in many cases, active avoidance of any activity that might lead their husbands in that direction. . . . [M]aybe we could speculate that if their husbands came on to them in just the right way and offered to help fold the laundry first, they may have warmed up to the idea. But our data suggests not. Many of these women said they would rather fold the laundry than have sex." Sims and Meana suggested that while the emphasis on relational connectedness is a welcome departure from viewing desire in chiefly biological terms, the pendulum may have swung too far. Intimacy is important—just not necessarily where it comes to sex.

How we define healthy desire has become a loaded question in recent years, especially as big pharma continues seeking to develop drugs to treat libido. Drug approvals hinge on how well they address a given set of symptoms, lending new urgency to the debates over what behaviors and attitudes should be classified as symptomatic. Brotto, who works closely with Basson, has been at the center of these deliberations. She says the "arousal first" model effectively skewers the idea that if women don't *want it* there must be something faulty with their libidos. Instead, sexual problems occur when women don't respond to sexual cues or advances—a subject at the heart of the mind-body dilemma that so captivates her.

In 2009, Brotto led the committee charged with defining low desire for the fifth, and most recent, edition of the DSM. The way the manual describes conditions has significant ramifications for how clinicians work with patients and bill their care and for how practitioners—and drug developers—think about effective treatment. Moreover, these categories influence how women regard their own sexuality, and whether they view themselves as being on a spectrum of healthy appetite or as disturbingly deficient.

The previous edition of the DSM included the category hypoactive sexual desire disorder (HSDD), which applied to men and women alike. It was described in brief as "persistently or recurrently deficient (or absent) sexual fantasies and desire for sexual activity" that causes "marked distress or interpersonal difficulty."

Under Brotto's lead, the DSM-5 created a new women-only condition, female sexual interest/arousal disorder, suggesting that appetite and excitement are dependent states in ongoing dialogue. Desire is not necessarily an internal force that comes to life when the moon and stars align, but a reaction triggered by external factors. Her definition gives a nod to Masters and Johnson before placing Basson's model at its heart.[16] In the revised treatment, low desire is characterized by neither initiating sex nor responding to a partner's solicitations.

▾▴▾▴▾

Brotto's revisions have caused no small amount of snarling from the medical researchers who have been running studies to test whether any compounds in the pipeline boost female libido. Her reformulation removed the illness category to which these drugs were pegged, meaning that the pharmaceutical industry is looking to treat a condition that no longer exists in the DSM.[17] But the idea of responsive desire courts controversy beyond definitional squabbles.[18] For one thing, HSDD remains on the books as a male condition, which implies that desire is fundamentally different for men and women. Male lust is conceived as a sort of spontaneous combustion, emerging from within, while for women it's more of an elusive visitation. The other troubling piece is that it casts women's erotic lives in dependent terms. Their lust is triggered by forces beyond themselves—by sights, by sounds, but mostly by their partners. What does this say about the nature of women's erotic motivations? And how should we think about sexual consent, let alone enthusiasm, if we assume that at baseline desire is largely imperceptible? It might be "normal" for women to have sex for reasons other than wanting to have sex, but surely it's not ideal.

As much as these questions gnawed at me, as I spoke with Brotto about her work with mindfulness interventions, I started to see responsive desire in a new light. Women who have participated in her program describe the restoration of desire in terms of a new ability to make innate connections. One woman reported, "I discovered that my sexual desire was always there, but I needed to pay attention to it."[19] It was not a matter of having to rely on the external world to turn them on; rather, it was a process of heightening their sensitivity to what was taking place around and within them. On an unconscious level, our bodies are constantly processing our environments. Our heart rates increase, our hormones make subtle shifts, lubrication gathers in our genitals. But consciously, we are not necessarily aware of all that.

Think of children, Brotto offers. They can be fully absorbed in a state of play, consumed by the task at hand. It is only with time that we start losing this pristine ability to focus, as the jabbering of doubt, self-consciousness, and competing obligations start nibbling away at our attention. It is as though our minds and bodies are forever trawling their own orbits. Brotto's allusion to our early states made me wonder whether sexuality in its most fulfilling form is the expression of a unified self, or if indeed such a thing exists beyond the realm of myth and metaphor. If sexuality plays out in the space of mind and body, perhaps moments of transcendent and trance-like pleasure are signs of a synchronous experience—skin and psyche humming along in unison, we become a perfect feedback machine. Our states of desire, whether keenly felt or imperceptibly muted, illuminate this inner orchestration.

BRIDGING THE MIND-BODY DISCONNECT

Psychologist Meredith Chivers explores the communication between mind and body and why these lines are so often fractured. In Chapter 5 we looked at her research on the relationship between physical arousal and subjective response, also known as sexual concordance. Studies in her lab have repeatedly shown significant differences in how men and women respond to sexual stimuli. For men, reactions have proven to be largely straightforward. If they noted, on a given keypad (an *arousometer*, as it's known in the sex studies world), that they felt turned on, their genitals tended to indicate agreement, and their responses, both physical and subjective, were in line with their sexual orientation. Not so with heterosexual women. Their genitals became engorged while watching men with men, women with men, women with women, and even, though to a lesser extent, bonobos with bonobos. And yet, these reactions were not in keeping with their self-reports.

Chivers's work underscored the striking idea that vaginal blood flow and lubrication—typical measures of arousal—do not necessarily align with women's feelings of desire or excitement; in other words, mind and body are not necessarily in step. The implications of this work are huge. It makes hash of the misogynistic assumption that if a woman gets wet, or has an orgasm during unwanted sex, she must have secretly wanted it. But it also suggests that female sexual response is very different from how it has typically been conceived. In the past, women's more muted expressions of desire have been read as evidence of their lower drive. Chivers's findings suggest that from a physiological stance, women's sexuality is stronger than generally appreciated.

Chivers urges against reading women's physical reactions as the ultimate barometer of their interest. She told me it's problematic to assert that what is occurring on a physical level is somehow more "real" than what a woman reports feeling. We need a more nuanced take on what low concordance really means. The idea that women are sexual omnivores is, in her mind, little more than a sensational headline beset by "conceptual incoherence." She and Brotto wrote, "If genital response is an objective indicator of women's 'true' sexual desires, then we are left with the disturbing and false conclusion that women are sexually aroused by depictions of sexual assault, even in the notable absence of self-reported feelings of sexual arousal."[20]

But what exactly is happening to produce these divergent reactions? Why is it that a woman might have a certain bodily reaction and a very different emotional response? And why don't we see this with men?

Chivers, like Brotto, is sensitive to the larger cultural factors that might create dissonance between women's minds and bodies, or conversely, make men especially sensitive to their physiology. Chivers tells me that women are commonly raised with negative messages about their bodies—that they're dirty, that their sexuality needs to be kept in check, that their very desires are dangerous. At the same time, however, they're bombarded with messages telling them to be pleasing, desirable, and sexy—all passive states.

While cultural suppression of women's sexuality plays a part, Chivers says, it does not fully explain why mind and body are misaligned. In 2010, she and four colleagues published a study looking at the relationship between genital response and self-reported measures of arousal.[21] Analyzing data published between 1969 and 2007, they found a far higher level of concordance in men than in women. The research further showed that low concordance is not affected by a woman's age, relationship status, or whether she has sexual dysfunction, suggesting that women consistently experience a rift between mind and body. So does that mean it's normal, or have other forces made this mind-body disconnect endemic?

One proposed explanation is that women's lubrication serves a protective function. The chilling theory holds that female genitals evolved in an ancestral environment rife with violence, and wetness was a way to stave off possible injury. As Chivers and her colleagues wrote, "ancestral women who did not show an automatic vaginal response to sexual cues may have been more likely to experience injuries that resulted in illness, infertility, or even death subsequent to unexpected or unwanted vaginal penetration, and thus would be less likely to have passed on this trait to their offspring."[22] It's hard, however, to accept the proposition that women's swift and marked arousal is little more than a byproduct of primitive rape culture.

A more likely theory is that men and women may differ with regard to interoception—that is, the awareness of physiological changes in their bodies. The extent to which we tune into cues like heart rate, blood pressure, and glucose levels feeds into how we label and experience emotional states, and a body of research suggests that men's emotions are more strongly tied to these internal changes.[23] Women's emotions, by contrast, may be more strongly influenced by external factors, making them less sensitive to what's taking place beneath the skin.

These findings fly in the face of centuries-long assumptions that women are wholly mired in their bodies. Men are the cerebral sex, we've long been told, while women are blood and moisture and swampy feelings. Ovulation was once considered such a strong determinant of female behavior that it was cited as a legitimate reason for women's exclusion from politics and other seats of power. (As a teenager I asked my father why there had never been a woman president, and he told me, with utter seriousness, that women were too prone to flying off the handle; they might very well press that big red button during *that* time of the month.) All this is not to say that women's emotional states are unrelated to ovulation or other physiological changes, but that it seems we have exaggerated their effects. Indeed, a disturbing amount of research indicates that women have moved so far in the opposite direction that they dismiss some of their bodies' most urgent signs. Women, for instance, tend to wave away early indicators of a heart attack. They chalk it up to stress or fatigue and continue on with whatever task is at hand, with potentially fatal consequences.

Part of the story here may be that it's a matter of conditioning. It's not simply that women are innately "out of touch" with their bodies, but that they have learned to silence its messages. If women speak out about their pain, or discomfort, or even their early symptoms of heart disease, they are all too often met with skepticism, dismissal, or paternalistic *there theres* meant to convey that they're *just being melodramatic*. It's impossible to say how much is learned behavior and how much is gendered biology; no human lives outside of culture. But it does seem fair to speculate that this kind of self-censoring is on the rise, especially as expectations for women's productivity and market participation shift. If, for instance, the implicit contract behind women's waged labor is that they need to act "more like men," then they face a lot of pressure to erase a lot of indicators that all is not well, and in particular, any indicators that their bodies might be out of step with the relentless pace of a 9-to-5 schedule with two weeks of annual vacation. Furthermore, if we look at the rise of female-headed households, and what's required to keep a family above water, it's no wonder that women train themselves to shoo away their aches and pains, and come, instead, to muffle the sensations within.

We can extend this line of thinking a bit further to consider sexuality directly. One woman I spoke with, a forty-year-old yoga instructor and grade school education director, described her sexual encounters as less than ideal because she routinely became caught up in judging her own actions, or became preoccupied with her male partner's pleasure. She shared that she could give a "great performance," but hardly ever experienced orgasm herself. She placed such pressure on herself to please, to come across as a sexy, open-minded lover, that she didn't speak up about what she actually wanted or needed, for fear that her partner would judge her, not like her, or resent any deviation from his own charted pleasure. She found herself shutting down and not attending to her own body's prompts, such as whether she was actually aroused enough for comfortable penetration. It's easy to imagine how our learned states might show up as a lack of bodily awareness, which makes it necessary to ask whether different levels of interoception reflect something fundamental about the sexes or something acquired.

▼▲▼▲▼

Over the past few years, Chivers and Brotto have teamed up to look more closely at concordance and how mindfulness might help with syncing up women's minds and bodies to improve symptoms of sexual dysfunction. They've found that as women become more aware of their physical selves—observing their physical reactions with care and compassion—the synchronicity between mind and body increase, and with it desire improves. Interoception may explain why this happens.

Researchers at Brown University have been investigating the effects of mindfulness on improving interoception as it relates to sexual function.[24] In one study, half the subjects participated in a meditation lab while the control group took a religion course. Before and after the training, the participants were shown a series of sexual and nonsexual images while the researchers recorded how quickly they rated their physical arousal. At the start of the study, the female participants were consistently slower in registering their reactions, and these delays were associated with higher rates of depression, anxiety, and self-judgment. After the course, however, the meditators were able to log their reactions far more quickly than the non-meditators. This improved timing was also associated with more self-acceptance and a greater sense of general well-being. To Brotto, these findings indicated that self-judgment, and related feelings of inner hostility and low self-worth, can interfere with bodily awareness. As women become more tuned into their bodies, they tend to lose the self-critical baggage. It is as though being explicitly aware of one's turn-on clears away the vapors of whether one is good, or right, or deserving.

▼▲▼▲▼

One of the most fascinating questions to emerge during Brotto's mindfulness session came out of a simple exercise in definition. "What is pleasure?" she asked the room. The women offered a number of expected answers: A bodily sensation that feels good. A nice touch.

Something that feels enjoyable. But everyone was stumped when Brotto pushed: "How do you *know* it's pleasure?"

What if something feels good, but we attach shame to the sensation? Or what about when something hurts, and yet that jolt of pain is not unwelcome?

The arc of Brotto's work angles toward the conclusion that pleasure may ultimately be less about feeling good than about learning to feel deeply: dispensing of anticipation, disentangling yourself from the gauze of time, hushing the yammer of the overactive mind.

Brotto says that when women in her groups share their experiences of incorporating mindfulness into their sexuality and intimacy, the details tend to vary, but one key theme runs through them: the person is present. It is not a matter of making notches on the bedpost. Acrobatics or marathon sessions don't matter nearly as much as being tuned into the moment. Perhaps pleasure is not just a matter of your body's particular sense proclivities, of wanting to be touched or stroked or penetrated in a particular way. There is a broader spectrum of sensation available, and feeling is the reward for your awareness.

8 THE LANGUAGE OF LANGUAGE AND THE LANGUAGE OF TOUCH

If we conceive of bodies as merely physiological organisms, subject to breakdown and repair, we miss all the joy our bodies can experience, claim, and reclaim. Our bodies are the repositories for memories, fears, secrets, hopes, and dreams. If you touch me in my secret places, will I lie to you? Will I lay myself bare and let you feel my joy? Why stop at orgasm when we can aim for ecstasy?

—*Peggy Kleinplatz,* New Directions in Sex Therapy, *2013*

PART ONE: REPAIRING THE CONJUGAL BED

PAM GREW UP not far from the town of Normal, Illinois. She references this general geography as a sort of shorthand for her upbringing: white, middle-class family, working parents, minimal sex education, some religious instruction—"nothing overbearing." She was a "late bloomer," she tells me, who "never broke rules." She didn't drink or do drugs or act out any of the typical young adult rebellions; she had her first kiss her senior year of high school. In college, she went with friends to the nondenominational church that played rock music and seemed cool. When the church passed around bracelets meant to declare one's pledge of abstinence until marriage, she casually slipped one on. Abstinence didn't necessarily strike her as a higher moral good. But "there was a part of me that was like, if there are rules to be followed, I'd better follow them," she says. And abstinence struck her as a "reasonable" tenet by which to abide.

Pledge aside, in college she met the man who would later become her husband. For six months, as they fooled around—"dry humping and stuff like that"—Pam was aware of a mounting excitement, like her body had "just come online." But when they eventually became sexually active, the sense of urgency dissipated. Complacency replaced hungry anticipation, though she didn't think it was problematic at the time. "We did sex the way I thought it was supposed to look, but I don't know how much I was really able to understand and articulate what I wanted." Pam points out that it's hard to know what's good, let alone what's great, in the absence of education. She'd never looked at herself, she tells me. But today, more than two decades later, she's been "playing around with this realization that there was never a focus on my pleasure, because I didn't know that there should have been, I didn't know what it would look like."

After they got married, Pam's lack of pleasure and accompanying sexual disinterest became more important. Her husband wanted sex more often than she did, a pattern that persisted for years and became a greater source of contention over time. Through the keen eyes of hindsight, she explains, "If it's not about your pleasure, it makes sense you wouldn't want it." Early on, this discrepancy was framed in terms of her having a problem, as it so often is with the partner who feels less desire. "It was a shitty space to be in," says Pam. They tried different tactics over the years, like having sex every Wednesday (which worked great, for a month), or agreeing to be sexier outside the bedroom (yielding a benefit for a few weeks). They told themselves it was the baby, or later, the birth control pills. Maybe after the vasectomy everything would be all right. Pam eventually got checked out by her gynecologist, who recommended a sex therapist. The therapist was all booked up, but referred her to six other professionals, none of whom were available—a frustrated search for care that speaks volumes about the current demand for such services. Pam was on the verge of giving up when her husband went online and came across Danielle Harel.

A sex coach, as opposed to a sex therapist, Harel is the cofounder of the Somatica Institute in the Bay Area, which we'll revisit in Chapter 12.

Working with both individuals and couples, Somatica addresses issues such as how to expand your erotic repertoire and revitalize a sexless union. Communication is typically not enough, say Harel and Somatica cofounder Celeste Hirschman. To help couples find their spark, they work experientially. They say that to sustain an active and satisfying sex life over the long haul, you can't settle for "good enough": you need to "shoot for the moon."

To Pam, the experience of seeing a coach proved momentous on several fronts. Unlike sex therapists, who are typically mum with regard to their personal histories, coaches will often show up as sexual beings for their clients, modeling what it is to be empathetic, empowered, and unashamed. Some will deliberately (and with these words) use their own *pussy* or *cock* as a barometer for what is going on in the room. In other words, they try to both assess and access the erotic range of their clients, sensing their turnoffs, their reticence, and their opportunities for opening. Pam told me about her first visits with Harel and shared her personal writings from the time. The first session focused on dismantling social messages. A lot of people going through the process might well stop there, Pam says—with simply realizing that you're not broken, but have imbibed a lot of garbage about an incredibly vulnerable part of life. She wrote at the time:

> [Danielle] comforted me and told me that as a female race, we've been taught OUR ENTIRE LIVES to keep it in our pants. She pointed out that that kind of brainwashing certainly makes it difficult to reconnect our mind with our pussy. . . . Whether it's that the initial infatuation period has worn off, or that work is stressful, or that the kids need attention, or that the dinner has to be made . . . it is SO EASY for us to focus on absolutely everything else other than our sexual needs and desires. She told me that most women have "low libido" which is just another way to say that we are disconnected from our sexuality.

The second session went into bodily connection, and Pam was thrown when Harel encouraged her to "breathe into her pussy." *That word*, she thought. But, with her husband beside her and Harel demonstrating what this might look like, Pam says she experienced a breakthrough. "You mean this part of me doesn't have to be shut down?" she recalls thinking at the time. "You mean I can be paying attention to it?" Pam says it was the first time she'd ever acknowledged her own genitals in terms of a personal connection. "It was for me, not for someone else—that was an important thing." The impact on her marriage was immediate. Simply put, she says, the permission to relate to her own body led to feeling more turned on. Of the next visit, she wrote:

> I'm not saying I automatically am thinking about sex a hundred times a day, it's much more subtle than that. But I did start to find that these small moments throughout the day helped me realize I might not only want sex for my husband's sake, or for logical reasons like connecting us more deeply, but I might want it for my own pleasure as well. My mantra is "This feels good." (A pretty big switch from my previous mantra which was more like "Oh man, he's looking at me that way again . . . he's going to want sex tonight.")

Pam says she is still learning about her own desire and what she wants. "It's a slow roll," she tells me. While there may be revelatory moments in the process of sexual awakening, they are more like passing lights on the road ahead than a brightly electrified destination. Learning to express desire—to engage, to feel, to connect—often requires understanding what one wants in the first place. Although I spoke with some women who knew the precise shape of their desires, most of them expressed a gradual—and not necessarily straightforward—uncovering. Like Pam, they had to remove layers of shame or dismissal or sheer unknowing before they could even begin to contemplate what, indeed, they craved. Their stories show that liberation is not a state but an unfolding. However, in the greater field of sexual help and therapy, there is a lot of uncertainty as to what that should mean.

▼▲▼▲▼

Given that sex therapy was an invention of the mid-twentieth century, it has traveled a long way in a short time: it has gone from a nonexistent field to a sprawling industry, whose many visions for success follow the changing social tide.[1] Alfred Kinsey's midcentury surveys of sexual behavior in the United States cracked open the facade of erotic decorum by capturing a notable gulf between what society deemed acceptable and what actually went on behind closed doors. Extramarital sex, homosexuality, and even bestiality were all apparently a part of the fabric of American life. In his 1953 book *Sexual Behavior in the Human Female*, Kinsey presented evidence that a majority of women masturbated, that more than half of them had engaged in premarital sex, and that a quarter had had sex outside of marriage. Ahead of his time in many ways, Kinsey believed that select sexual behaviors did not signal moral right or opprobrium. Rather, natural variations were so great that any effort to define "normal" was essentially meaningless.

These exposed realities aside, America at midcentury was marked by conservatism. When William Masters first tried publishing some of his initial data on human sexuality in 1960, his work was rejected for being pornographic. But the country was on the cusp of cataclysmic change, and when Masters and Johnson published the landmark text *Human Sexual Response* in 1966, the *Journal of the American Medical Association* asked, "Why was this study so long in coming?"[2] The book, which used lab data from over ten thousand orgasms reached by nearly seven hundred men and women, was, among other things, a triumph of perfect timing. To one observer in the 1970s, their work took place at a time "in which the 'diabolical' body became a 'glorious' body—a tabernacle of all positive sensations and energies."[3] The mass media at the time was busily promoting ideas of sensual enhancement, while new self-help manuals, such as *The Joy of Sex*, by Alex Comfort, presented intimacy as something that could be endlessly refined and savored. The value of sex itself was evolving from the currency of sanctioned unions to the individual pursuit of pleasure, and Masters and Johnson were figureheads of this transformation.[4]

In the intervening years, critics have questioned aspects of Masters and Johnson's work, including how they selected the research subjects whose orgasms would become the basis of their explication of the human sexual response cycle. That sexual function is natural became the pair's steady sound bite, and natural meant following the "universal" pattern of excitement, plateau, orgasm, and resolution. But as some have pointed out, the men and women who had sex for science were predominantly white, middle to upper middle class, and highly educated. They enjoyed sex (not to mention exhibitionism) and could readily climax from "effective sexual stimulation."[5] This latter point especially has raised ire. The sex therapist and scholar Leonore Tiefer has argued that the alleged gender equity of the model was built in favor of men's sexual interests and assumed that everyone both possesses and craves the same sort of sexuality. "Yet," she noted, "social realities dictate that we are not all the same sexually—not in our socially shaped wishes, in our sexual self-development, or in our interpersonal sexual meanings."[6]

Masters and Johnson did acknowledge that women internalized "prevailing psychosocial influences" that might interfere with their natural function. But then, they were so convinced of women's sexual athleticism—that their capacity "infinitely surpasses that of man"— that they supposed a bit of regulation might be needed to curtail what would otherwise be a voracious appetite. In their 1970 book *Human Sexual Inadequacy*, they mused, "Indeed, her significantly greater susceptibility to negatively based psychosocial influences may imply the existence of a natural state of psycho-sexual-social balance between the sexes that has been culturally established to neutralize women's biophysical superiority."[7]

These controversies notwithstanding, their work launched the field of sex therapy—and their status as celebrities. The pair appeared on a 1970 *Time* magazine cover describing them as scientists "repairing the conjugal bed." By defining adequate function, Masters and Johnson established the basis for treating deviations from the norm. In their view, problems like premature ejaculation or women's lack of orgasm were not mired in inner angst, as early theorists like Freud supposed. Rather, men and women simply required straightforward education and technical finesse. They treated specific sexual concerns in intensive two-week-long interventions. These were oriented toward behavior and introduced techniques designed to help patients (re)discover their bodies and their potential for sensual pleasure.[8] The centerpiece of their therapeutic program was "sensate focus," touch-based exercises intended to help both the diagnosis and resolution of sexual issues. Sensate focus, also called "nondemand pleasuring," aimed to redirect patients' attention to sensory feeling, encouraging them to experience, in a nonjudgmental way, what it is to both give and receive touch.[9] It's hard to overstate their appeal at a time when Americans were for the first time openly enthusiastic about sex. Even though *Human Sexual Response* was written in a deliberately antiseptic style (making clear—much like its authors' public uniform of white lab coats—that this was not smut, but science), it became a best seller. In *Human Sexual Inadequacy*, they described remarkable results from their programs—an overall cure rate of 80 percent—leading to a wide embrace of their work by professionals. Here was an approach to sexuality in which everyone possessed a reserve of hidden lust that could be brought to the surface with changes in performance and positioning. It seemed market ready.

In Masters and Johnson's day, the typical person seeking help was young and well educated and presented with (what were at least considered) straightforward issues. But over time, the patient profile began to change. Men and women began showing up with harder-to-treat problems—leading some therapists to bemoan, "Where have all the good cases gone?"[10] To some, this shift reflected a success in the field and in society at large. With quality information available to the masses—by the 1980s Dr. Ruth was piping her sex advice into America's living rooms—the earlier types of issues, springing from a lack of education, were no longer so widespread. But some believed the more complex patient profile offered a truer reflection of human intimacy. Sex therapist Marty Klein told me that in the decades immediately following Masters and Johnson, professionals "learned more and more about a pretty narrow thing: how people's bodies work during sex. But of course there are people attached to those bodies and the field has been trying to understand people. That turns out to be a lot more complicated."

Helen Singer Kaplan, who trained as both a psychologist and a psychiatrist, was at the forefront of this more intricate landscape. When she opened the country's first dedicated sex therapy clinic in 1973, she found that Masters and Johnson's tremendous results did not translate as well into an outpatient context. She believed that many sexual struggles stemmed from issues clouding desire itself, and also that these kinds of issues were the ones that were the most difficult to resolve. "Patients with sexual desire disorders tend to have more serious underlying emotional and marital problems," she wrote in her book *The Sexual*

Desire Disorders.[11] Whereas sexually healthy people "accentuate the positives and decentuate the negatives" to maximize their pleasure, she said, people with low desire effectively "turn themselves off."[12] In her thinking, desire disorders represented an essential motivation "gone awry." In her "new" sex therapy model, Kaplan examined how psychological experiences like trauma, guilt, insecurity, and the fear of being selfish could derail libido.[13] She later led the way in using medications, specifically SSRIs, to treat sexual aversions. She also experimented with eclectic models of care that included sensate focus, marital therapy, directed masturbation, and group therapy.

But other factors were also changing how Americans conceived of successful and satisfying intimacy. Chief among them were growing expectations for high-quality sex. The new generation of patients wasn't necessarily seeking help with basic functioning; they were looking to augment passion and eroticism. Writing in the late 1970s, sex therapists Joe LoPiccolo and Julia Heiman observed that the bounty of circulating information was not assuaging Americans' sexual anxieties, but exacerbating them. "Somehow the popular media have transformed 'women are sexual and can have multiple orgasms' into 'real women must be hypersexual and must have multiple orgasms,'" they wrote.[14] In tandem, social roles for women were undergoing rapid changes, including both a snarl of hope and a backlash about the meaning and expression of autonomy. Insofar as women were coming forward with "complex" issues like low desire, it was hard to determine how much of it was due to changing gender norms: perhaps women were simply trying to navigate a path between their newfound public power and continued expectations for their subordination in the home.

The 1980s marked the beginning of a new era in how we understand both sex and the human psyche—an era that continues today. Problems of all stripes, from male impotence to depression, vaginismus, and premenstrual syndrome (PMS), have been recast as biological maladies requiring medical—as opposed to behavioral or psychological—solutions. From Prozac's introduction in 1987 to Viagra's debut in 1998, advances in medical treatments and knowledge have tracked changes in how the public consumes care. In looking to the popular appeal of the medical model, some have speculated that Americans prefer to be diagnosed with a "no-fault" biological disorder rather than to carry the "stigma" of a psychological one. And yet this view rests on a troubled division, as it is impossible to separate mind from body.

The medical community has surged ahead with new interventions to address dysfunction even as sex therapists have engaged in a protracted self-appraisal; meanwhile, innovations such as mindfulness have gained traction.[15] Against the medical tide of quantifying deviations from the norm, sex therapists have been wrestling with elemental questions, including how, in our endlessly variable world, we decide whether something is a sexual problem, and if it is, how we determine whether we've fixed it. Is it ethical to promote function without attending to the emotional universe in which sex exists? Does helping women become more sexually receptive, for example, suggest that others are entitled to their bodies? The Canadian psychologist and sexologist Peggy Kleinplatz has said that sex therapy can end up perpetuating some of the very problems it aims to dispel. By "quietly treating the causalities" of troubled sex and gender norms, it can avoid challenging the status quo that "engenders the sexual problems" to begin with.[16]

The late sex therapist Gina Ogden similarly reflected on her discipline's aims, criticizing, in particular, the focus on function and quantity—how many times did you have intercourse in the last week/month/year? How many times did you orgasm? Despite their limitations, she observed, "performance outcomes remain a fixed idea in much of sex research and sex therapy training today, too often inhibiting what we ask clients about the depth and breadth of sexual healing, pleasure, and potential."[17]

Experts have been pressed to say what success means in this more complicated landscape. Part of the issue is how the problem is framed; professionals and their clients have been left to wrestle with whether it is realistic to attempt to restore what has passed, or indeed whether it is healthy to strive for the *extraordinary* states promised by the media, as well as by some practitioners. Against the yearning for mind-blowing eroticism, some therapists have urged a tamping down of expectations. Maybe sex does not have to be earth-shaking, suggests sex therapist Barry McCarthy, who champions a goal of "good enough sex." Performance is both variable and vulnerable, he maintains. Accepting that sexual quality can range from "very good to mediocre or even dysfunctional" is an important feature of maintaining satisfaction and "inoculating the couple from disappointment and sexual problems in the future."[18]

And yet irrespective of uncertain outcomes—Does sex therapy lead to better sex, improved self-acceptance, greater pleasure, stronger pairs?—the field has seen incredible growth and widening breadth. From medical interventions to spiritual guidance, from polyamory counseling to kink-informed treatment, the niches in the field have bourgeoned. To some, the acceleration of experts on the edges reflects a commitment to embracing diversity. To others, it runs the risk of neglecting a sizable center. To Marty Klein, the splintering of special-izations has not been a positive trend. Citing the high number of un-intended pregnancies in the United States, alongside the prevalence of sexual pain, anatomical ignorance, extreme body consciousness, and other problems, he said, "as a field, we have completely abandoned the everyday American public." There is tension between attending to intersectional inclusivity and speaking to the common ground—a pain point in progressive politics more generally. Another sex therapist told me that "modern alphabet soup movements have distracted sex therapy away from concerns about plain old heterosexual intimacy in long-term committed partnerships," which is what most clients seek help for.

With the mushrooming of specializations, one of the most gnaw-ing questions for practitioners and the public alike has become, *Who gets to be an expert?* As the numbers of credentialed, uncredentialed, and self-proclaimed specialists bloom, it's easier than ever to get lost in the brambles of promise, an increasingly noisome crowd that's keeping stride with our own longings. In our "OK Google" age, help seekers are just as likely to find someone with little training and lots of opin-ions as they are to find a seasoned professional with years of clinical insight. That said, doctors are also a big part of the Internet's amped-up culture of entrepreneurialism, making it all the more difficult to deci-pher sound science from a good hook. As psychologist Leonore Tiefer has observed, in the popular mind, practices considered fringe from a medical standpoint have been granted equal footing with mainstream therapies: "Searching online for sexual advice, enhancement, enter-tainment, or remedy can instantly lead to explicit videos, surgeries, supplements, medical treatments, instructional videos, sex coaching or weekend workshops, all seemingly on a level playing field."[19]

But maybe having all these in- and out-of-the-box options is a good thing. Perhaps what we're seeing now looks more like sex therapy in its early heyday, when treatments were more experimental and experiential. Tiefer describes the 1960s and 1970s as a time when "humanistic sex therapy" flourished. Bringing together elements of the California counterculture, the human potential movement, and new practices like Gestalt therapy and bodywork, the era's approaches included group therapy, the use of surrogate partners, nudism, and sexual touch. These offerings were sometimes practiced under the mantle of medicine, but not always. Instead, their "major goals were 'empowerment' via peer exchange and 'authenticity' in self-disclosure and body acceptance."[20] She argues that many of these practices lost out due to "embarrassment about sex itself," which led to a professional focus on function at the expense of "the respectability of sexual pleasure."[21]

PART TWO: SHOOT FOR THE MOON

It is within this increasingly multipart and unverified landscape that the industry of sex coaching has come to prominence. Since the 2000s, sex coaches, as well as love, intimacy, dating, and divorce coaches, have been popping up all over the place. Capturing the industry in a succinct description is a challenge because it is so wide ranging. On the one hand, coaching can be an adjunct or alternative to sex therapy, one psychologist told me. On the other hand, it is a serpentine lock on the Medusa head of self-help, offering to satiate our every hope and need while pushing us to further professionalize our inner worlds.

The beauty of it—or the problem, depending on your view—is that anyone can become a sex coach. Under that title, practitioners administer a variety of services, from online workshops to in-person classes. Sessions can look like psychotherapy, or they can look like sex work. Some coaches—though not many—have intercourse with their clients; others work with sexual surrogates. Some coaches, calling themselves "sexperts," have a sizable digital presence. Some are licensed in other fields, such as counseling; others have degrees but have let their licenses lapse in order to engage in practices like intimate touch, which would jeopardize their professional standing. Klein told me he views coaching as a sort of "Wild West" composed of "outrageous promises and potentially harmful interventions for people" alongside "efforts that seem to be much more focused and assert an air of regulation." He says the rise of coaching goes hand in hand with the heightened level of sexual expectation in contemporary life. "Coaching is one of the things that attempts to address that chronic hunger the population has."

Unbound by the licensing requirements or the ethical codes of medicine or psychotherapy, coaches can facilitate some pretty radical opportunities for healing and self-discovery. This is the field's boon as well as its ballast. While there are now several sex-coach training programs out there, none of them offer credentials recognized by any regulatory body. Nor are there standard qualifications for joining the field: some programs advertise to prospective students with claims that you—yes, you!—should consider this lucrative, *extraordinary* career. Though some of the established psychotherapists I interviewed dismissed sex coaching as "small potatoes," others suggested it has been a useful development. I am writing about it here because among the women I spoke with, the subject came up numerous times as an approach they had personally tried or were curious about.

By most accounts, a sexologist and educator named Patti Britton is the creator of sex coaching—though something between *grande dame* and den mother might be a more fitting attribution. "I am a mother hen and you're my chicks," she told a group of protégés at a workshop I attended. Britton held leadership roles at Planned Parenthood and the Sexuality Information and Education Council of the United States before shifting gears and obtaining a doctoral degree at San Francisco's now defunct Institute for Advanced Study of Human Sexuality—aka "the Institute" to its trainees, aka "Fuck U" to its critics. Despite graduating most of the sexologists working in the United States today, as well as veritable heroes of the sex-positive world, among them Betty Dodson, Carol Queen, and Annie Sprinkle, the for-profit school was unable to attain an accreditation status. Its founder, the late Rev. Dr. Ted McIlvenna, claimed that the school didn't want to be "handcuffed" by taking federal money, and therefore be limited in terms of what it could do, say, or teach. The institute's training included erotology, nudity, and erotic exchange. In an interview, McIlvenna once said, "We have only one rule here—that you couldn't solicit in front of the building to raise [money for] your tuition."[22]

Britton is a proud torchbearer of the institute's ethos, and accordingly views sexology as the humanistic investigation into what people do sexually and how they feel about it. Sexology is not, she tells me, a sex-based subdiscipline of psychology or any other realm of social science. It is, in the lineage of Havelock Ellis and Kinsey, a discipline unto itself, concerned with the range of human sexual behavior and its countless contexts and meanings. In 2005 Britton authored the first (and to my knowledge only) practitioner's guide on the subject, *The Art of Sex Coaching*, and later she founded the training symposium Sex Coach U. Meeting her in 2019, I was struck by the sheer adoration she inspires in her followers and her zeal for certifying as many sex coaches as she can. To train under Britton, it occurred to me, was not simply to get schooled on anatomy and healing methodologies; it was to strive to embody the very principles of radical acceptance, self-expansion, possibility, and sex positivity she aims to convey to her clients. She peppers her exchanges with the word "love," frequently telling her students, "I love you" and "You are loved here." In the original brochure for her services, she defined her philosophy as follows:

> We are all affected by the increasingly sex-negative cultural climate. Sex coaching is a way for you to share sex positivity, get the sexfacts, and celebrate your sexual power.
>
> Sexual fears, ignorance, confusion, and the many stressful pressures on our lives today are killing sexual pleasure. Sex coaching offers a safe space where you can heal your pain, reclaim your birthright to enjoy sex as pleasure, and regain mastery for your own success.[23]

In her book, Britton presents sex coaching as a paradigm shift. She writes, "More creative and flexible than traditional therapy methods, sex coaching is an art." However, to understand what sex coaching really is, it is perhaps easiest to lay out what it is not. First off and most importantly, it's not therapy. As one coach put it to me, therapists tend to be great at talking the language of language, but coaches also approach intimacy from the language of touch. Sex coaching is not pathologizing, that is, it doesn't proceed from the label of dysfunction and endeavor to restore "normalcy." It doesn't designate certain behaviors or longings as unhealthy, but aims rather to normalize what individuals are already feeling and doing. It is forward-looking rather than focused on untangling the past. And unlike traditional therapy, in which professionals rarely reveal any personal information, coaches tend to be self-referential, modeling empowerment through their personal demeanor and selective disclosures about their own life histories (or, in the case of Somatica, their own genitals). Coaching comes from an *I* place, Britton said. She readily shares, for instance, that she has traveled the spectrum of human experience. She has lived in a sexless relationship, felt the "ravages" of menopause, and lost her daughter to HIV/AIDS, and yet, she says, she moved from grief to ecstasy.

As I surveyed the field and talked to some of its practitioners and clients, one of the chief distinctions I saw between sex therapy and sex coaching was around the personal value of sex—and what we believe we can aim for. Therapists may readily concede that sex is life energy, a creative power, but at the same time they acknowledge that it's as much about the plumbing as it is about transcendence. In their emphasis on the naturalness of sex, therapists maintain that intimacy and sensuality should be enjoyable, playful, and satisfying, but they also say it's perfectly normal for sex to be marked by mediocrity or complacency, or to be just "good enough." The coaching industry, by contrast, stresses excellence. The word "extraordinary" makes routine appearances in coaching materials. In some respects, this orientation is a return to the Age of Aquarius and the human potential movement. But in others, it is thoroughly of the current moment and our culture's bleating faith in self-optimization (another term, "sex hacks," also floats in the coaching vernacular). As in other areas of today's culture, the restless individual takes center stage.

As the founder of sex coaching, Britton is attuned to the rapid growth in her field, and she is particularly sensitive to the competing programs that certify new coaches. "I'm concerned about protecting professionalism in a world where anyone can say, I do sex coaching, and then slap up a website and start collecting money in the shopping cart," she told me.

Britton is not just concerned about protecting professionalism; for her, the bigger issue is safeguarding consumers from self-proclaimed coaches who lack the needed skills, and potentially the ethics, to properly help their clients. Most people who come to sex coaching have already tried some of the orthodox routes, such as consulting with doctors and therapists. "They're not tabula rasa," Britton said. Rather, the very systems that purported to be able to help them have often failed them. "I worry about people not being competent," she said. "The sexual soul is a very delicate membrane. And to open that up and not have the wherewithal and proper training to help that client become whole—that's what healing means—that to me is immoral and egregious."

Over the course of our first conversation, Britton referred to flagging desire as both a "crisis" and an "epidemic." Beyond the struggles of long-term monogamy and poor body image, she pointed an accusing finger at the ubiquity of technology, which has "hijacked our presenceness." Our constant connectivity is, ironically, undermining our human connectedness—"We're having relationships in which there is no touch," which further condemns us to a "neck-up" existence. One of the other prime culprits in her view is the media, which has been a double-edged sword in that it promotes sexual potential while also feeding our anxieties. But perhaps, above all, she said, the crisis of desire stems from our reluctance to investigate what our desires really are. We're cut off from our innermost selves and need to be brought home. Britton thinks that through its dual emphasis on embodiment and self-acceptance, sex coaching is uniquely poised to address these issues. While part of becoming more connected sexually may be as simple as "put down the fucking phone," effective sex coaches can also help clients come back into their own bodies and realize what they really want without feeling shame, engaging in unrealistic, self-flagellating aspirations, or succumbing to the fear that genuine erotic expression will fracture the safety of their existing social world. "The sex coach goes to the inside and brings the person out," Britton told me.

▼▲▼▲▼

When I spoke with women who had tried sex coaching, I came away with a scattershot impression of the field. One had turned to coaching because her sex life with her husband had come to feel "like drudgery." Another sought a sex coach to help with her unease surrounding her body. She said that most of her sessions were devoted to guided meditations intended to help her reconnect with her inner and outer beauty.

Another consulted a coach because she was upset that her sex life had tapered off. She told me that she and her coach had established a set of goals for her, such as more frequent intimacy and improved communication. She had then checked in weekly with the coach to assess her progress and tweak the approach. She described the process as "effective," but quickly added, "It was a ton of work."

Still, I wanted a more solid understanding of sex coaching. In order to get a taste of some of its many flavors, I decided to try three different practitioners for myself. In keeping with the focus of this book, I told them I was interested in increasing my sexual desire and that I would be writing about our sessions. The first coach offered sessions over Skype, and we chatted several times between her home office in Colorado and mine in Brooklyn. She had trained as a professional coach and picked up certificates in different somatic, emotional, and relational therapy methods. In her promotional materials she stressed her use of neuroscience and guided visualizations. Her current work stemmed from her own experience of living in a sexless marriage and her efforts to reignite her sense of passion. Doing so, in her framework, was largely a matter of staying curious—about oneself and one's partner. It was not approaching sexuality with the same ho-hum sense that you know all there is to know. Rather, the aim was to try to harness a beginner's mind-set in intimacy: relinquishing everything you think you know in order to discover how it is you actually feel. She underscored the vicious cycle through which absent pleasure erodes women's desire. When you don't feel good, your body will retreat from what's on offer, she said, even if you continue to say yes, and that results in a punishing split. Desire, she told me, was the language of my soul, and so it was my fundamental duty to revere its wishes. If its siren call had been blotted out, I was to become an intrepid hunter of buried pleasure. "Do you feel an animal inside you?" she asked me more than once. "What sound might it make?" Uncertain as to what my inner beast might be, I contemplated ending our discussion, but instead emitted a soft roar, rather like a dysthymic cat. It was a good start, she said, but neither of us were convinced.

The second coach I consulted with was in recovery from a sexless marriage of two decades. We met just once, in her home in Northern

California, and she told me that most women never come close to realizing their orgasmic potential because so much of the sex they have is second rate. Women put up with touch that is not actually the kind of touch they crave—they may long for domination, but instead tolerate soft, puppy-like affections that leave them feeling frustrated and turned off, or vice versa. Moreover, women routinely consent to penetration well before they are actually ready; as a result, they endure sex that is painful, but they grit their teeth and bear it. Our session revolved around a guided visualization. Much to my surprise, I was rapidly led to confront a former assailant and to rewrite the script of our encounter so that, theoretically, I could leave the situation empowered and unharmed. I had hardly anticipated doing something of this depth right off the bat, and it left me physically shaking. And so I was jarred by our session's abrupt conclusion immediately thereafter, which combined an embrace ("May I give you a hug?") with a rather heavy-handed sales pitch for continued work in the future. The experience made me think of what Britton calls the "Humpty Dumpty effect." She teaches her protégés to "avoid cracking open another human being and not having the wherewithal to facilitate their putting themselves back together again."

My third sex-coaching experiment was with Dimitry Yakoushkin, who is affiliated with the Somatica Institute. We met for one in-person session in an apartment in San Francisco, and I interviewed him by phone thereafter. Aware of his large and strong presence, he told me that a lot of women use him to act out their desires for and aggressions toward men. He told me, "A big part of the work is to be human—not to be a therapist or pretending you have it all together, but looking at the person in front of you and wondering, what's keeping this relationship from deepening. That's what I do, I sit and think why aren't we making out right now, why aren't we falling in love?" Admitting his own erotic energy into the space is a big part of it. He is, as he describes himself, of the dominant paradigm: tall, blue eyed, handsome, muscular. He exudes power: he can play the father, the lover, the nameless object of rage. When I asked whether his clients fell for him, he shrugged. I pressed him, "You must get off on doing this work—how do you manage your own excitement?" To which he replied, "I'll tell you the secret to succeeding in this field: you have to get off in doing it."

His take is that women tend to have massively unaddressed sexual needs. Even though the media all but assaults women with tips about how to be better in bed, he said, "women don't need skills-building on how to be better lovers to men. They need skills on how to be better lovers to themselves, to find the voice to ask for what they want." He said he's "shocked" that there are indeed women who know how to have great sex and focus on their own pleasure when "the cultural current, the flow of water is toward men's pleasure, and men's orgasm. No one sits girls down and says your body is beautiful, you deserve all the pleasure you could possibly experience, if it feels good keep doing it. No, the message is sex is dangerous, men can't help themselves, and you need to guard yourself."

Our session involved a conversational prompt about what I enjoy in my sexuality and my best erotic experiences to date. After a while, he said, "Okay, I think I have everything I need." He stood up, dimmed the lights, and walked to the bed on the other side of the room, sprawling on its surface. I didn't know what to expect, but I understood there would be no sex, no nudity, no kissing, no penetration or other explicit acts. It was to be a container of erotic experience meant to get me in touch with my own sensual pulse. "Dimitry is going to take care of you," he said, "you can let go." I placed my head on his chest, per his instruction, and for a while we just breathed together. Just as I was relaxing into it, the scene abruptly changed. He climbed on top of me, and for the next half-hour or so proceeded to praise me, whisper in my ears, pull my hair, flip me around, spank my behind, and smell my armpits. It was, frankly, exhilarating. But as I pulled out my credit card to pay for our time together, I wondered what service it was I had just procured.

Even though I left my session with Yakoushkin wondering whether I had unwittingly engaged in infidelity, as I considered our encounter I believe I got a better sense of what sex coaching might offer. I had been turned on, and yet, as opposed to my normal experiences of intimacy, there was no emotional "other" to which my thoughts rallied. The sensations of my body had nothing to do with my feelings for this man, or anyone else. Nor, significantly, did I have to *do* anything with them. Instead, I simply felt lit up, electrified by my own body and its pulse.

LIBERATING THE EROTIC IMAGINATION

In her introduction to the first edition of *New Directions in Sex Therapy*, published in 2001, psychologist Peggy Kleinplatz highlighted the limits she saw besetting her field. Therapists' own understanding of what is right or wrong or normal, she said, can interfere with how they practice. "We tell clients that all the 'shoulds' they inflict upon themselves are hazardous to their well-being—but only when we disagree with them. (We might say, 'You shouldn't feel guilty about self-stimulating,' but we would be very unlikely to say, 'You shouldn't feel guilty about stimulating your dog's genitals.')"[24]

This line came back to me as I thought about the chief differences between sex therapy and sex coaching. If therapy tends to be about removing symptoms to restore function, coaching, as Britton explained it to me, was about helping the individual uncover their erotic truth within. In the world of the latter, premised as it is on viewing all behavior with an eye toward normalization, practitioners might not look askance at something like bestial urges. To wit, when the professional sex coach leading an educational seminar I attended told the class that her secret fantasy was to "make love to a panther," no one batted an eyelash. The room yearned, like grass to sky, toward radical acceptance. So long as it does not carry harm, no sex act or craving is thought too obscene, too risqué, too weird, or too wrong to be excluded from the wondrous mess of human intimacy.

To get a better sense of how sex therapists, as well as Britton's coaches-in-training, approach the task of normalization, I attended a training session known as SAR, for Sexual Attitude Reassessment (sometimes the "R" is for "Readjustment" or "Restructuring"). It's a requirement for Britton's coaching program as well as for those obtaining certification in the American Association of Sexuality Educators, Counselors and Therapists (AASECT), a regulatory body for sex therapists. The SAR process was developed in the 1960s at the Institute for Advanced Study of Human Sexuality in San Francisco. Over the course of two days (originally it was a sixty-hour intensive delivered over six days), individuals are encouraged to confront their own judgments so that they can become more tolerant of diverse sexual behavior. According to one definition, "SAR is designed to inundate participants with sexual material in order to bring awareness to areas of discomfort or bias, and through exploration and discussion, ease the participants into a place of greater comfort and confidence in approaching this work with clients and in life."[25] One component of the original training was dubbed "Fuck-O-Rama" because it entailed extensive pornographic saturation with numerous screens blaring simultaneously. Explicit content was also a major component of the session I attended, which, because of the confidentiality agreement I signed, I will not write about in detail. My weekend in a West Coast hotel featured CBT (which, while watching a wincing scene involving a typewriter and a miniature cactus, I learned stood for "cock and ball torture"), a gay head-shaving fetish (though we were reminded that a *fetish* also means an object of magical worship that transports you to another time and place), a medical-latex threesome with labial clamps, and a grandmotherly figure administering a prostate massage to her septuagenarian consort. It also included frank confessionals from people whose bodies and lifestyles don't necessarily accord with our rigidly gendered and ableist stereotypes—like what it's like for a trans woman to experience pleasure, or how a little person (the preferred term for adults with dwarfism) self-stimulates when his or her fingers cannot reach the genitals. The idea, beyond highlighting all the "inscrutable, mystical loveliness" of sex, in the words of one facilitator, is to get participants to identify their own discomforts, seek out what turns them on—"It's okay to get aroused"—or disgusts them, or both. We were told to examine our triggers so that we could work toward breaking down our prejudices. But we were not to respond with our cognitive selves; the goal was to allow the reactions to percolate below the skin. The true professional—when met, say, "with a client who declares that his greatest passion is to smear his partner's menstrual blood all over himself"—will not balk, but simply nod and say okay. The only unnatural act, we are reminded in reference to *The Happy Hooker*, is one that cannot be performed.

At the SAR session I attended, there was a sort of rah-rah attitude around all things non-vanilla. Sex workers in attendance were commended for their integrity, as were any who professed to plumb the depths of fantasy in constructing their waking lives. There was almost a certain pressure to act blasé about what elsewhere would register as extreme, as when the room smiled politely as an unassuming middle-aged woman stated that she had had a gang-bang the night before. When another woman reported that she was arranging a similarly multitudinous scene for her trans lover, the room all but broke out in applause.

In my recollection, the word "dysfunction" never surfaced over the course of the weekend. Rather, sexuality was framed in terms of accessing delight and accepting nonconformity. The subject of low desire was not viewed as a matter of sexual disinterest, but rather a result of how, owing to the greater culture, we hold ourselves back, condemn our fantasies, foreclose on what we really want, and sell ourselves short on the idea that sex and love must look a certain way. We push ourselves toward physical encounters that we either do not want or for which we have not allowed desire to adequately develop. I came away with the impression that sexual healing and erotic growth had little to do with tricks or techniques, or even how we choose to configure our connections, and almost everything to do with liberating the imagination, with sensing an internal flicker of *I want that*—whether *that* was painting with body fluids, being dominated, or just having missionary-style sex that lasts longer than three to seven minutes—and feeling empowered to act accordingly.

▼▲▼▲▼

Of course, one could argue, the project of inner liberation does not necessarily shift the levers of the larger system. But Britton, along with her trainees and colleagues, views person-by-person healing as a piece of a greater turn toward equality. To learn to listen to the body, to find comfort in demarcating what it craves or consents to, is to challenge on a fundamental level the world we have inherited.

Pam wound her way toward a similar conclusion. Following her first three sessions with Danielle Harel, she started a group for women in her social circle to discuss the issues she was suddenly coming up against. Her girlfriends were enthused about the forum. "Oh my god, we haven't talked about this with anyone," is how she described their general reaction. Pam's curiosity was piqued. She began reading up and using her vacation days from her job at Facebook to attend some of the national conferences on sexuality, including AASECT's annual meeting.

Watching her pursue these interests, Harel encouraged her to join Somatica's coaching program. After a brief hesitation, Pam enrolled, and shortly thereafter she decided to remake her career. "I came home and I told my husband, 'This is amazing. I want to quit my job,'" she told me. So she did. And while she was going through the coaching program, she also got a degree in counseling.

Today, three years into her new profession, Pam has her own waitlist of eager clients. But professional clarity aside, she told me she is still in the process of understanding what she wants. "It took me how long—forty years to get here?" she said. "It's gonna take a while to unwind. I am still learning about what turns me on." It's a matter of refinement, she said. "It's about getting more and more clear on exactly what works for me." One of the issues coming into focus is what it is to feel desire. For a lot of men and women who are partnered to someone with a higher drive, they don't get to steep in the sensations of mounting interest and arousal. This is a major deficit. Pam likens the experience to being perpetually force-fed and then suddenly being able to work up an appetite. "That feeling of hunger is amazing." Even though she describes herself as a traveler on a longer journey, she says she now appreciates the centrality of sex in her life. "I didn't understand that before. But sexuality has made all of my life so much richer, physically, emotionally. I definitely now believe it is a cornerstone to me feeling alive and joyful in the world. And, I would love to have that part of me alive and turned on until the day I die."

9 HUMAN POTENTIAL ON THE OPEN MARKET

> There is one way to awaken this world, and it is
> not through your hard work, it is not through
> your suffering. It is through your pussy.
>
> —*Regena Thomashauer,* Pussy: A Reclamation, *2016*

IT'S A FREEZING Saturday in February, but inside the Tribeca auditorium temperatures are running high. Having removed their puffy outer layers, women are stripping down to lingerie and nightclub wear. Pink feather boas punctuate the aisles, along with T-shirts reading, "8,000 Nerve Endings at Your Service." Some women dance together in cloistered circles, others sway before their chairs, and many sit quietly, just taking it all in: this teeming sea of give-or-take one thousand ladies. Dreadlocks jostle with gleaming blowouts, brocade jackets and fold-out fans perch beside lacquered nails and leopard prints. Knitted ovary caps are out in spades. And all around, *pussy* buzzes in the air—not as a charged noun, but, confoundingly, as an adjective. *That haircut is so pussy! What a pussy top!*

The turn of speech is an exercise in reclamation proposed by the weekend's headliner, Regena Thomashauer, or Mama Gena, as she is known to her "Sister Goddess" devotees. Women have traveled from as far as Alaska, New Zealand, Poland, and Nigeria for "the Experience," a weekend-long introduction to Mama Gena's School of Womanly Arts that promises to help a woman "connect with her desires, find her voice, and create a life she deserves." "Pussy" is a degraded term, Thomashauer explains. It connotes shame, weakness, women as objects, and bodies as unclean. But this is all wrong. Pussy should be a site of worship: it is the wellspring of life, of creativity, of strength and power. We should all raise our hands to the Great Pussy in the Sky.

"She's like a priest," whispers my seatmate, Carrie, a freckled doctor clad in a black lace bodysuit and expensively tattered jeans, as a barefoot middle-aged woman makes her way through the roar and waving arms. The atmosphere is charged with all the hype and hope of a Tony Robbins pageant.

Thomashauer takes the stage and breathlessly welcomes the crowd to "the greatest, most spectacular celebration of women that has ever existed": "We've been waiting for you," she adds, "and you've shown the fuck up!" And who is she? Thomashauer declares, "I am sacred. I am sassy. And I swear like a truck driver." Of us, the teeming audience, she determines, "Something stands between you and your dreams and I'm going to get that fucking bastard out of the way."

The crowd hangs on her every word, pouring faith into her prancing form: radical transformation is within reach and pleasure can set you free. To Thomashauer, society is all mixed up where it comes to desire. Desire should not be buried or denied, but held aloft like a guiding torch. Women feel stressed, depleted, empty, and angry because they have learned to subdue their sexuality, but in doing so they have cut themselves off from the core of their being. The erotic, she says, is a woman's connection to the most sacred part of herself. It is "the part of her that is both timeless and eternal, that never diminishes, but only intensifies, the more she pays attention to it. When a woman is in constant investigation of her erotic landscape, her well never empties, her cup is always full."

We audience members, she continues, slowly catching her breath, we are women who yearn for more. Our sex lives are lamentable. Our libidos have flatlined. Our orgasms are little more than "crotch sneezes." We're stuck. We're filled with doubt. We're struggling—with money, with men, with meaning. We feel trapped in a man's world—we've manned up so much we're more masculine than they are. We are, in short, collective victims of the great Patriarchy, and she is here to liberate us. The crowd thunders.

Thomashauer explains that her own life is living proof. Long before she became Mama Gena and joined the ranks of other self-fashioned gurus of personal improvement, Thomashauer was a struggling actress trying to make ends meet by waiting tables in New York City. "But in truth my life was slowly grinding to a halt," she wrote in her 2016 book, *Pussy: A Reclamation.*[1] "I was an actress who was not acting, a singer who was not singing, a young woman who was not dating or developing socially. . . . I was waiting tables and hiding from everyone whose expectations I was so conscious I was disappointing." A turn to therapy led to a self-directed course on mythology, where she began to see that early religions commonly revered a female creator, rather than a great Father on High. Her journey eventually brought her to a class on sensuality run through an organization called More University. The class taught "how our culture restricts us from experiencing pleasure," and Thomashauer recalls leaving one of the workshops with instructions for a unique task: to prepare herself and her home as if the most important person in the world were coming to pay a call—with the catch being that that person was herself. "I bought myself pink roses, Pellegrino, dark chocolate with almonds, French bread, gruyere cheese, and strawberries," she wrote in her book. "Then I scurried home . . . and took a long, delicious bath with music playing, my little tray of treats spread out by the tub."

She stepped out of the bath and continued with the prescribed exercise, gazing at her naked form in the mirror. "I realized in that moment that women have no clue about our own beauty; no clue about the connection between pleasure and time; no clue about this deep, delicious, endlessly replenishing source of divinity within each of us. All these years I had been looking for the Goddess. Suddenly I had stumbled upon her—in the last pace I would ever think to look. She was here, inside of *me.*" Thomashauer became more involved with More University, living briefly in an affiliated intentional community in New York. Eventually she traveled across the country to study with its founder.

Victor Baranco, a former appliance salesman, started Lafayette Morehouse, Inc., in the late 1960s in Lafayette, California. It was to be a place for research in communications, sensuality, and relationships. The university doled out masters and doctoral degrees in lifestyles and sensuality until the State of California cracked down on private, for-profit, nonaccredited universities ("worthless diploma schools," is how the *New York Times* put it in 1994).[2] His wife had long struggled with orgasm, and after consulting with all manner of doctors, Baranco developed a technique of clitoral stroking intended to help women experience pleasure without any burden of reciprocity. Lafayette Morehouse became known for putting on live demonstrations of the technique, a practice Baranco and his followers called Deliberate Orgasm (or Extended Orgasm). Thomashauer references the practice in her teachings. Baranco, who died in 2002, called his philosophy "responsible hedonism." Although some followers still revere him, others have criticized him for using coercive methods on his acolytes. "It was a huge ego-crushing machine," said one man, who lived at Morehouse for twenty years, in an interview with the *New York Times* in 2009.[3] Baranco was featured alongside Charles Manson in *Mindfuckers*, a 1972 book about the rise of "acid fascism" and the darkness that "lurks beyond the Aquarian Age."[4]

Nicole Daedone, the founder of OneTaste, which until 2018 taught Orgasmic Meditation, or OM, also trained at the ranch in Lafayette. In a lecture on her experience of being stroked, Daedone said: "I found myself lying there . . . with my legs open. . . . All of a sudden, the traffic jam that was my mind broke open, and it was like I was on the open road, and there was not a thought in sight. There was only pure feeling. And, for the first time in my life, I felt like I had access to that hunger that was underneath all of my other hungers . . . a fundamental hunger to connect with another human being."[5]

When a woman is connected to her pussy, Thomashauer says, she taps into her body, her innate sensuousness, and her creativity. Women's bodies are built for pleasure, but we forget this in our busy world. "When she ignores her pleasure, a woman can mistake her purpose and believe her function is to enslave herself to her job, or live only to serve her husband, her kids, her family," she wrote in her book. "The omission of pussy has created a legacy: generations of women who live as victims, always blaming others for our own unhappiness and not knowing how to generate joy, pleasure and satisfaction of our own."

Thomashauer began her self-help career by offering intimacy workshops with her former husband, Bruce Thomashauer, through their company Relationship Technologies. It was after the birth of her daughter at the start of the millennium that she christened herself Mama Gena and began her School of Womanly Arts. The workshops, run out of her New York City brownstone, were originally small affairs, covering topics such as "Training Your Man," "Hexing," and "Trust Your Pussy." However, after she started getting press, demand for the courses grew significantly. Though the fee for the Experience itself is modest, until recently it functioned in part as an elaborate sales pitch for her "Mastery" course, a workshop that was held over three weekends that required a "personal investment" of nearly $6,000. Graduates were then eligible to join in the nine-month "Creation" course, which ran about $12,000 and included trips to Tulum in Mexico's Yucatán Peninsula, Paris, and Miami's South Beach.[6]

That her book, *Pussy*, reached the best-seller list certainly contributes to Thomashauer's current popularity. It was an unlikely hit: even its publisher, the self-improvement empire Hay House, was squeamish about going to print under that title. It was released in September 2016, and not three weeks later, an unedited transcript of Donald Trump in conversation with the Access Hollywood personality Billy Bush captured America's president-to-be gloating over groping: "Grab 'em by the pussy. You can do anything."

Trump's remarks became the number-one trending topic on Facebook. The next day, Thomashauer's book hit the *New York Times* best-seller list, coming in just below Sebastian Junger's meditation on modern society's loss of meaning and above Claudia Rankine's poetic examination of race and racism. As the *Washington Post* put it, "If there's any woman in America—besides Hillary Clinton—who stands to benefit from Donald Trump's utterance of the word "p—y," it is Regena Thomashauer."[7]

These days, the School of Womanly Arts aims to help women make pleasure a priority, whether that's through engaging in rituals of self-care and pampering, learning how to brag about themselves, improving the quality of their orgasms, or elevating their own needs above those of everyone else. And the central part of that task is to guide women to connect emotionally and physically to that most neglected and defiled of body parts. Thomashauer teaches self-literacy, or *cliteracy*, as it's known, a process that encourages beautification, being outrageous, and a practice she calls *swamping*, accomplished by wearing a garbage bag like a dress and thrashing about until you expend all your miserable feelings. Thomashauer fully embodies the character of her creation.

Her speech is laden with third-person references—"Mama Gena is here"—and her claims make clear the room's hierarchy of womanly wisdom clear—"I am a pussy whisperer."

"Mama Gena," four women from Lagos stand up. "Mama Gena, we traveled sixteen hours by way of Heathrow to come here."

One young Chinese woman shares, "My pussy is always on the journey to set me free." She is at the Experience with her boyfriend's mother, who was also born in China. The older woman rises. She is a single mother who saw her son through college and into a successful entrepreneurial career. "I've finished with my parenting and have no excuses. My pussy is all dried and it needs to be wet."

Another woman shares with the group that her introduction to sex came from her father, who told her as a child that men experience erections when they see beautiful women, and that they endure terrible pain if they can't subsequently ejaculate. It's of the utmost importance, therefore, that they get off. She grew up thinking, "Poor men, what a terrible affliction."

Carrie, the freckled doctor, confides in me over lunch that before finding Mama Gena she was convinced she was broken. Now she sees that she was merely disappointed—"My whole soul was disappointed." This is her second time at the Experience, and she is considering enrolling in Mastery for another go-round.

She offers a brief narrative of opportunities curtailed. She had attended medical school with the intention of working with pregnant women. But when her boyfriend started to complain of the long and unpredictable hours required of working in obstetrics, she switched gears and moved into dermatology, which she found to be safe but not nearly as satisfying. She helped support her boyfriend through law school, hanging on to his promise that once he passed the bar they would get married. After the wedding, he became consumed with his career, working late each night and demanding that Carrie be on call to help him unwind. He sulked when she went to weekend yoga classes, and he steamed for weeks when she took a three-day trip with her college friends. "You owe me," he said on more than one occasion, when she returned home late from after-work drinks. And, dutifully, she would placate him, "because that's how it worked."

Over the years he would come to chastise her for not getting more into it. She almost never orgasmed during sex, and the rare times when she did speak up, explaining that it wasn't working for her, he quickly shut her down. "I'm the doctor and I still believed him when he said I was broken," she told me. "But then I found Mama Gena, and everything started to change for me." For Carrie, the opportunity to talk about sex and desire and social injustice with a large group of women was catalytic. She eventually filed for separation and moved into a new apartment.

My other seatmate is a white-haired and conservatively dressed woman from the Upper East Side; she would fit right in at Bergdorf's, were it not for the beadwork bracelet on her wrist. She received it from her shaman after *seeing*, under the influence of a traditional South American hallucinogenic brew, *ayahuasca*, that her life-long sexual problems stemmed from early abuses at the hands of her father and uncle. She is a calm presence for much of the day, until an overweight, cripplingly shy African American woman takes the stage. "You're so fucking brave!" my seatmate screams, as the woman reluctantly hauls back and forth to the urging that she move to the mantra, "I have a gorgeous pussy." The woman onstage had issued a half-hearted hand when Thomashauer had asked the audience if anyone wasn't feeling "into it." Her initial saunter is painfully stiff, closefisted, her legs stutter rather than stride. Thomashauer tells her that it is a "wonderful" walk, because it completely expresses how the patriarchy has dominated her body.

Women announce wanting to "live the wet life." "I want to make time every day to fuck god." "I want to live without apology, anchored in my body."

A song by the hip-hop artist Khia blares, and the audience gets up to dance—"My neck, my back. Lick my pussy and my crack." Women undulate and fist pump, twirl and grind in front of their seats.

What follows is the power of positive thinking—the idea that your thoughts shape your reality—as applied to sexuality. Desire is given a bad rap—you're supposed to be a cheap date. You don't want to be seen as greedy, needy, selfish, or high-maintenance. Thomashauer shakes her head: "Desire is the interface between you and that which is greater than you. It is nameless, faceless longing, calling you forward to an unnamed destiny. Desires are transformative."

REMAKING THE SELF

For all their modern gloss, Thomashauer and her ilk have their roots in the generative soils of the 1960s human potential movement. This broad camp held as its premise that humankind sits on a reserve of untapped resources, including sexual energy, that when properly harnessed can produce happiness, creativity, and fulfillment. Drawing liberally from the era's counterculture and from principles of Gestalt therapy, the many branches of the movement stemmed from the idea that self-actualization was our highest purpose. Around the country, hundreds of centers devoted to personal transformation cropped up to teach men and women how to harvest the buried emotions and libidinal instincts that clogged the path to inner growth. Writing critically in 1976 for *New York* magazine, Tom Wolfe observed: "The new alchemical dream is: changing one's personality—remaking, remodeling, elevating, and polishing one's very *self* . . . and observing, studying, and doting on it. (Me!)"[8]

Critics have long observed that interest in self-help peaks when the social contract reveals its fault lines. The gilded ranks acquire greater luster as the means to join them corrode away. Worry not, the experts tell us: happiness, wealth, and belonging are still attainable—with the right mix of attitude, ritual, and faith. As consumers in a free market, we are enjoined to become *entrepreneurs of the self*, striving to iterate better versions of ourselves by cultivating grit, resilience, gratitude, and other such attributes. I believe something similar is happening these days around sexuality. We're inundated with seductive sexual ideals—perfect bodies, gushing orgasms, lasting passion—and as these messages seep deeper into our days, we confront what feels like mounting poverty in our own erotic lives. In the realm of sex, self-help references a Gilded Eros.

The sprawling genre of personal betterment provides a constant background noise as women go about investigating, fretting over, and seeking to alter or enhance their sexuality. Living at a time when most people are looking to the market for answers and reassurances, as opposed to talking to their mothers or getting the facts through formal learning, self-help, whether in the form of books, workshops, or brand-conscious editorials, winds up informing how women conceive of their struggles and how they try to resolve them. A large number of the women I spoke with had at one point or another either deliberately waded into the self-improvement industry or unconsciously imbibed some of its ample offerings. And its offerings are ample indeed—the self-improvement market is valued at $10 billion in the United States alone. Countless book titles now offer surefire solutions for women who want to rev up their sexuality and enliven their relationships. *Red Hot Monogamy* promises to make your marriage "sizzle"; *Have a New Sex Life by Friday* declares that your marriage "can't wait until Monday"; *Reclaiming Desire* is for the woman who asks, "How can I go from mommy one minute to passionate lover the next?" Meanwhile, *The Tired Woman's Guide to Passionate Sex* offers a road map to overcoming your exhaustion, while *No More Headaches* enjoins you to give up the old rouse.

The world of workshops like the Experience offers a dizzying spread, often making salvatory claims. From anatomical tutorials to squirting intensives and retreat weekends devoted to themes of rage, infidelity, and orgasm, these sessions promise radical results in just days. For some women, Mama Gena represents but a stop on a wider personal improvement circuit. I spoke with women who had also attended workshops with the sex coach Pamela Madsen, who helps women "explore the landscape of their erotic soul" at her Back to the Body retreats. Others have traveled to exotic locales in Hawaii, even Bali, for programs that promise "endless bliss," "life shifting sex," and "insight into the meaning of desire, love, sensual awakening, sexual wholeness and cultivation of our own inner marriage." As we saw in the previous chapter, there is now such a hot market for these types of services that savvy service providers offer numerous programs for aspiring personal improvement professionals. It all has the effect of absorbing women into self-help not merely as a tool, but as an all-encompassing lifestyle. There are even workshops devoted to helping participants get more out of workshops.

However, one need not sign up for a retreat or drift into the section of the bookstore that houses *Pussy* and its parallels to run up against self-help. Above and beyond discrete products, the improvement ethos has come to be a defining feature of our culture. We have on the one hand a pervasive sense of disenchantment. We're sad, we want for meaning, secret discontent corrugates our otherwise contented lives. The more we have, the more ardent our quest for satisfaction becomes, but, mirage-like, it remains ever out of reach. And yet accompanying this pervasive dismay is the oddest corollary: our faith in the possibility of fulfillment. If we strive for more, or to be different, or if we diligently renovate what we even mean by *more* or *different*, one day we will come home to the promised land of our imaginations.

Where it concerns sex, the members of the consuming public keep stacking up their realities beside their expectations and favoring the latter. They are convinced that their sex lives are lacking in major and disruptive ways: they don't enjoy sex enough, they certainly don't have enough of it, they're opting for sleep over wild nights and begrudging themselves that choice. Their orgasms aren't as big or as important as they would like them to be, and somehow, even though they're in love, date night still feels like something of a chore. It looks so easy in the movies. Others, surely, don't struggle with these mundane indignities. We are uniformly and yet uniquely deprived, and that is what necessitates our entitlement: we deserve so much more. Convinced that we, too, can and should have dynamic, lustful, creative, energizing, life-affirming, spiritually transcendent, turned-on-in-perpetuity-regardless-of-the-boorish-partner sexual fulfillment, our discontent becomes our crucible.

THE PERSONAL AND THE POLITICAL, REVISITED

Thomashauer views the state of women's sexuality as part of a vast cultural web. In her schema, it's all connected: women's depression, the gender wage gap, #MeToo, human trafficking, human history, the suppression of feelings, misogyny. Her program aims to surface a logic of linkages. The uninspired sex pairs with the faltering career ambitions. The low body confidence stems from the absent spirituality. The lackluster orgasms accompany the empty bank account. In some respects, it is a welcome framework, departing as it does from the tendency to isolate sex from everything else. *How's your sex life?* so often runs as a separate line of inquiry, suggesting that even as other aspects of your life flourish, this area can be a big dark stain on your overall level of achievement. According to Thomashauer, chances are good that if your sex life is floundering, it's not floundering in isolation—it's either been bogged down by some other low-functioning part of your life, or it's dragging down the high performers. She encourages her followers to pay attention to the greater connective tissue, which she would probably call *pussy*.

To Thomashauer, erotic awakening underpins larger political, social, and personal engagement. To "turn on," in her words, is not just to listen and respond to the sexual pleas of your own body; it is the critical first step in taking one's full place in the world. It sounds a bit like magic. But this genre of personal improvement is giddy with such assertions that, taken together, radically reframe how feminism has long viewed women's problems.

Instead of challenging the external structures that limit sexual autonomy and self-determined pleasure (as well as social inequalities more broadly), this breed of self-improvement encourages women to transform their sexuality and thereby improve their well-being and elevate their worldly stature. It is, to reference Gloria Steinem, very much a "revolution from within." This idea marks a major turn from how feminism was once conceived. Instead of vying to topple the systems of inequity that keep us down, Thomashauer and many others espouse liberation by means of altering the self—and specifically, it is one's sexuality that engenders change. In place of agitating for legal gains and better social policies, this approach urges women to remake their interior reality. Women are to rummage through their psyches to unearth and then divest themselves of the baggage they've inherited: the low self-esteem, the gnawing feeling of being undeserving, the distant relationship to their own bodies. Empowerment then becomes not a social project but a personal achievement. Catherine Rottenberg, a critic of so-called neoliberal feminism, has argued that we've gotten rid of the wider goals of emancipation by substituting positive affect, the semblance of contentment, for genuine change. The emergent form of feminism places the onus of responsibility on the individual woman, contracting her vision and guiding her attention ever more "intensively inward."[9]

Thomashauer has spoken to this shift. "The feminist movement was really sourced by anger," she once told the press. "The problem with anger, though, is that it never leads to happiness. We thought that if women could step into a new dimension of feminism that was a celebration of womanhood, they would learn how to treasure themselves, which is a more fun game than being angry or seeking revenge."[10]

Fun was certainly a prominent theme at the Experience. It was a riotous affair. At one point, Thomashauer and her former students performed a burlesque routine over stiletto heels and straddled chairs to the song "Pink Is My Favorite Color." Heartfelt, at times teary confessionals followed fist-pumping interludes. We were excavating our very souls because ultimately we wanted to have a good time. After the choreographed interstitial, Thomashauer told the audience that if we chose Mastery, maybe next time we could join her on the stage.

A number of scholars have looked witheringly at the self-improvement industry and the mediated messages directed at women. Some have pointed out that while prevailing social models encourage women to *free oneself, please oneself,* and even *choose oneself,* this behest disguises the constraints on achieving those very ends. The British sociologist Rosalind Gill writes, "A grammar of individualism underpins all these notions—such that even experiences of racism or homophobia or domestic violence are framed in exclusively personal terms in a way that turns the idea of the personal as political on its head."[11] Related to the premium on choice, Gill argues, is the notion of self-monitoring. She maintains that close personal scrutiny has long been a feature of public femininity: consider, for example, the way women's magazines portray femininity as "contingent—requiring constant anxious attention, work and vigilance, from touching up your makeup, to packing the perfect capsule wardrobe, from hiding 'unsightly' pimples, wrinkles, age spots, or stains to hosting a successful dinner party." But this watchfulness has swelled in scope, she says. Today, self-surveillance extends more deeply into intimate life, taking stock of our psychology as we try to regulate our beliefs, attitudes, and feelings.

What's more, Gill says, is that there has been "an extraordinary ideological sleight of hand." Instead of viewing self-improvement regimens as *work,* they have been repackaged as acts of leisure, pampering, and indulgence. Women are encouraged to undergo a "mental makeover" in order to feel sexy and enjoy their erotic lives.[12] These compounding pressures to monitor and correct one's body, one's career, one's ambitions, and one's sexual desires enlist women into a state of ongoing watchfulness. She writes:

> From the sending of a brief text message to the ordering of the drink, no area of a woman's life is immune from the requirement to self surveil and work on the self. And more and more aspects of the body come under surveillance: you thought you were comfortable with your body? Well think again! When was the last time you checked your "upper arm definition"? Have you been neglecting your armpits or the soles of your feet? Do you sometimes have (ahem) unpleasant odours?
>
> But it is not only the surface of the body that needs ongoing vigilance—there is also the self: what kind of friend/lover/daughter/colleague are you? Do you laugh enough? How well do you communicate? Have you got emotional intelligence? In a culture saturated by individualistic self-help discourses, the self has become a project to be evaluated, advised, disciplined and improved or brought "into recovery."[13]

Thanks to my research for this book and signing up for countless newsletters and the like, my inbox is now flooded with opportunities to discover, renew, and optimize my sexuality. I am invited to unblock the barriers to my "deep vagina." I am urged to reckon with why I have been starving myself of the full variety of orgasms I should be experiencing (clitoral, vaginal, G-spot, cervical, nipple, partnered, solo, induced by thought alone, mystical, multiple, continuous, reverberant with the beaming cosmos from whose dust we are formed). Maybe it's because I've internalized a deprivation logic and should reconsider my relationship to abundance. One post that I glanced over at dawn, as I prepped breakfast for my toddlers, enumerated the reasons why orgasm should be incorporated into my morning ritual. By becoming more orgasmic, I would reap rewards across my life. I would open myself to newfound avenues of wealth, meet my inner goddess and *fempreneur* (maybe I, too, should be a sex coach!), glow, grow slim, and magnetize strangers as I danced-like-nobody-was-looking down the street. Years would vanish from my face. And I had best fire my prescriber, because the "well-fucked woman" has no need for pharmacopeia. The "underfucked woman," as one successful sex coach reported to my email box, is short fused, broken, depressed, and "flipping out at shop clerks and road-raging her way across town." So I was invited to *be my best vagina*. Not only would I enjoy "dramatic, life-changing, jaw-dropping results," but "happy, satisfied vaginas make more cash."

What I find so remarkable about this rhetoric is the way it empowers and undermines all at once. In crude terms, it used to be that social conditions were at least partially responsible for bad sex, and improving matters required some level of dismantling the patriarchy—or at least advocating for better treatment in the workplace and at home. But here, sex, and specifically female sexuality, is what moves the needle. Want more money? Have more orgasms. As Thomashauer declares, the one way to awaken the world "is through your pussy." On one level, there is huge appeal to this patently sex-positive and *cliterate* approach to erotic empowerment. Where I falter in my enthusiasm is over whether erotic empowerment is an adequate substitute for empowerment overall. Moreover, I see in this message not only an inducement to work relent-lessly and pay lots of money to improve the quality of your libido, but also an implication that failure to do so is part of what holds you back. It's your own fault for casting a vote against fun.

I've found myself drawn repeatedly to the question, well, does it work? And in service of answering that query I have read widely and enlisted in both in-person and online workshops to strengthen my rela-tionships, hone my self-love, and amp up my climactic bliss. I also reg-istered a number of willing interviewees in a pay-to-play app designed to teach women skills for boosting pleasure. And yes, I've found that by devoting more conscious time to one's own satisfaction, pleasure does appear to grow. If you dedicate a portion of every day or week or even month strictly to the investigation of your own body, it responds favor-ably. Earth-shattering changes, not necessarily. Will you springboard from office grunt to CEO? Less likely still. But there is absolutely noth-ing to suggest that a concerted focus on intimate self-discovery works against you. Indeed, taking a disarmed approach to appreciating your anatomy, considering the ways personal experiences have derailed your entitlement, and viewing pleasure as a birthright rather than an acci-dent are all enormously important. Plenty of self-help critics have even conceded that it can effect some change. While it is unlikely to midwife a wholly remodeled self into existence, it can help people reorient their general outlook.

The bigger issue, I believe, is not whether self-help actually helps, or even whether all that throbbing verbage changes how women experience reality. It is rather an issue of consumer demand, and the cycle of reinforcement between desire and promise. We feed our hopes to the personal growth industry, and it grows plump with ways to court our aspirations. It may be easy to slip into skepticism at this juncture: the Experience, after all, was also a spectacular exercise in branding. But to do so runs the risk of missing out on the voracious appetite for this kind of messaging. Irrespective of whether programs like Thomashauer's result in astonishing transformation, the fact that women by the thousands are flocking to them for help, for community, for reassurance, for guidance, and for healing is worth attending to.

▼▲▼▲▼

Taking in the pageantry of the Experience, I found myself indulging a nostalgia for a time of bottom-up approaches to consciousness-raising. Not the pussy whisperer inciting us to live our best, most outrageous, most dripping wet lives, but a circle of peers who could normalize our hopes and experiences. I thought, perhaps naively, of the groups of the 1970s, and before that, of the forums of feminine exchange within communities that have existed and disappeared and been resurrected and suppressed through much of history. I wondered, is this what it takes to connect women to their genitals? Do we require spectacle to appreciate the private virtues of, say, masturbation and self-care? Swept away as I was by the booming oratory of how disenfranchised we are from our power—our *pussies*—and our potential for greatness in the world, I found myself concluding that Thomashauer, above all, is a commentary: this is what happens when we cede our private lives to the market, when we don't have quality sex education, when we shame our bodies, and when we teach women to stay small.

But in the weeks and months after the weekend concluded, as my inbox filled with urges to make the "self-investment" in Mastery, and as I talked to a number of Thomashauer's students, my perception changed. The women here *do* by and large understand the value of self-pleasuring, they often *are* among the ranks of the socially advantaged, and, moreover, they *are* generally giving voice to their opinions and pursuing what they want. So why, I wondered, the emphasis on overcoming our oppression?

In order to sell us diet pills, or cleaning fluids, or high-tech home security devices, we must first be convinced that our bodies aren't as comely as they should be, and that our homes are neither clean nor safe. And in self-help, too, we are invited to feast on our shared deficiencies, so the experts can deliver us to what we truly need. I am certainly not trying to make a case against flaunting desire or having great sex. Rather, I want to trouble the idea of using our oppression as a market hook. Like a revival camp that comes together over declaring the known features of the enemy, self-help makes the case for overcoming in order to give us what we may already have.

10 OPENING TO CHOICE

Yes, I am a Free Lover. I have an inalienable, constitutional
and natural right to love whom I may, to love as long
or as short a period as I can; to change that love every
day if I please, and with that right neither you nor
any law you can frame have any right to interfere.

—*Victoria Woodhull, "The Principles of Social Freedom," 1871*

When we see love as the will to nurture one's own or
another's spiritual growth, revealed through acts of
care, respect, knowing, and assuming responsibility,
the foundation of all love in our life is the same. There
is no special love exclusively reserved for romantic
partners. Genuine love is the foundation of our
engagement with ourselves, with family, with friends,
with partners, with everyone we choose to love.

—*bell hooks,* All About Love, *1999*

WHEN THEY FIRST began dating in college, friends used to joke that Vic
and Barton looked similar enough to be brother and sister. More than
a quarter-century later, the resemblance remains, strengthened perhaps
in the way some couples begin to take on each other's features over the
years, expressions following the same worn grooves, mannerisms mir-
rored. In the light of the diner where we are having lunch, their pale
faces are composed of the same texture and shade. On each head straw-
berry blond waves are fading to gray.

They're bickering this afternoon. It's all earnest smiles when they're speaking to me, but the current between them thrums with displeasure. The problem, explains Barton, is that Vic has fallen for someone else. "I didn't think that would happen," he admits with a sigh.

Four years earlier, Barton had met Cheryl when he was traveling for business. His work takes him on the road a fair amount, but this was the first time the opportunity for infidelity had presented itself so plainly. His description of this meeting and the relationship that followed is thick with terms like *chemistry, energy,* and *electricity,* which is perhaps unsurprising given that he is, by profession, an engineer. At home, his life with Vic was stable, but largely platonic. They attributed some of the loss of passion to Vic going through menopause, and with it the unwelcome development of vaginal pain. "But if we're going to be honest," Vic elaborated, "sex stopped happening before that." It had been years since she had felt much desire for sex, and though they continued to have scheduled sessions of intimacy every other week or so, for Vic it was mostly just going through the motions. She describes how she used to tie herself up with chores in the evening, hoping that Barton would be asleep by the time she came to bed.

Vic is a Christian—she wears a dainty gold cross around her neck—and according to her take on the faith, a wife has a duty to satisfy her husband. "Men have a physical need for sex," she tells me, a statement delivered as unblinking fact. According to that doctrine, male sexuality is strong by design—*God's design*—but it is also meant to be a gift to her, the wife. It is her responsibility to honor that duty, because otherwise he'll stray. For years, Vic half-heartedly embraced the "just do it" strategy of sexual activity, though often she would have preferred to read a magazine or watch a show on TV.

Enter Cheryl. When Barton returned from a business trip, Vic remembers him seeming "really up." She did not know yet that he was texting with Cheryl or calling her from his office, or thinking about her while he lay in their bed at night. For his part, Barton knew that he should cut it off, but he didn't want to. It was so invigorating to flirt and exchange confidences with another person. To Barton, these communications took place in a gray area. He tried to assure himself that it was all right because *technically* he hadn't cheated. It was no worse, really, than fantasizing.

Vic eventually found out. The volume of Barton's texting was puzzling to her—he'd never been much of a texter. When she asked him what was going on, Barton was surprised by his own candor. "I said, more or less, that I had met this woman, I was excited by her, I thought we had a connection, and I wanted to see her again." He was flabbergasted by Vic's response. "I had 110 percent assumed that she would get really upset. Maybe she would throw me out. Maybe that was *it*." This, he says, was a scary proposition, because he did not want his marriage to end. "But she just said, okay, maybe you should see her again."

Vic says she was also startled by her reaction. However, she explains that while she was hardly enthusiastic about Barton developing feelings for someone else, it seemed unreasonable to simply shuck the life they had built together. Besides, men have needs, and she felt like it was a sign of respect that he told her rather than just carrying on behind her back. And so, Barton started seeing Cheryl. Vic preferred not to know any of the details. She didn't want to know when Barton had dates; nor did she care to learn more about this other woman. She insisted that he be safe and discreet. Vic and Barton have two teenage sons, one of whom is autistic, and it was extremely important to her that neither their kids nor their community found out. It created a lot of tension on the home front: whenever Barton appeared to be more solicitous than usual, Vic was quick to attribute it to compensation, which caused a lot of ugly fights. But part of her also felt relief. She no longer felt obliged to have sex when she didn't want to. She also felt a greater liberty to engage in activities without him, like socializing with members of her church.

It was there, in this least suspect of places, that Hank came into Vic's life. Recently widowed, he was a newer member of their congregation. "He had this softness to him, kind of hangdog. He was so grateful, like an orphan," says Vic. They got to know each other while volunteering for different church-sponsored projects in their New Jersey suburb. Eventually, Vic told Hank about Barton's arrangement with Cheryl, which was something she kept secret from everyone else, save for one close friend, whom she'd confided in because she didn't live in the area. It was good to talk about everything. When she told Hank about it, Vic felt she was heard without judgment or pity. He disclosed that he had slept with other women before his wife's death from cancer, and that she had encouraged him to move on and find love again.

In some ways, it seemed natural, given Barton's relationship with
Cheryl, that Vic should have someone too. But Barton did not see it
that way. Both he and Vic had assumed that Vic's low appetite for sex
was just the way things were. Barton was deeply uncomfortable with
the idea that another man could stoke her interest. Vic insisted that if
he could have another partner, then she could, too. Barton's displeasure aside, she started seeing Hank. They were going slow, she says. "It's
mostly tenderness. Closeness." Most of the time, they go on outings or
have long conversations. But she tells me, when we are alone, that she
finds sex with Hank exciting: she feels "turned on" for the first time in
years. She wonders aloud whether it wasn't so much that she lost interest in sex, but that she was no longer interested in sex with her husband.

I met Barton and Vic at a conference in Philadelphia that its sponsors advertised under the moniker of "bringing together people who
love more." Held in a drab hotel not far from the airport, the weekend's
diverse programming catered to both veterans and newcomers to consensual nonmonogamy as they navigated a terrain splintered by desire,
jealousy, disclosure, and "new relationship energy" (NRE)—a term attendees used, sometimes eye-rollingly, to describe the gurgling thrill
of a fresh partner. While open love may ring free and easy, it is often
more structured than monogamy, where the only rule is that you won't
have sex with anyone else. Nonmonogamists, by contrast, tend to be
highly rule bound, even elaborating goals for what individuals want out
of sex and partnership. Insiders make plain that there are major differences between open love, flexible relationships, and polyamory. Rather
than wade into the distinctions here, I will refer to these practices under the rather clunky umbrella term of consensual nonmonogamy because it underscores its chief quality, which is that these relationships
are known and consensual for all parties involved. For some, it is permission to have one-night stands, with the understanding that further
emotional intimacy is off limits. For others, it is partner-approved Tinder profiles and divulged details at the end of an extracurricular date.
Others still want to vet potential partners before consenting to share
their mates. Some maintain complex calendars balancing families with
secondary, and sometimes tertiary, partners.

Most of the conference weekend was given over to dialogue, with
workshops and role-playing sessions intended to equip existing or

would-be lovers with tools for managing expectations and heartbreak.
If there was an objective, it would be helping those at hand to make
their own choices, to respect those made by the ones they love, and to
manage the suffering that often ensues. "Open love is hard work" is a
phrase I heard repeatedly, along with variations on "ongoing process,"
"personal journey," and "balancing act."

The subject of nonmonogamy can incite unease. It explodes our
most beloved fable of partnered eternity. And as we saw in Chapter 5,
even though marriage may be losing some of its statistical relevance, the
idea of the monogamous soul mate holds powerful sway over the popular imagination. Indeed, we expect more from our intimates than ever
before. These days, the demands on unions are expansive: marriage—
with monogamy as its main expression—is supposed to serve as a vehicle for spiritual growth and personal betterment. Andrew Cherlin,
a sociologist who has been chronicling the country's patterns of marriage, divorce, and remarriage for decades, has argued that compared
to other Western nations, where the institution is markedly on the decline, Americans have unique conjugal patterns stamped by a contra-
dictory valorization of the married ideal and expressive individualism.
The end result is what he terms a "carousel of intimate partnerships."
Americans, and their children, cycle through rounds of upheaval in
their search for greater satisfaction.[1]

British sociologist Anthony Giddens has described these trends as
part of the "transformation of intimacy." Older norms of romantic love
premised on *till death do us part* have been displaced by the pursuit
of personal fulfillment through coupledom. Such modern partnerships
auger greater happiness and autonomy, he argued, but they also breed
insecurity: nothing is lasting, all love is contingent.[2] The higher we pile
our needs onto marriage, the more we risk running out of oxygen at its
summit. That, at least, is the takeaway from a group of researchers from
Northwestern University who elaborated the "*suffocation model* of marriage in America." Led by Eli Finkel, they noted that our soaring demands for marriage have produced a supremely fragile "all-or-nothing
state."[3]

And perhaps the most supreme—and thus most contested—virtue
of all is sexual fidelity. As the terms of marriage center increasingly on
individual choice, as opposed to social obligation, the expectation that

partners will remain faithful has amassed unprecedented weight. "Monogamy is the sacred cow of the romantic ideal, for it confirms our specialness," wrote psychologist Esther Perel in her 2017 book on infidelity, *The State of Affairs*. "By turning our backs on other loves, we confirm the uniqueness of our 'significant other.' . . . Miraculously, our desire for others is supposed to evaporate, vanquished by the power of this singular attraction. In a world where it is so easy to feel insignificant— to be laid off, disposable, deleted with a click, unfriended—being chosen has taken on an importance it never had before."[4]

In contrast to the security that monogamy is said to sustain, nonmonogamy raises the nasty specter of living with ongoing jealousy and its raging retinue of inadequacy, fear, and loneliness. It forces partners to confront the possibility that they are not always the most cherished, and it foists a lot of choice into areas where there was formerly none. And yet, its proponents have described consensual nonmonogamy to me as a higher calling, saying it requires a depth of honesty and emotional inquiry that is frequently unrivaled by monogamous pairings. After all, the statistics make clear that most monogamists struggle with their binding precept, but choose to encroach on those limitations with secrecy—or pain. But research routinely lays bare a discomfiting paradox.

Even though monogamy is upheld as the cultural ideal, a lot of people cheat. On the high end, statistics suggest that roughly half of Americans may have engaged in infidelity at some point in their lives, and about one-fifth are currently stepping out.[5] Infidelity is a leading cause of divorce as well as the dissolution of nonmarital heterosexual relationships. Alarmingly, real or suspected cheating is also a leading factor in spousal and household abuse in the United States and Canada.[6] As one research team from the University of New Brunswick said in 2018, "in most Western countries, belief in the importance of monogamy is strong, yet relatively few individuals actually discuss with their partner what monogamy must entail."[7] On all these counts, nonmonogamy endeavors to follow a different path. Opening up, one of the women leading the conference tells me, is an act of "emotional maturity." It is taking responsibility for your desire and your choices and realizing that your satisfaction lies in your own hands.

For Vic, the experience had been fraught with doubt and volatile feelings, but she thinks that the erotic connection she has with Hank

may even be good for her relationship with Barton. In addition to communicating more openly, she has begun on occasion to enjoy sex with
him again. Though she says it's motivated in part by guilt, she has also
initiated intimacy with her husband—something she had not done in
years. The very notion of choice, that she could decide when and with
whom to be intimate, is new to her. In opening up her relationship,
she is confronting for the first time the idea that her needs exist independently of her role as wife, and that even if her actions cause pain,
they are honest expressions of what she truly wants. The idea of want is
in itself new and raw. More importantly, though, Vic feels a new sense
of autonomy in her sexuality, a budding appreciation that it is hers to
give rather than his to take. "I can hear my desire," she says. "Like it has
learned to speak."

▼▲▼▲▼

Like Vic, Ellen, a New Yorker in her late forties, came to rethink monogamy later in life. Married now for more than twenty-five years, she says
her sexuality "got pretty quiet" early on in her relationship. It was hard
to tease out what was causing her muted interest: there was the prolonged bout of anxiety in her twenties, the years spent wrestling with
infertility and subsequent in vitro cycles, and then her later experiences
of carrying and mothering a set of twins. But she was hardly alone in
her indifference. Her friends—many of whom, like her, worked in the
legal field—admitted to having sex only about once a month, or even
just a couple times a year. Ellen reasoned she must be "frigid" or into
women, but that didn't bother her.

It wasn't until her sons were around seven that she started to feel less
comfortable with the persistent hush in her erotic life. She suggested to
her husband that they do something about it, and so they went to see
a sex therapist. Ten years later, they still see this therapist from time
to time. Initially, they worked on their sex life, scheduling times for
intimacy, while Ellen tried to forge an identity apart from "momness."
Of her husband, she says, "We happen to have an incredibly strong,
beautiful, peaceful relationship, where we really, really enjoy each other
and we communicate well." And yet, "the chemistry just wasn't there."
She began to think that the problem had to do with the limitations
of monogamy. She explains, "It's just what happens when people become familiar and there's no separateness. I think that living on top of

somebody may not be great for sexuality." So together they decided to see what other arrangements might look like. Ellen stresses that she had no guides or role models. "We knew nothing about any kind of creative relating; all my friends were conventional. I wore flat shoes, I showed no cleavage, I was a typical mom."

Her husband suggested swinging, and with the help of their therapist, they tried it. Ellen says it was not her cup of tea—it was "horrible," in fact—but right away she met someone and "fell really hard . . . which was not part of the plan." What ensued was complicated, she says. The other man ended up divorcing his wife, and the three of them—Ellen, her husband, and her new boyfriend—all became very close. It made her realize that while her husband enjoyed the freedom of swinging, and the ability to have sex with whomever he chose, she needed intimacy and emotional connection in order to be sexual. Her boyfriend, she says, provided "the feeling of really being seen" that had been lacking in her marriage.

The relationship with her boyfriend eventually ended, but Ellen was now rethinking her sexuality and the forms that love could take. It was all about opening herself up to choice and realizing that she had the freedom to do whatever she wanted. "It didn't happen overnight. It was a bit of a roller coaster," she says. "It takes time to feel you have the space to do whatever you want, to create whatever relationship structure you want, to have whatever kind of sex you want. And then, oh my god, it's like the bottom drops out." The process has not been without its pains, not the least of which is the stigma her lifestyle presents in the day to day. But now she has a strong community of like-minded people with similar lifestyles supporting her, and as a result she feels very clear in expressing what she wants from her sexuality and how she wants to inhabit the world more generally. "I guess, in retrospect, it feels like a big shift. But it is so genuine to me that it seems like a shame that this *me*, who I believe was under there, was being masked for so long."

Today, even though she is immersed in the "poly lifestyle"—"whatever that means"—she has one boyfriend with whom she is "monogamish." She is still married, and her marriage remains important to her—"I feel really proud of what my husband and I created together"—but it is her boyfriend who provides the intimacy she craves. Ellen enjoys activities like yoga and chanting, and she likes to eye-gaze with her partners—all things that made her husband laugh, but which she shares with her other partner. In place of her previously conservative uniform, she now dresses seductively and makes her own costumes. She's lost all the shame from the societal and religious values that once dictated how she thought she should behave (she's a Reform Jew), and her sexuality is "off the charts." She thinks a lot of women use open relationships as a way to "cobble together what they need." But ultimately for Ellen, it comes back to the issue of choice. Nonmonogamy was not, for her, about having multiple lovers, but about finding herself in a space of freedom. Moreover, she says, it's brought into focus the fact that sexuality is always in a state of flux. "I think it's just about having the confidence in yourself to create whatever it is that you need at a given point in time," she says, "and realizing that you can create relationships and have a sexuality that looks totally different from the way you've been taught to think it should."

▼▲▼▲▼

The subjects of nonmonogamy, new monogamy, open marriage, and polyamory have received increasing attention in recent years, with a spate of how-to manuals now available for the curious. Meditations on the social meaning of the phenomena have appeared in major publications, from *Rolling Stone* to *The New York Times Magazine*.[8] There has also been an explosion of scholarly fascination with the implications for mental and physical health, social justice, family structure, law, and housing.[9] A body of therapists and coaches now specializes in helping couples navigate the promises and pitfalls of nonmonogamy, with further training courses available for professionals who want to add this area of specialization to their practices. It would seem that the demand for information is growing.

However, it is far from clear just how many people participate in some variation of nonmonogamy, or whether numbers are actually on the rise. The census doesn't poll these figures, which are also difficult to capture, since nonmonogamy can take a blurry range of forms. But research based on the 2012 National Survey of Sexual Health and Behavior, conducted by the Center for Sexual Health Promotion at the Indiana University School of Public Health, found that 4 percent of the population identified as being in an open relationship (an additional

8 percent reported being in a nonconsensual nonmonogamous relationship—i.e., cheating).[10] Other findings suggest that as many as one
in five adults have experimented with some form of consensual nonmonogamy in their lifetimes.[11] And there are indications that these
numbers may grow as millennials cart new values into the mainstream.
A 2016 survey by YouGov, a market research and analytics firm based
in London, found that only about half of Americans under the age of
thirty thought of their ideal relationship as "completely monogamous,"
compared to more than 60 percent of those aged forty-five to sixty-
four.[12] Meanwhile, data analyzed by the research firm GlobalWebIndex,
also based in London, showed that 42 percent of Tinder users were
married or in relationships.[13]

According to the behavioral psychologist Heath Schechinger at the
University of California, Berkeley, consensual nonmonogamists constitute a "sexual minority" deserving of options for informed health-care
services and social protections. Schechinger is helping to lead a new
American Psychological Association task force to study the topic. Too
often, clinicians assume their clients are in sexually exclusive partnerships, and Schechinger believes "it's time to make asking about relationship structure a standard practice."[14] In his own research, he has
observed that nonmonogamy is associated with unique benefits not
shared by fidelity, including "diversified need fulfillment" and robust
opportunities for "individual growth and development."[15]

Other researchers are also peering into the inner workings of non-
monogamous relationships, including family life.[16] While public perceptions often regard those not sticking to the dyadic script as less
trustworthy, more likely to court health risks, and less likely to be sexually satisfied, the emerging data suggests that the opposite may well be
the case.[17] A spate of recent studies indicates that the nonmonogamous
are more transparent than their monogamous peers, more inclined to
use contraception, and more sexually satisfied; they also apparently
have more orgasms—perhaps, as one research team speculated, because
they escape the rut of habituation.[18] But to even ask these questions is
to wade into thickets of controversy. Terri Conley of the University of
Michigan found in her studies of nonmonogamous relationships that
in most respects they function much the same as sexually exclusive
ones. And yet presenting nonmonogamy in a favorable light is to open

oneself to controversy. She told me that researching nonmonogamy is inherently challenging: our belief in the pair bond is so ingrained that usually we don't even think to talk about it. "It's not a matter of being morally right or wrong. It's that people are so hell bent on the idea that nonmonogamous relationships don't work," she said. When she tried to publish a paper looking at safer sex practices among nonmonogamous people, the reviewers expressed pronounced hostility, deriding the data and assuming it must have been a master's thesis. She went back and reframed her paper, and although she did not touch the data, but only repositioned the research as a comparison of cheaters and consensual nonmonogamists, the journal accepted the work.

▼▲▼▲▼

Media buzz notwithstanding, the "new" part of the "new monogamy" is actually something of a misnomer. What's taking place today may be better understood as an updated version of ideas that have come in and out of vogue for the past two hundred years. Early feminist thinkers took aim at marriage as an institution that rendered women the property of their husbands and foreclosed on their intellectual and economic freedom. Mary Wollstonecraft saw marriage as a form of tyranny, while the free-love advocate Mary Gove Nichols described it as the "annihilation of women." The activist and suffragette Victoria Woodhull, who was the first woman to run for US president, was also an advocate of open love, viewing it as part and parcel with women's autonomy.

The early free-love movement continued into the beginning of the twentieth century, most prominently with the bohemians of New York's Greenwich Village. There, figures like Edna St. Vincent Millay, Emma Goldman, and Mabel Dodge championed sexual freedom in their lives and work. In the United Kingdom, philosopher Bertrand Russell critiqued prevailing notions of sex in his 1929 book *Marriage and Morals*, arguing that the advent of contraception meant that sex could be separated from reproduction: in the absence of children, men and women should be free to pursue sexual activity at will.

But it was not until the 1960s and 1970s that ideas of free love reached deep into the public psyche. Ready access to birth control pills, relaxing mores around premarital sex, and steadily climbing divorce rates created an atmosphere of unprecedented experimentation. The human potential movement posited sexuality as a source of individual development, and its leaders, at venues like Esalen and the Human Awareness Institute, espoused free love. Around the same time, the women's movement began to foreground female sexuality: an entire generation had suddenly been freed of fears of pregnancy, a success with massive implications for their education, careers, and romantic lives. For some feminists at the time, the critique of monogamy was a crucial arm of the era's challenge to male privilege.[19] For others it was part of an anticapitalist appraisal of marriage as a form of private property in which mates claimed sole ownership of their partners' erotic lives. Breaking with monogamy was seen as both a political counter to tradition and a strategy for women to gain greater sexual and social autonomy. Looking back on the era's goals, feminist researchers Stevi Jackson and Sue Scott wrote in 2004 that marriage was variously viewed as "a patriarchal institution that granted men rights to the sexual, reproductive and domestic services of a wife, and a bourgeois institution founded on a hypocritical morality and the protection of ruling class men's property and inheritance rights." The solution, they claimed, was not to demand equal rights within a lopsided system, "but to challenge the ideology itself."[20]

Some critics at the time, including Shulamith Firestone, argued that cultural expectations left women socially impoverished. At issue in particular was the expectation that women should invest the bulk of their time and mental energies into sustaining love and the nuclear family. Firestone went so far as to call for the elimination of the biological family, so that Eros could freely "diffuse throughout and humanize the entire culture."[21] Meanwhile, others, including Kate Millett and Adrienne Rich, railed against the ways in which marriage subordinated women into domestic and reproductive service as well as "compulsory heterosexuality."[22]

Popular culture was sensitive to the shifting of the sands. In their 1972 book *Open Marriage: A New Life Style for Couples*, Nena and George O'Neill brought a new term into the popular lexicon. The book stayed on the best-seller list for forty weeks and has since sold some thirty-five million copies. At the book's core, they made the case for sustaining personal growth in long-term partnerships, dwelling largely on the issues of trust, communication, flexibility, and equality. Although some lines stood out as license to roam—"Sexual fidelity is

the false god of closed marriage"—the authors devoted just one chapter to sexuality with other partners. "The whole area of extramarital
sex is touchy," Nena O'Neill told the *New York Times* in 1977. "I don't
think we ever saw it as a concept for the majority, and certainly it has
not proved to be."[23]

Journalist Gay Talese captured the era's frisson in his 1980 book *Thy
Neighbor's Wife*. In his account of freedom-extolling wife swappers,
couples tumble through audacious acts in the name of liberation, often
leaving trails of torment in their wake. In the pages of his book, women
use extramarital sex to overcome dependence, cast off the shackles of
their Catholic upbringings, and resurrect passion from their chore-like
bedroom lives. Their escapades empower them, but all the while, their
husbands are left quaking with possessiveness and pain.

▼▲▼▲▼

The very anticipation of jealousy is sometimes enough to dissuade the
curious from venturing into such a lifestyle, as we'll see below. But for
some of those who have practiced nonmonogamy for a while—or, perhaps especially, are just in the throes of opening up for the first time—
jealousy can take on what they describe as a spiritual dimension. For
them, it is an invitation to harvest their own fears and expectations, to
confront the fundamental temporariness and mystery of human feelings that they feel marriage vehemently tries to pave over.

Several years ago, I spent two weeks writing about an intentional
community outside of Berlin that was founded on the principles of
emotional transparency, a euphemism for open love. In midsummer,
they hosted a camp for the amorously inquisitive. Hundreds of participants, from all over the world, came to engage philosophically, and
practically, with nonmonogamy. Coming from a background that up-
holds two-person partnerships as the most holy, right, and natural form
of togetherness, I struggled at the time to make sense of why people
would wittingly court the very forms of pain most couples try their best
to inoculate against. So I started asking people. One exchange stands
out.[24]

"When my woman goes to bed with another man, this is good," said
a man named Thomas. We were sitting on a bench and drinking coffee; he was smoking an endless chain of cigarettes. His face was hardly

attractive, but it was utterly compelling in its expressiveness. He was tall, indeed gigantic, with long brown limbs and wild gray hair swept into a messy bun. His eyes bulged behind his wire-framed glasses. At forty-two, he looked older than his years, although his body had a jangly, boyish quality to it.

When we spoke, he had been living in the community for several years and had chosen to remain there indefinitely. He believed that his new life was helping him to know himself better. After marrying in the early 1990s, he had lived a quiet life, maintaining a small house and raising three boys. After several years, however, his wife started to feel restless. They were materially successful, well educated, and socially active, but something seemed to be missing. Uprooting their family, they went in search of a new environment, and eventually they found themselves in southern Portugal. It was there that Thomas's wife met another man, and the couple was confronted with the prospect of opening their marriage. Thomas and his wife decided to turn their relationship into an experiment: Thomas, his wife, and her lover all moved into an apartment and lived together for several largely harmonious years. I confess here my own ready retreat to assumption. Talking with Thomas, my questions betrayed their own biases; repeatedly, I seemed to be trying to touch on some nerve that simply wasn't there. "It was one of the best experiences of my life," he told me. "It was certainly one of the most important experiences." His wife now lives with her boyfriend in Portugal, while Thomas lives at the community with a girlfriend and an orbit of other partners.

"It is good when my woman goes with another man," Thomas said, "because so much comes up." *Phew*, he let out a loud sigh. "And I have to see where it is coming from. My head, my heart, sometimes just from right here," he added, gripping at himself through his jeans. "That is good, yes? It's peeling away another layer of delusion so that I can see myself and others more clearly. I have to ask myself, why am I bothered by this, what do these feelings really mean?"

In our conversations we circled around the question of why one would choose to live in this manner when it could cause such pain. But Thomas—and others—had an attitude that struck me as being almost Zen-like in its regard for suffering. All love relations, whether "normal" or exploratory, are trapped by facts of hurt. What touched me was that despite the conclusion that torment likely was inevitable, Thomas and so many others I met remained committed to openness. "I just keep peeling off the layers," Thomas said, speaking with his enormous hands. "Like a Band-Aid, it hurts, but there I am, deeper in myself, one more layer free of bullshit."

▼▲▼▲▼

Talese's *Thy Neighbor's Wife* was released just as AIDS was emerging and the Reagan era's crusades for conservatism were taking hold. Reacting against the social freedoms of the 1960s and 1970s, the country whipsawed, igniting "moral panic" and pleas for traditional values to be restored. As Susan Faludi described in her classic book *Backlash*, women's liberation was recast as a social ill, responsible for the collapse of the family, the rise in mental illness, and mounting tensions between the sexes. A number of leading feminists in the 1970s and 1980s also started to depict intercourse through the lens of female subordination. They viewed sexual liberalization as an extension of male privilege. Taking aim at pornography, sex work, and BDSM (bondage/dominance, sadism/masochism), critics underscored themes of force and exploitation and championed a sexuality based on compassion and companionship rather than lust. Against this background, the subject of nonmonogamy went into retreat, and it did not really resurface until the end of the twentieth century.

Sociologist Elisabeth Sheff, author of *The Polyamorists Next Door*, describes the renewed interest in the late 1990s as the "third wave of nonmonogamy," counting the nineteenth century's transcendental movement as the first, and the counterculture of the 1960s and 1970s as the second. She speculates that the Internet gave new visibility to the lifestyle.[25] When I asked Terri Conley why she thought nonmonogamy was getting more attention than in the past, she suggested that we're seeing a return to a pre-AIDS world. Think of the *Mad Men* era, she offered, referring to a TV drama set in the 1960s, during which it was all but assumed that men would have affairs. In the early days of AIDS, "men were expected to tow the monogamy line as well," but as the threat of AIDS subsided, these patterns started to resurface.

At the same time, a new generation of sex-positive writers and activists were countering the idea that sex equated with violence, oppression, and inequity. Sexual liberation was a key aspect of feminism, they argued, and women should be free to pursue their erotic interests, whatever form they took. In 1997, marriage and family therapist Dossie Easton and her occasional lover Janet Hardy published *The Ethical Slut: A Practical Guide to Polyamory, Open Relationships and Other Adventures*, which one practicing nonmonogamist I met in the Bay Area described to me as "the bible for opening up." The text lays out ground rules for transparency and communication, suggesting that open love can be managed with etiquette and care. Moreover, the authors argue that acknowledging an individual's many passions paves the way for both better relationships and a better society. The problem, they say, is that monogamy is presented as the default setting, making it not "much of a choice when you are forbidden to choose anything else." They write, "We believe sexual freedom helps us to see our lives as they really are, with the honesty to perceive ourselves clearly and the fluidity to let us move onward as our needs alter, as a changing and growing self with changing and growing partners in a changing and growing world. . . . In expanding our sexual lives, we foresee the development of an advanced sexuality, where we can become both more natural and more human."[26]

In recent years, a number of scholars and public figures have begun to present consensual nonmonogamy as a rational way to manage the sexual strain of long-term partnership. To the claim that modern marriage is "suffocating," Conley and a colleague have proposed that nonmonogamy can help to "oxygenate" coupledom, writing, "We believe that high altitude needs"—like personal fulfillment—"can be met through swinging or through independent relationships pursued in open relationship arrangements."[27] Internationally syndicated advice columnist Dan Savage popularized the term "monogamish" to describe his own variations on sexual exclusivity. To Savage, monogamy does not work for everyone. Rather than cast blame on unbidden urges—or celebrate false virtue—we would all be well served, he says, to have frank conversations about our desires, respectfully granting ourselves and our partners the space to engage in amorous experiments as needed.

Psychologist Esther Perel rose to celebrity status on the back of her 2006 book *Mating in Captivity*, in which she argues that keeping Eros alive is a feat of sustaining distance. The cozy closeness of contemporary marriage is the bane of desire. "Intimacy becomes cruel when it excludes any possibility of discovery," she writes.[28] In *The State of Affairs*, Perel extends this argument to look at infidelity and how it can, paradoxically, bring a couple closer together. An affair, she explains, is often an expression of curiosity, a desire to know oneself better, a quest for self-discovery. "Sometimes," she writes, "when we seek the gaze of another, it isn't our partner we are turning away from, but the person we have become. We are not looking for another lover so much as another version of ourselves." Referencing Octavio Paz's description of eroticism as "a thirst for otherness," Perel offers: "So often, the most intoxicating other that people discover in the affair is not a new partner; it's a new self."[29]

Perel is in every sense a voice of our current individualistic moment. We feel entitled to desire; we are expectant of ecstasy. Our sexual woes acquire tremendous gravitas—and it is worth it, perhaps even necessary, as a hungry, deserving populace, to seek out the thrills that give life more meaning. Perel, who also maintains a private therapy practice in New York, is quick to defend the nonmonogamists on her couch. "Today's romantic pluralists have done more thinking about the meaning of fidelity, sexuality, love, and commitment than many monogamous couples ever do, and are often closer to each other as a result," she writes. "Contrary to the stereotypes of bored, immature, commitment-phobic people engaging in a licentious romp, these experiments in living are built on thoughtful communication and careful consideration."

In looking to this landscape, sex therapist Tammy Nelson suggests that what's taking place is a fundamental shift in how women and men design and maintain togetherness.[30] Nelson, who runs a private practice in Connecticut, says that in her experience, many women are content in their marriages—they like their partners, they enjoy the companionship—but are sexually dissatisfied. Sex with outside partners "fills a need that is not being met in the marriage." Instead of blaming themselves or their partners when their needs aren't met, as in the past, women today feel a new entitlement around pursuing a sexuality that isn't dependent on their partners. They are guided by an ethos of: "I want it and I'm going to get it."

Other sex therapists have told me, however, that if a marriage is on the rocks, consensual nonmonogamy is unlikely to make things better. "It's taking a problem and making it a lot more complicated," one told me. However, others have suggested that if the problem between a couple is a sexual one—as when one of the partners has a higher drive or wants a different kind of sex than the other—then nonmonogamy may be a fruitful option.

▼▲▼▲▼

Nelson told me she has observed a general pattern in her practice. For a lot of heterosexual couples, men drive the decision to open up, but women are the champions of lasting change. "Men want to do it and the women are hesitant, but then they get on board with it," she says. Eventually, the men get it out of their systems and have had enough. But, she says, "the women are like, are you kidding? I'm just getting started, this is great. We're doing this forever."

A few of the women I spoke with shared a similar narrative. Jo and her husband decided to open up their relationship after reckoning with the painful reality that their sex life had more or less ground to a halt. Her husband eventually wound up with a girlfriend, while Jo flitted "like a hummingbird" between new engagements. For her husband, the arrangement quickly lost its novelty; he was repeating the same patterns that had furrowed his marriage. But for Jo, the experience was thrilling. Having spent her whole life angling toward coupledom, to not think of herself as part of a pair was revelatory. She says, "For the first time ever I started asking, what do *I* want? Rather than always starting with what does he want, what does the relationship need?"

Nadia is an Indian American woman in her mid-thirties whom I met at a monthly gathering called Poly Cocktails in New York. Born into what she describes as a strict family that placed a heavy emphasis on marriage, she spent much of her adulthood struggling against her parents' insistence that she marry an Indian man and settle into the expected life of work and children. Her mother and aunts would introduce her to eligible men, several of whom she dated for a while; but with each man, she would eventually feel herself "shut down." "There was always a point when I would start to have trouble, no matter how nice or generous he was. I couldn't imagine *this* being it," she says. Later in our conversation, she remarks, "We make ourselves sick on the fairy tale that you need to hunt for your perfect match and then stick with this person through everything, no matter how you change."

Breaking with her family's expectations that she limit her romantic activities to fellow Indians, she started dating Sean, an African American man she met through friends. "My parents aren't racist but they are very close-minded about these things," she says. Nadia kept the relationship hidden—she even lived with Sean in secret for over a year. The clandestineness was burdensome. When her mother came to visit, she had to "flash renovate" the apartment to hide any traces of her partner, who would obligingly relocate. She couldn't bring Sean to family events, and when questioned, she spun off elaborate lies about her dating life. Fearing that she would be outed, she carefully policed her social media presence, lest some careless friend tag them together in a post.

But she also found a certain joy in living this other *forbidden* life and the space it gave her to consider new dimensions of herself. Sean had been in an open relationship before, and when Nadia told him about her own history of losing interest, he suggested that she consider seeing other people as well. It was a radical proposal, she says. "I always felt like men ultimately wanted me in a fancy cage. They would be all like, oh I love your mind, I love your independence, but they still just wanted to own me." Dipping her toes into other sexual relationships left her "totally freaked out," she says. "There was so much out there, like I was standing in this river and the current might sweep me away."

Her hesitation did not last long, and Nadia soon began dating other people, filling up her weeks with encounters that ran the gamut from casual flings to heady connections. Ultimately, the pursuit and maintenance of these outside relationships became more important to her than keeping things going with Sean, and they broke up on peaceable terms. "Once I felt like I didn't have to limit myself, to always come back home and play the girlfriend part, I became too big for our relationship," she says. "I literally outgrew it." Like many of the nonmonogamists I spoke with, Nadia points out that she doesn't have just one friend—she doesn't expect a single person to service the full spectrum of her interests—so why would it be any different in her intimate life?

All the same, Nadia says, it can be difficult to form meaningful relationships in her current lifestyle. It can sow a lot of confusion and dismay for men and women who come into her orbit from outside the poly community. "I think there is this sense, this hope, that I'll grow out of it. Like a Cinderella story, if the person is just right then that will be it," she explains. "It's hard to make people see that this isn't about a lack of love or some kind of deficit. I've tried to explain it as being like a sexual orientation—some are straight, some are gay, some love many—to make it clear that this is really about who I am."

▼▲▼▲▼

Most of the women I spoke to for this book did not practice consensual nonmonogamy. But, especially among younger women, the idea cropped up repeatedly. Some told me they could not envision sleeping only with one person for the rest of their lives. Most of the partnered women had had other loves before settling down with "the One," and they pined, at least occasionally, for the excitement they had experienced in the past. A number of them had sustained mild flirtations with old flings, or had identified a Plan B—that is, someone on the wings they imagined taking up with if their current relationship did not work out. Several shared that they had engaged in sex outside of their partnerships but balked at the thought of coming clean to their significant others for fear that doing so would be ruinous. In these conversations I was struck by how women consciously tempered their own longings for adventure and variety; the fulfillment of these appetites was often presented as a far second to preserving the security of their relationships. "My husband and I have talked about it, and it makes sense," one woman said of opening up her marriage. But she was quick to clarify: "I don't think I could handle him having sex with someone else or starting to care for someone else." And yet, the possibility of other men, other lovers, continued to hover.

What struck me most in these discussions was the general shift in thinking that has developed as nonmonogamy has become more prominent in popular culture. This shift tracks the visibility of LGBTQ lifestyles and with it a more dynamic range of what modern love and sexuality can look like. A number of younger women approached the subject of nonmonogamy as something they felt they *should* be considering, against their presumption that fidelity was unlikely, unreasonable, or bound to require major compromise at the expense of essential aspects of themselves and their mates. It was presented as a tantalizing (and yet sometimes terrifying) prospect. But it also emerged as part of a larger inquiry into the nature of marriage and other partnerships that are soldered together by routine expectations for monogamy. Women were frequently skeptical about the feasibility of faithful devotion in the long term; I heard a lot of variations on *How can it possibly work?* And it would seem, from my discussions and from social trends more generally, that sexual exclusivity only works until it doesn't. The bigger question is how, individually and culturally, we can contend with that. As Tammy Nelson, Esther Perel, and others imply, affairs and self-denial can harm ourselves and others; the more humane response may be to alter the shape of our institutions—and the ideals that underpin them—to allow for change. If desires can only be contained, and not extinguished, perhaps it would be a collective kindness to adjust the parameters of intimacy so that monogamy becomes but one of many choices, rather than the sole, and sometimes stifling, vessel for all our wild range.

11 PLAYING WITH POWER

Asking is difficult for most women. Especially for those
of us who've been socialized to take care of everyone else
before we begin to think about ourselves. But where are
we if we don't ask? We're stuck in a perpetual cultural
missionary position—possibly underneath a well-
socialized man who's perfectly willing to stay on top.

—*Gina Ogden,* The Return of Desire, *2008*

Our erotic knowledge empowers us, becomes a lens
through which we scrutinize all aspects of our existence,
forcing us to evaluate those aspects honestly in terms
of their relative meaning within our lives. And this
is a grave responsibility, projected from within each
of us, not to settle for the convenient, the shoddy,
the conventionally expected, nor the merely safe.

—*Audre Lorde, "Uses of the Erotic: The Erotic as Power," 1978*

IN AN ORNATE ballroom in midtown Manhattan, Kasia Urbaniak stands
on a low raised stage with her hands on her hips and her pelvis jut-
ted forward. It's midafternoon in late September, and the light slant-
ing through the windows above Bryant Park carves pools behind her
clavicles and beneath her deep-set eyes. A half-smile sits between two
ever-present dimples. It is impossible to get a read on what she might
be feeling, whether she is pleased or displeased, and maybe that is why
the room rustles with agitation. Or maybe the shifting tension is due

to the events of two days prior, when Christine Blasey Ford testified against then US Supreme Court nominee Brett Kavanaugh, and all this shuffling is really the low-wattage thrum of rage. "Who's feeling angry?" Urbaniak calls out, nodding as the women roar back in response. But perhaps the immediate political context is superfluous. After all, we hundred or so women are attending "Power with Men," a workshop run by "The Academy," which aims to teach women how to harvest their fury as a source of personal transformation.

Urbaniak is a former dominatrix—one of the highest-paid dommes in the world, she likes to say—and as she speaks, she struts and beams her laser stare and wields a riding crop to masterly effect. "People say that women ask for too much," she lectures, "but they're wrong. We don't ask for enough. We settle for crumbs." She gestures to a brown-haired woman in the audience and requests—or rather commands—her to talk about her *Ask*, that is, what she wants from one of the men in her life.

The woman, startled, flushes briefly and then complies. She wants her ex to know the pain he caused her, she explains, and then elaborates that in her fantasy her abusive former partner is made to dress up in a tutu and enter a gay bar, where he'll be locked inside and anally raped for the next thirty days. As the woman shares this vision, the muscles of her jaw clench visibly. But Urbaniak, whose followers call her "Mistress," isn't satisfied.

"Then what?" she asks, her whole attention centered on the woman. "Now he knows what it is to be sexually traumatized. What do you want to happen next?"

The brown-haired woman fumbles. "Then . . ." she searches. "Then I want him to write a letter of apology."

"To whom?" Urbaniak asks. "To you? To the world?"

"A public letter. To everyone."

"Okay. He's confessed. He's a stripped, raw, and vulnerable man who thanks you for taking the burden of his misguided ways away from him. Now what?"

When the woman hesitates, Urbaniak offers a signature theory: victims know what their perpetrators need better than anyone. "What should his atonement be?"

The woman offers, "I want him to work for rape victims."

"Right away?"

"No, no he needs to study first. He needs to be qualified."

"Okay. So he studies and then works for victims. He is in direct contact with the most vulnerable wounds that he was responsible for creating. Is that enough?"

The woman shakes her head. "He needs to write a book," she says, and as she speaks something in her aspect shifts. It's as if she fills more space, and her voice finds its direction. "He'll teach other men."

Urbaniak nods approvingly. The woman gets it: the path from rage to redemption. "Your vindictive hatred of him is so generous," Urbaniak says. "He'll chart the journey from monster to reformer. He'll become a champion for other men and show that it's possible to move from terrorizer to savior."

Urbaniak refocuses her attention on the rapt room. "In designing a path for our rage," she explains, "we're offering salvation. We can rescue men, not just for them, but for our benefit. Why the fuck not?"

"We have to start with revenge and devastation," she states, "because that is where we are. All of us have been traumatized many times. By men, by patriarchy, by scared little boys and irresponsible motherfuckers." We women, she says, are sitting on a mountain of rage. But we're told to be pleasant, and so we end up, unawares, choking on our own anger. But this rage is crucial, she tells us, punctuating the air with the riding crop. It contains our passion, our vision for a world that does not yet exist. "We move from vengeance to reparation to elevation," she says, lifting her hand as she speaks. "Anger is a path of redemption."

DISPENSING WITH THE CRUMBS

A few years ago, Urbaniak gave up her career in the dungeon and told her boyfriend at the time, Ruben Flores, to give up his job with Doctors Without Borders and help her start a school to teach power to women. Her appeal to him, as he recalls it to those of us attending "Power with Men," went something like this:

Dear Ruben,

I know I've been asking for a lot lately. You've been asking for more too, which is legitimate. But I'm going to ask you for even more. Leave Doctors Without Borders and make this dream of mine the number one thing in your life. In return I can offer you absolutely nothing, because if we succeed I don't know if I'll have anything more to give to you. But if we don't do this, we'll die a slow and silent death.

According to Flores, who now codirects the Academy, but is no longer Urbaniak's boyfriend, "Her ask was what I needed." His replacement in the field was killed on the mission, and so Flores expands on his original statement: "Her ask saved my life." At the time, however, he was a bit thrown by Urbaniak's scheme. "I have a revolutionary idea," she told him: "We are going to get women to ask for what they want." Flores remembers thinking, *That's it?* If that was all they had to go on, they were doomed. But, as gradually became apparent, "the Ask" is not a complete curriculum; rather, it is a diagnostic tool for helping women assess how they approach their own desire. Do they treat it with curiosity? Or do they immediately label it as bad or selfish or impossible and quash it down?

The idea for the exercise came from Urbaniak growing bored as a dominatrix. Some clients were just too easy: sit, stand, bend over. There was no resistance. It was *Yes, Mistress* all the way. So she started making more outlandish requests: wear this curtain like a dress and sing an opera in falsetto while giving me a foot massage. She wanted to probe just how big a demand she could make before she started rubbing up against *no.*

The experience sensitized Urbaniak to how women tend to box in their own requests in everyday life, tamping down what they ask of their partners, families, and jobs—and of themselves. Accustomed to hearing a consistent chorus of *no*, women whittle themselves down— so much so that they no longer even know what it is they want. Their desires are deformed by the confines in which they're kept. What does manage to escape is often just a fragment that's mistaken for the whole, and thus women settle for minor dreams, not sure why the subterranean yearnings rumble on. "We were all raised by women with fewer oppor-tunities," Urbaniak says. "We keep bumping up against invisible *no's* that we inherited, cultural norms built in favor of men." Mothers, con-sciously or not, teach their daughters compromise. Girlfriends and col-leagues, having been burned by overstepping the boundaries imposed on them, urge one another to take caution. The media and educators make bold claims of gender equality while casting humans according to rigid scripts. Even as matters improve in the social scheme of things, women begin to learn from the start to think small. They are encour-aged to settle, to concede, and then to be *grateful* for what they get. And they are encouraged to fear rejection, to avoid seeming too needy, too bitchy, too demanding, too determined, or too manly. This tendency, Urbaniak maintains, is so deeply ingrained that it becomes almost im-possible for women to reach beyond their meager allotment to consider the vast reservoir of desire that remains buried underneath.

As Urbaniak inveighs against the greater culture, I find myself sneer-ing along, particularly at the mention of gratitude. It is a pointedly fe-male directive in today's wellness-inflected zeitgeist. All those prompts to just breathe, relax, take it easy, and say *Namaste* in the face of anger or upset. There is arguably a place for these messages in our easy-to-escalate age. And, of course, in these self-conscious times, gratitude provides a ready mantra when confronting the lopsided cornucopia of con-sumerism. But I've come recently to see it as a more bullish injunction than I'd realized, one that feeds the very problems it is meant to allay.

I have a dear friend: an artist, an art teacher, a wife, a mother of two. She is stretched as thin as she can make herself but scarcely notices because this is just the way things are. Inevitably, every once in a while, a rent appears in the fabric. And just as she starts to give voice to her frustration—the impossible demands, the racist political climate, the unrelenting schedule, the money that evaporates before it's even ap-peared in the bank—she flanks herself in merciless caveats. "I have so much to be thankful for," she says, thus putting an abrupt end to her complaints instead of railing against anything that could legitimately be called a problem.

Gratitude is not an antidote for our real frustrations and injustices, and telling women to promote inner peace when they are angry does nothing to promote serenity in the long run. On the contrary, it reinforces the idea that women should be uneasy when confronted with their own dissatisfaction. I see this principle at work in my daily life, and I saw it in evidence over my weekend at The Academy. No sooner does a woman start to ask for something—a more thoughtful sexual partner, a deserved promotion—than she badgers away the impulse with a flurry of thankfuls, suffocating her longing even as she is trying to express it. *Who am I to ask?* a little voice pipes up. It is as though the seeming plenty in one aspect of one's life is meant to compensate for the absence she perceives in another. One woman I spoke with is agitating for a raise. She has worked hard and is good at what she does, but midstream, in articulating this desire, she interrupts with a counter litany: "I really can't complain, I have a house, my kids are in good schools, we're going on vacation." The little voice clambers away: you don't deserve more. Another woman at The Academy explains that she wants more from her partner. She wants more support in managing the million details, more recognition for how she keeps all the balls miraculously spinning, and for him to be a more skilled lover. "Oh but he's kind and means well, I can't really ask for more." To which Urbaniak replies, "You are not asking for nearly enough."

This tendency to rim our wishes in conciliation affects all aspects of our lives, from ordering a meal to pursuing a career. But it perhaps lands nowhere quite so heavily as on how we structure our most intimate interactions. This is where the rage comes in. In Urbaniak's view, it is like the central artery to desire. Our anger, our dissatisfaction, is the friction of reality rubbing against our longing. But overwhelmingly, when women feel rage, they immediately pivot to dampen it, which has the twofold effect of making women choke on unarticulated feelings and lose sight of what they really wanted in the first place. We are encouraged to festoon our pain in silver linings and ram it back down our own throats. "You have no say in what you want," Urbaniak maintains. "Desire won't go away until it's satisfied. You can stuff it down, and it will kill you. But give it energy, and you can create beautiful things in life."

Hence the asking practice is meant to serve as a line of self-inquiry, helping women get a sense of just how small they have made themselves.

If they can get a whiff of the magnitude of their desire, a whole new reality cracks open. Urbaniak is unabashed in claiming that she wants to start "an army." That, she says, is part of what The Academy is all about: teaching women to access their untapped desires and cultivate the power to realize them. She says, "We're imagining a world that does not yet exist."

THE POTENCY OF WOMEN'S RAGE

The media gushingly dubbed 2018 the Year of the Woman (without any sort of reflection on what we're then to make of other years, with the exception of 1992, which was assigned the same tag line). It might more rightly, however, have been termed the Year of Women's Rage. Between the indignities of the Oval Office, renewed attacks on reproductive freedoms, Brett Kavanaugh, unabashed displays of toxic masculinity, and the unfolding fallout of #MeToo, alongside the internecine feminist battles all of this has spawned, women are furious, and publicly so. As the writer Ijeoma Oluo said in an article in *Elle*, "To the men scratching their heads in concern and confusion: The rage you see right now, the rage bringing down previously invulnerable men today, barely scratches the surface. You think we might be angry? You have no idea how angry we are."[1]

We once again seemed to have reached a breaking point. The principles endorsed by the sexual revolution—autonomy, the presumed value of consent, the social-emotional value of sex itself—heaved up against the stalwart figure of male privilege as encoded in both public policy and indiscriminate persons. Some suggest we have crashed on shores of our own making, and that the erotic laissez-faire that has defined the past few decades has come to a head: the permissive atmosphere has at last, inevitably, encountered boundaries.[2] To others, we are finally starting to complicate sex beyond the most obvious instances of transgression. The boundaries between sex that is good and sex that is bad are not the same as those between consent and coercion. The power dynamics underpinning almost all of erotic life have been coming into view. "Sex is *feminist*. And empowered women are supposed to enjoy the hell out of it," wrote the journalist Rebecca Traister. Except, as she noted, most of us don't, because the game is "rigged."[3]

Today we're in the throes of a renewed effort to unify the personal and the political, and coming to appreciate at a whole new level that women's vulnerability in the streets, in the workforce, and in the home are all of a piece. Calls ring out to overhaul the entire system: the gendered order as it now exists is making everyone sick. Liberated from the gender studies lexicon, patriarchy is now a subject of mainstream commentary. Reckonings are astir.

Just as 2018 brought in new faces of female political power, some writers declared that the time had come to unite that power with rage. A succession of books, most notably Soraya Chemaly's *Rage Becomes Her: The Power of Women's Anger*, Traister's *Good and Mad: The Revolutionary Power of Women's Anger*, and Brittany Cooper's *Eloquent Rage: A Black Feminist Discovers Her Superpower*, highlighted the value of female fury and bemoaned the way women are socialized to keep it in check. "American women were a tinder box and the Weinstein story was an extremely hot match," Traister wrote of the Harvey Weinstein case that catapulted the broad reality of sexual assault and harassment into public view. The ensuing torrent of #MeToo stories amounted, she said, to "a conflagration, an eruption of so much that had been held back, hidden from view for decades, for centuries."[4]

▼▲▼▲

Against this backdrop, Urbaniak appears tailor-made for the present. The Academy was almost a secret before the convulsions of #MeToo—a word-of-mouth, invite-only affair. But in early 2018, she held a class aptly titled "Cornering Harvey," to help equip women with tactics for confronting male privilege and predation. Ever since, her popularity has skyrocketed. She and Flores admit they are blown away by the level of attention they've received. Her signature "Power with Men" course routinely sells out, and interest in her teachings has surged to international proportions. Business schools, the US military, and medical gatherings have brought her in for lectures. As a coach, she is now sought out by the rich and famous.

In the Bryant Park ballroom, her appeal was palpable, and many women in attendance appeared in thrall. "Rage Witch" was the title that came to mind when she first stalked onto the stage in towering heels and ruffles playing to her earlobes, an inscrutable half-smile hanging between its dimpled frame. There was a particular authority to her pronouncements—"You're not asking for enough"—that made you believe with certainty what you'd long suspected to be true. Some of the women I spoke with over the weekend and in the weeks thereafter enthused that Urbaniak was not just their teacher but their emblem: they wanted to *be her*. They saw in her the embodiment of principle: the riding crop, the fuck-me boots, the spell-like language laced with proud irreverence, the alt persona of prim finishing-school headmistress.

But when I met Urbaniak for coffee a few weeks later, there was a gushing, call-your-girlfriend quality to her. Even as we talked about power and shame and self-actualization, I felt an impulse to toss it all aside and gab. Urbaniak said the material she teaches represents the qualities she most struggles with herself. "I created this curriculum because this is exactly what I suck at," she said. "I used to not be able to ask for a glass of water in a restaurant." And as though to demonstrate her own transformation, she snapped at a passing waiter.

If Urbaniak is a figure of the current moment, she is also a rare voice in calling out why our current strategies to help women say no—or say yes—fall far short of their aims. "You can command all the words you want, but they mean nothing if they are not matched by inner states," she told me. In Urbaniak's view, sex, along with almost all other kinds of human interactions, is fundamentally defined by power. And power is not something that exists at the level of language. Rather, it slips in and out of words, it rests in our bodies, it shapes our beliefs and our impressions. Accordingly, mastering power is about learning to inhabit different states of being, getting into what she calls "the animal of the body." The phrase, she admits, is a work in progress, but it is meant to convey the unspoken dynamics that lead someone to feel at ease with or overpowered by another person. These undercurrents encompass eye contact, posture, and tone of voice, as well as what's taking place inside when someone cuts you off midsentence, or places an unwelcome hand on your knee. They further call upon your social legacy, like whether you're accustomed to dealing with creeps or jerks—or "shit worms," as Urbaniak describes a broad class of men.

So to help women play the part of power, she teaches them the roles of the dominant and the submissive—the domme and the sub—to help them get to what they want. Like robes to slip on and off, these roles are available for as-needed use. The domme directs her attention outward to express her will, while the sub's resolute desire carries all the gravity of a black hole. I saw, sipping coffee across from her mischievous eyes, how it could all just be a game. I'm not sure whether this is because her years in the dungeon have rubbed off to such a degree that everything had become a matter of toying with control, of mocking privilege, or whether she is onto something in a greater, perhaps even spiritual sense.

"You have no say in what you want," Urbaniak said repeatedly. "You can only control whether you stay present in it." In her view, there is a mystical dimension to desire: it is the essence of the life force. "Desire is legitimate, complete, and choiceless. It comes through you." It is not for us to question its origin; we only need to heed its message. There are places in Urbaniak's unfolding mythos where she wades into decidedly self-helpy territory. She is fond of the word "alchemical." She talks about how the universe knows to give us what we need, lines that sound a lot like they're drawn from *The Power of Attraction* or other stews of positive thinking. The trick, Urbaniak says, is to act like what you want has already happened, to treat your desire like it already exists in the world. As much as these utterances send my red flags soaring, I found myself nodding along as she elaborated on the underlying problem. We women, she said, are so accustomed to hearing *no* that we go around asking other people to validate our desires and give us permission to want and long as we do. Her lesson, essentially, is *Stop that and own what's already yours.*

OF KINK AND CONSENT

During our coffee date, Urbaniak and I circled around a thorny question: If women have learned to be uncomfortable in the presence of their desire, what are the implications for consent? We might be saying yes, but what is the value of that assent if we are only half attuned to what it is we truly want?

Now more than ever, consent is vaunted as *the* political expression for how we obtain pleasure, or at least how we're told we should. There is bad sex—forced, transgressive, *nonconsensual*—and then there is sex in which consent serves as a permissive balm. Its presence is meant to erase the inequities fundamentally at work. (The game is *rigged*, after all.) Given this underlying tension, it's unsurprising that consent is presented in anachronistic terms, with repercussions that go far beyond the theoretical. Consent is considered our best-in-class strategy for dealing with unsolicited attention, and so how we think and teach about it bears on our behavior. The underlying assumption is that the male, or other dominant figure, wants access to as much as possible, while the female, or less dominant figure, wants to limit that access. It is an outmoded model of interaction that pits appetite against reserve; one party exists through will, the other through limit-setting. The very verb, "to consent," is reactive.

Consent matters all the more as we broaden the spheres of our sexuality to encompass people and encounters for which there is little precedent for how we should behave. And as we have opened up our sexual lives to a widening range of players, we have turned to the law to arbitrate our intimacy, seeking clear boundaries for some of our most blurred interactions. The resulting quandary has to do with whether consent is really part of our erotic vocabulary or is simply a legal term. And the law, being only human-made, spins out its own varied interpretations. California, for instance, defines sexual consent as "positive cooperation in act or attitude." Washington, DC, holds that it requires "words or overt actions indicating a freely given agreement to the sexual act or contact in question." And in Florida, consent is "intelligent, knowing and voluntary."[5] But none of this gets at underlying motivation, which is the domain where desire resides. One can say yes, but that does not guarantee the sex is wanted, or good.

As I parted ways with Urbaniak, it struck me that the world she previously occupied—that of BDSM—is what informs her nuanced views of yes and no. In the dungeon, power is the erotic medium, and the subject of consent is approached with a perhaps unrivaled degree of inquiry.

I admit that as a writer I initially shied away from BDSM because it is so mired in misunderstanding. Its very mention often prompts reactions like, "Why would someone want that? What's wrong with them?" But to riff off sex therapist Marty Klein, we are best served to remember that *normal* is in essence an ideological designation, and it has little to do with health or sanity. The women I spoke to who engaged in BDSM, either routinely or occasionally, described their practices in terms of expanded sensation, catharsis, and nurturance. Critically, they also underscored the role of security and trust—submissives, in particular, stressed how they were able to exercise control by determining the conditions of their own surrender.

For all the varieties of kink they enjoyed, from bondage and role-playing to flogging and exploring sensory extremes, the women I spoke to uniformly described the erotic thrill of toying with power itself, of assuming, subverting, or relinquishing authority. Our social virtues maintain that intimacy should be democratic, and yet tender sex between two equals is rarely the fodder of our fantasies. Our imaginations stray instead to friction-lined encounters: most of us crave a bit of conflict or tension, some struggle that we must first surmount. In the greater culture, this idea seeds discomfort, because we are all too accustomed to seeing the eroticization of inequality; this is not playing with power, but rather an abuse of privilege. Whether through sexualizing nonwhite bodies, or endlessly recycling some of our favored pornographic tropes—boss and secretary, doctor and nurse, headmaster and schoolgirl, predatory father/uncle/step-relative to nubile kin—it is the abuse of existing social difference that is the source of titillation.

BDSM, as I understand it, does much to resolve this unease by creating conditions of consensual power differentials. It explores the edges of agreed-upon imbalances. Unlike the crude forms of domination that pervade pornography (and hum in the background of daily life), wherein force overcomes refusal, BDSM entails a conscious level of complicity. When players negotiate a given scene, the domme must first investigate what the sub wants to experience or attain. Writing on the nature of this interaction, psychologist Peggy Kleinplatz avers, "The dominatrix may be the ultimate phenomenologist." In order to service the sub, the domme needs to survey the landscape of his or her desires, inquiring into whether the sub craves an unyielding disciplinarian, a figure of doting love, or an insatiable companion. "The devil is in the details," as Kleinplatz puts it.[6]

Among the women I talked to who had played with submission, control and vulnerability typically went hand in hand, a pairing made possible because they possessed a detailed internal map. They could elaborate on which boundaries were to be breached or held firm, which orifices attended, and the quality of touch they craved. They could detail how they wished to be treated afterward—whether with sweet-toned coddling, for instance, or with wordless dismissal. I observed several scenes in person, and one exchange in particular made a deep impression. A male domme asked a female client, "How will I know that you're enjoying yourself? What will I see and hear?" The question floored me, as it did the woman to whom it was directed. This refined approach to consent encompassed not only permission, but also sustained pleasure. How much lousy sex might be avoided, I wondered, if that sort of compassionate inquiry was a standard feature of foreplay.

It is partly because of this possibility of locating agency in submission that so many claim BDSM offers therapeutic relief. Researchers have underscored the "healing narratives" in circulation in the BDSM community.[7] One sociologist, Danielle Lindemann, even noted the propensity among dommes to refer to themselves as therapists.[8] Summing up her interviews with professional dominatrices, she described their sessions as "healthful alternatives to sexual repression, as atonement rituals, as mechanisms for gaining control over prior trauma, and (in the case of 'humiliation sessions') as processes through which clients experience psychological revitalization through shame." A male domme I spoke with described himself as a healer whose motto is radical acceptance. "I provide my absolute presence," he said. "I crack women open, dump in new information—I'll tell them the things that every woman needs to hear, then seal them back up." A female dominatrix told me, "It's not just about pain. It's emotionally connecting with what's in your soul."

For one woman I spoke with, BDSM has been a way to recover from being molested as an adolescent. I met Heidi, a white woman in her thirties who lives in Los Angeles, through a personal connection. For years her sexuality was a source of confusion and distress for her. She had always had a high sex drive, she told me, but the experience of turning on or having an orgasm was persistently bound up in guilt and negative self-judgment. "I would be coming and telling myself, you're so fucked up, you're disgusting," she said. "Even though it felt good, the *feeling* was really bad." Heidi has been in serious relationships over the years, but maintaining healthy relationships, as she put it, was challenging, a problem she attributed to the love-hate struggle playing out around her pleasure. All the same, she dated regularly—"mostly because I'd get horny." One night she wound up with a man who explained that he enjoyed domination. "I was like, huh, no shit, you're a man," she recalled. "But he said, 'No, no, we're going to talk about all the things I will do to you.'" To Heidi, it was the first time she had considered sex as a menu she could pick and choose from. She described their conversation. "Can I kiss you? Sure. Can I kiss your lips? Okay. Can I touch your breasts? All right. Can I twist your nipples? Ehhh." Heidi said that although the night was not a great sexual experience, it set off a flare in her mind.

Fortunately, Los Angeles is a good place to be if you are curious about kink, and Heidi had no trouble finding play parties open to "newbies." She also linked up with a "kink-friendly and trauma-informed" therapist who helped her understand how she could "reclaim the pleasure that had been stolen" from her. Thanks to therapy, she said, she understands that her arousal was a source of grief because her orgasm had routinely been a part of her early violations. To address that, she does scenes where she is the submissive and gets to establish beforehand the ways in which she is both dominated and pleasured. She told me, "I needed to go back to those times and find my power. It's really given me a part of my life back."

While BDSM narratives frequently reference its therapeutic potential, members of the community point out that it would be a mistake to look at play strictly in terms of resolving trauma or exhuming haunting pathos. For many, it's sheer recreation or a means to sensual enhancement. (However, I have to mention here the heterosexual male domme who told me about the favorite pastime of his straight male clientele: to dress up in "slutty sequins" and "fuck-me heels" and reenact "some #MeToo shit." They want to be told they're "filthy cumhole sluts," he told me, musing that they got off from enacting degradation. He wants more female clients, he continued, because "men are total dicks"—and women, by contrast, can use this work to find themselves.)

For Jenn, a former lawyer in New York, playing with power was a way to rekindle her sex life with her husband. She described him as a gentle man who was "very sensitive to, you know, never harming a woman," adding, "His father really hammered in that message: you treat women like you would your mother." As a result, his touch was light and timid. Early on, this didn't bother her, "probably because I had hormones on my side," she said. But over time it started to feel "icky," and she was perpetually turned off. Jenn wasn't prepared to give up on her sex life, though. "It took me a while to realize that I still wanted sex, but I needed more force," she said. She started by asking her husband to do things like pull her hair and spank her, and quickly found that she enjoyed the heightened sensation it provided. "I had a tendency to kind of drift during sex—it would all become kind of soupy—but just that little bit of force would bring me back into the moment." When I asked whether that desire made her uncomfortable, she countered, "Not at all. It made me feel so much stronger, because I was finally putting into words what I wanted, and that is his undivided attention, and his masculine energy, and to help me really feel myself, feel my body, when we're making love." She said they've enjoyed a steep learning curve: while they still have "regular sex," they also have sessions devoted to bondage, paddling, and role-playing, elements that had all been there in her fantasy life. She further stressed that now "sex means so much more than sex," noting that when they play, intercourse is often not on the table. "It's brought us closer together," she told me. "I honestly believe it's saved our marriage."

Psychologist Esther Perel has observed along similar lines that some of America's most rightly celebrated features, such as fairness and equality, can, when carried to the bedroom, "result in very boring sex." Sexual excitement, she argues, is not politically correct. To Jenn, the desire for dominance did not mean she wanted to dismantle the respectful companionship she prizes in her marriage, just that in her erotic life, she did not wish to be constrained by the same polite deference that guides their financial planning or childrearing decisions. Perel maintains that the "emphasis on egalitarian and respectful sex—purged of any expressions of power, aggression, and transgression—is antithetical to erotic desire, for men and women alike."[9]

For Shayna, a fellow participant at the Sexual Attitude Reassessment I attended—the one who announced to the group that she had been "gang-banged" (by a group of twenty men) just the night before—transgression has been central to pleasure. A conservatively dressed blond with limpid blue eyes—in her daily life, she works as a school counselor—she did not falter in the slightest when sharing this information. There was even a sense of triumph. She later told me that her partner, a polyamorous man whom she calls *my Sir*, had arranged the encounter. Her ex-husband had been a "cheater," and though she had previously only known "vanilla" relationships, she was immediately drawn to her Sir's unwavering openness and commitment to servicing her desire. Today they live in a state of 24/7 power exchange, and he routinely orchestrates scenes to suit her sexual imagination. "I love a gang-bang," she said, noting, "for the record," that it's a common female fantasy, and that she has participated in several of them. Even though it's physically arduous, she described it as "rejuvenating mentally." She went on to share that there is a sort of protocol among the men, whom her Sir preselects. Everyone must get a turn, but no one can be seen as taking more than his fair share. At the end, she reconnects with her partner by making love to him. What she most enjoys about it, she said, is that all the details have been worked out in advance. She doesn't have to think about the who, the what, or the how. She has delivered the contents of her fantasy to her Sir down to the condoms, the angle of penetration, and how the men should stand by so that during the experience she can focus entirely on receiving. By surrendering fully, she explained, she can enter a trance-like state.

While I initially had a hard time digesting this information, what I came to see in Shayna's account was a statement of pure desire followed by a willingness to turn her vision into reality. She fantasized about being taken by twenty men, and her partner, "as an act of love," and made that possible. "I never imagined that I would want or be capable of what I'm doing now," she told me. "What seemed extreme has become the norm."

The other women with whom I spoke did not share stories that were nearly so intense. Rather, they played with bondage, costumes, and at times, pain. But they all stressed again and again how their submission fed their sense of control: it was enacted on their own terms and ultimately put them more in touch with their bodies, their passions, and their power.

FINDING POWER IN THE BODY

Around midway through Urbaniak's weekend seminar, three men came onstage. Nice enough looking guys, they part-shuffled, part-strode to their chairs, their faces showing affable terror. Their arrival was met with an audible gasp, as if invaders had been allowed into the room. So much of the program had been poised on an underlying antipathy between the sexes—"Power with Men" assumes a sort of zero-sum game in which we women must wrest control through verbal force or covert conniving—and yet here were the brazen adversaries! Later we would be told that there had been nearly a thousand applicants for the role—that of sitting in impassive silence while women tried out their new skills of pleading, berating, and getting their way.

The resulting scenes unloosed a lifetime's worth of *esprit d'escalier*. Grievances never shared with the shitty boss. Invectives never snarled at the philandering spouse. Requests never made because the women had not dared. But there was something happening beyond merely giving voice to the long unsaid. These were restorative fantasies. The women were not trying to undo the facts of the past—the cruelties, the degradations, the sloppy maltreatment. Rather, by reenacting their experiences, they were harnessing memory and its reverberations.

Watching as women took to the stage and began to make demands, I was reminded of the work of the somatic therapist Pat Ogden, who specializes in trauma. "The story told by the 'somatic narrative' of gesture, posture, prosody, facial expression, eye gaze, and movement is arguably more significant than the story told by the words," she wrote in 2015.[10] Ogden encourages therapists to abandon the verbal recounting of whatever has happened to the client and to work instead with the body, with the goal of helping the client release sensations of having been trapped or belittled or overwhelmed. Instead of slogging through past emotions, she says, you can alter what the body believes.[11] Urbaniak grasps this intuitively. Onstage she had the women try out different poses; here, command a towering height; here, mewl like an abandoned kitten—and in each moment try to access that burning sense of want.

A tall black woman, who for the purposes of this book selected the pseudonym Circe, climbed up to the stage and selected a trim, suited man with a kempt beard. He was to be a stand-in for her boss, whose attention, she said, she craved.

"What sort of attention? What do you want him to do?" Urbaniak asked her. In her world, specificity is key.

"Well," the woman admitted, "I like him."

"Okay, so you want him to ask you for coffee, to go out for dinner?"

"Yes," the woman said, "that would be nice. I'd like to get to know him."

"You have a coffee and you find out you like him, then what?"

The woman paused, then said, "I'm married."

The balance onstage began to shift, as if the players were slowly realizing they'd been working off the wrong script. What followed was like watching a drill bore through stubborn layers of earth.

The compact man then became a stand-in for the husband. "I want an open marriage," Circe practiced saying, alternately domming him with a riding crop and a no-nonsense tone and approaching the subject matter-of-factly: "I know what's best for us and our marriage."

"But," she said, breaking character to explain, "This is just about me. I want to be free to see other people, not him."

Circe rehearsed accordingly, becoming both more regal and more outrageous as she started to inhabit the dimensions of this request, her height extending as she stood over the man, her wrist snapping with confidence as she flicked the crop against his chest. "I am going to see other people and you are going to support me in doing that," she told him. With her eyes locked on his, her voice uncompromising, she owned the interaction.

"Now stop," Urbaniak ordered. "Do it again from a sub state."

To be submissive is not, Urbaniak explained again, to be weak or impassive. It is to be the essence of immovable desire. It is to become a void sucking the other person into your conviction.

Circe got to her knees in front of the man, her head level with his lap. It was a powerful vision to behold: a groveling black woman and an impassive white man. She started to beg and plead; she whined and whimpered: "Please? I want to see other people. Please?" And then the drill bored deeper. Her tone softened: "When you married me, I was a different woman. I was beautiful and wild and free. I want you to see me as wild and free. I want to be wild and free." She was almost crying as she said it, as if she'd just remembered what had been on the tip of her tongue. "Wild and free, wild and free."

Later, when the men debriefed on their experience, Circe's scene partner addressed the audience: "Take this out into the world," he said. "It needs you. Most men really want to serve. We're dying for something meaningful to do."

Later still, when the men retreated, Urbaniak stated, "Most men secretly feel like shit worms who don't know what the fuck to do."

▼▲▼▲▼

In the weeks after "Power with Men," I found myself returning to the image of Circe onstage, her "wild and free" lodged in my mind like an anthem of recovery. But I was curious to know whether that declarative moment proved to be anything more than just that, a moment. Some two months later, I was able to connect with her by phone. We spoke late at night, her voice low as her baby cooed audibly in the background. "I'm still trying to figure myself out," she told me. Circe had grown up in another country, one that I am not going to identify here for the sake of her privacy. Her home was an extremely religious environment, and at no point was there any discussion of positive sexuality or "things like that." She did not have any boyfriends growing up, but did contend with instances of unwanted contact. A cousin used to lurk outside the shower while Circe was in it and would occasionally barge in and try to touch her. Usually she fought him off, but sometimes he would manage to grab away her towel. One time, another young man came to their house when her mother was out and touched her inappropriately. She never shared these experiences with her family, though they haunted her. "I thought I would be accused of something," she said. "We talked about sex like, it's wrong, don't do it."

Circe later moved to the United States and launched a career in medicine. She was in her late twenties when she lost her virginity to the man who eventually became her husband. "I never set out to be a virgin," she said. "I just was not comfortable enough in myself, in my body, to be in a sexual relationship." When I asked what had motivated her to become sexually active, she said, "It felt crazy to me, how can you not have had sex at twenty-seven? So it was something I wanted." But, she recalled, the experience was not enjoyable. It left her filled with shameful feelings that she could not discuss with anyone. She and her future husband began to have sex "every once in a while" despite the fact that she didn't want to. "I don't think I knew enough about it to enjoy it," she told me.

When I asked about the open relationship she had practiced asking for, Circe said she had since raised the matter with her husband. She explained, though, that her husband had cheated on her a few years ago, and since then, their sexual relationship had "broken down." Maybe, she mused, if she knew how to be in an open relationship, she would be inoculated from the kind of pain she was suffering. Or maybe, she later offered, she really just wanted a divorce.

Recently, Circe had been exploring sexuality on her own terms. She'd read Regena Thomashauer's *Pussy* and Soraya Chemaly's treatise on rage. These books, along with communities she had found online, had gotten her thinking about how her life could be different. These steps had provided her with an important sense of connection that had otherwise been missing. "It is so isolating as a professional black female, because there are not a lot of people like me," she said. "Others can't fathom what's really happening." She noted that she has to rely on herself alone in "making and understanding [her] own truth." Her process of discovery had been one of getting back to basics and learning what she wanted. "I used to be other-directed," she said. "A lot of times I did stuff because I was used to being obedient. I didn't want to break the rules—I didn't know where my desires were." Now she was starting to "acknowledge [her] emotions, owning them, being in touch with them, processing them."

There was no grand, combustive change in circumstances following her weekend at The Academy. As much as self-empowerment figures might like us to believe that we can change our whole lives—our very souls!—in a revelatory flash, the impact of a "life-altering" seminar tends to fizzle quickly. But Circe told me the experience had fed into a larger process of self-actualization for her. When I asked what that entailed, she said, "It means being okay with who I am and having a voice. It means being able to show up in the world in my power and in my own skin."

12 THE LIMITS OF TALK

Sex is really only touch, the closest of all
touch. And it's touch we're afraid of.

—*D. H. Lawrence*, Lady Chatterley's Lover, *1932*

If you bring your car into the garage because
something's not working, you don't sit around
drinking tea and speculating as to what the problem
is. You go under the hood and see what's going on.

—*Namita Caen, PhD, sexological bodyworker and*
intimacy coach, personal communication, 2016

IT WAS NOT until several months after the divorce that Mona's rage blossomed in full. At first, it was just an unrelenting sadness; she'd rise each morning to feel the wind had been knocked from her. The ordered days had lost their footing. "Who gets divorced when you're nearly seventy? You've made it this far, why stop now?" she asked when I spoke with her.

Her life before her husband announced his intent to leave had been "pretty content, pretty satisfied." She enjoyed a close circle of friends, grandchildren, and a home in Northern California, and she continued to see the occasional patient, though she had otherwise largely wound down her private therapy practice. Hugh's declaration threw her out of orbit. "I was convinced that there was someone else—there had to be." Why else would someone walk away from over forty years of marriage?

Hugh had "stepped out" in the past. There were small incidents: business trips from which he'd return too cagey or too effusive;

suspicions, unconfirmed, like that coworker who used to look at her so pointedly. But to her knowledge, there had never been any big affairs. Mona is stoic about these incidents: they're what happens over the course of a decades-long marriage. "Men have needs," she told me, without pausing to consider that women, too, have needs.

It was after their vacation to Guatemala, Mona thinks, that the changes began. No sooner did they return home than he was already researching opportunities to go back as a volunteer. They had always been a sensible couple, making safe, steady decisions about their financial, personal, and professional lives. Many of those choices had been made with the intention of moving through these late decades without worry or strain. But now that they had arrived, this was not what Hugh wanted. He was keen for adventure, more wide-ranging experiences. So he started on a junket of solo trips, which at first she thought was a good way for him to spend his retirement from a financial services firm. But the stints grew longer and more elaborate. He said he wanted to spend a year in Cambodia—or was it Colombia? He said he wanted to get rid of the house.

Mona hardly recognized the person speaking these intentions. This wasn't part of the script. They had their life, the days settled around their comfortable routines and rhythms. It may not have been thrilling, but that hardly seemed reason to chuck it away.

Hugh insisted to the contrary. They reached an impasse and split up. It was amicable, she said. But all the same, his departure hollowed her out. A "dark and frantic" time followed. Sleepless nights found her combing through memories, feeling for signs that her life could have been heading this way. For how long had Hugh been restless? How deep did his dissatisfaction run? "Was I not a good wife?" the question gnawed at her.

But then the rage began edging in. It came in the form of postcards from the freshly traveled wild. It showed up in old photos, in friends' passing comments, in the tidy labeled cupboards, in the worn but sensible sheets. This nice life that was their co-creation was now a museum of evidence. The house choked on stillness. Was it possible that she had been too tempered, that for the sake of their quiet marriage she had silenced the woman she believed to be incompatible with the wife?

Looking back, she was struck by a hoary habit of compromise. Across all those years she had never pursued her own satisfaction. She had put her husband first, and for years it was all about the children, then the demands of her work, then the grandkids. Anytime her desires had veered off the path of sensibility, she'd laughed them aside. She hadn't permitted herself any pleasures that seemed out of character. And through it all, her neglect of her own sexuality was so complete, so assured, that she didn't wonder that it might be otherwise.

Until now.

As if in a flood, ailments beset her. Headaches came, stomach troubles, aching joints: her very bones felt tired. She supposed it must be depression and eventually went to see a therapist. The doctor encouraged her to talk about her marriage, her expectations, the way she communicated, her relationships with her children, her own mother. It was productive, Mona said. But all the while, her physical anguish only grew. She felt numb. Some days it was like her head was floating atop a disconnected body. As much as talking helped to soften the jabs of grief, it did nothing to divert the course of sadness flowing through her limbs.

It was a friend who recommended her to Judith, a specialist in somatic healing, and it was through Judith that I met Mona. A brilliant-eyed and disarming middle-aged woman, Judith gave up her license in counseling to help men and women "reach their full expression." What this means, in practice, is touching people for a living, often in ways that place her activities in a legal gray zone between physical therapy and sex work. Judith is among a network of such practitioners in the western United States and Canada, some of whom I visited, interviewed, and researched over the course of several months. To protect her and the privacy of her clients, I am not using Judith's real name.

Judith believes that a disproportionate share of human suffering is directly linked to our muzzled sexuality. Whether overtly or covertly, by our own designs or as a result of violent force, "this vital and expansive energy," as she calls sex, gets derailed, reshaped, and, most often, subdued—by culture, family, education, religion, and lackluster experience. The result is not just sexual disappointment but a far more encompassing failure to thrive. Judith works with a number of women in their fifties and older who are in the process of reassessing their sex lives and realizing they may have long settled for compromise. While many of today's leading researchers are hashing it out over whether sex and desire are based in the mind or lodged in the body, Judith and her fellow practitioners ignore such distinctions altogether. Mind and body are not merely linked but of a piece.

In their first session, Judith held Mona's hand. The next week, she stroked her face. By the end of the month, Mona was lying on a table as Judith instructed her to follow the sensations of her hands as they moved, first gently, then firmly, up and down the length of her body. Midway into these sessions, Mona would inevitably start crying. It felt good, this touch, but it also felt foreign, like fingers traipsing across a surface that did not quite belong to her. She began talking more: about her mother, who had spurned touch; about being afraid to tell her husband she had not been a virgin; about how her own body had rarely had a place in her marriage; about feeling utilitarian. "I was always in service of something—having children, pleasing him, caring for the house," she said when I spoke with her. But this was part of the routine, so she "never thought anything was wrong." Mona said she'd enjoyed the sense of closeness when she had sex with her husband. She'd enjoyed kissing and the feel of his skin on hers, and she'd always enjoyed his excitement. But her own pleasure had not really been a part of it. "I was hard to please," she told me. Then, "Maybe we both just stopped trying."

It was around the sixth or seventh session that Judith began touching Mona's genitals. It was vaguely terrifying—no one but her husband had seen this part of her body for decades, and certainly not a woman. "I don't think anyone had ever touched me before with that kind of concentrated attention," she said. It felt painful before it felt good. Judith told her to breathe, to listen in to her own skin, her nerves, to examine why it was that she felt squeamish, rather than simply running away from the sensation. She was sent home with instructions to practice masturbating—and as good as it felt, she continued to find herself back on a familiar threshold, unable to let go.

Meanwhile, she had begun to rethink her marriage—its arc and ultimate dissolution. Whereas before she had always found peaceable compatibility, she now saw all the ways she had shut herself down over the years, a collage of self-denials, some of the episodes so small as to barely be perceptible. And yet it was as though they had carved deep channels by way of repetition. She mourned. It was terrible to see her life in this way. But, she said, "It wasn't as if anyone else was shutting me down or saying I could or couldn't behave in certain ways. This came from me."

One afternoon Judith asked Mona to masturbate in front of her. She noticed that Mona tensed and lay still, only moving one hand, scarcely breathing. Try like this, Judith demonstrated, writhing, curling, sucking in big gulps of air, using both hands, clenching, stretching. Shoving her self-consciousness aside, Mona gave it a try, and as she breathed she became aware of a giddy sensation that curled up from her toes. A knot in her belly began to dissolve. "My fingers started talking to my brain," she recalled. She stopped thinking. And at seventy-two, weeping, laughing, Mona realized she could experience full-body pleasure.

▼▲▼▲▼

For most of the human body's problems and malfunctions, a trip to the mechanic holds a decent analogy: as at the garage, medical practitioners look directly to the body to diagnose and treat the physiological source of the complaint. Women's sexual function, however, is a common outlier. While men's sexual complaints are often treated as problems with the plumbing, women are repeatedly told that it's all in their heads. This perspective is acquiring nuance, as we've seen throughout this book, but even these refined views frequently hold the nebulous workings of the mind at a distance from the body's drives.

For all that our culture is obsessed with women's sexuality, it is remarkably standoffish about women's genitals. They're considered messy, smelly, bafflingly intricate, even frightening. Their purpose? Uncertain, as we have seen with the history of the clitoris, whose occlusions and denials historian Thomas Laqueur described as a "parable of culture."[1] (In both the original and revised editions of *The Joy of Sex*, author Alex Comfort describes the vulva thusly: "'The part of you,' as the advertisement used to say, 'that is most girl,' but also as magic as the penis, and to children, primitives, and males generally, slightly scary: it looks like a castrating wound and bleeds regularly, it swallows the penis and regurgitates it limp, it can probably bite and so on."[2]) These skewed notions inflect science, too, largely in the form of persistent ignorance and avoidance. And just as individual women imbibe variations on the idea that their unmentionables are, well, unmentionable, so, too, are many doctors ill-equipped to respond meaningfully when women report feelings of sexual shame, numbness, or displeasure.[3] Perhaps the problem relates to hormones, or maybe diet? Find ways to reduce your stress, try an antidepressant. All of these factors may place limits on a woman's sexual possibilities. But sometimes the problem may be that she does not know her own body, or her own preferences and capabilities. It may be that through habituation, boredom, unknowing, denial, or violence, she has been shut off from actually *feeling*.

The field in which Judith practices represents a little-known but steadily growing curative to the common mind-body rift. Called *sexual somatic therapy* or *sexological bodywork*, the approach entails touching and stimulating the entire body, including the genitals, as a means of addressing persistent sexual problems, from absent pleasure and inability to orgasm to trauma-related fears of and aversions to sex. It can also be used to help women and men access greater states of erotic pleasure, even trance-like experiences of ecstasy.

Internationally, the field has some traction, with practitioners operating—with varying degrees of legality—in Canada, Europe, the United Kingdom, and Australia. In the United States, the practice is legal only in California. Strict regulations prevent most therapists from physical contact with their patients, and for good reason, and thus this field is almost entirely outside the law and licensing. Caffyn Jesse, a prominent sexual somatic therapist based in British Columbia, talked to me about the blurred boundaries between sex work and somatic healing, noting that there are those out there who, whether deliberately or not, may end up exploiting their clientele. She co-teaches training programs in somatic sex education and sexological bodywork, and tells me that learning to clearly uphold boundaries and ethics is a major component of the education she and her colleagues provide. But, she told me, "You have to be a creative edge walker to do this work," especially since most practitioners work in places that criminalize the exchange of money for erotic touch. Jesse refers to it as a vocation, emphasizing that for many who seek help it is "the missing piece" in sexual healing and discovery.

CONFRONTING THE PLAGUE OF DISEMBODIMENT

The originator of sexological bodywork is a gentle-seeming, soft-edged former Jesuit priest-in-training now in his seventies. Joseph Kramer was raised in a Catholic household and was aware from an early age that he was gay. He soon perceived the constraints around how his adulthood might take shape. There was the path of family and fatherhood, which didn't at the time seem like the right choice for a homosexual man. There was a life of being single, which, during the mid-twentieth century, carried connotations of loneliness, even perversion. And there was the church. Kramer pauses frequently over the course of our video conference call, occasionally touching his heart. "I escaped from coupledom," he tells me when we spoke in 2016.

After high school, Kramer committed to the Jesuits and spent ten years as a celibate member of the Society of Jesus. He loved the rituals of prayer, meditation, and self-awareness, the summons to discern God in the world around us, the life of the mind in service. He relished living in community, freed largely from financial considerations. He also was happy to be free of all the assumptions in the wider society that maturity requires the formation of a two-by-two partnership. But when he happened to experience a full-body massage, something within him sprang to life. "That massage woke up such extraordinary new levels of consciousness in me that I thought, 'That was the most important two hours of my life!,'" he once said.[4]

Although we are accustomed to describing the priesthood—or, say, law or medicine—in terms of "vocation," rarely do we use the term in relation to sexuality. But that is how Kramer, like Jesse, saw it: as a calling. The Ignatian spiritual charge, he says, referring to St. Ignatius of Loyola, founder of the Jesuits, is to "find God in all things"—and Kramer found it in the body ecstatic. He speaks of it as a *charism*—an extraordinary power, in the Catholic sense. "They say celibacy is a gift—well, so is not being celibate. I have more of that gift. I felt comfortable leaving the Jesuits because I had a calling elsewhere," he told me.

He exchanged the priesthood for the gay scene in New York. This was the early 1980s, and AIDS had begun making its dire claims on the community. Men, says Kramer, were scared of sex, avoiding intimacy, and yet the need for physical, sensual connection was greater than ever.

So he began giving erotic massages. What might spring to mind at this point are salacious, cheap encounters. But what Kramer and his trainees—including Caffyn Jesse—offer is of a very different order, a vision of sexual pleasure based on health and elevated consciousness. Kramer describes his work as being that of a sexual monk or shaman, creating space for vulnerability, compassion, and erotic fulfillment to help others grow and heal.

The Jesuits focus on education. Accordingly, Kramer has spent his life creating schools. After giving "more than a thousand" erotic massages, he opened a school in 1984 to train others in the techniques of touch he had developed, the Body Electric School based in Oakland, California. He went on to obtain a doctorate in human sexuality at the Institute for Advanced Study of Human Sexuality in San Francisco in 2002, and there, the next year, he established the first professional sexological bodywork training program. The school, which called itself the "Harvard" of human sexology, is now defunct, as I noted in Chapter 8. It was one of the only places in the United States where students could obtain graduate training in sexology. It was also the only place in the country to offer a legal certification program devoted to erotic touch.

Kramer aims to fill a pronounced gap: while we can nobly undertake courses of study in practically every other domain pertaining to the physical body, where it comes to our own sexual expression there is stunning—and insistent—absence. According to Kramer, the goal of sexological bodywork is to help develop erotic self-mastery by bringing awareness to the body. For Judith, success with clients like Mona does not necessarily mean getting them to reach orgasm, but imparting tools for basic self-care. Our cultural attentions rest easily on achievements like weight loss or athleticism, but we can hardly conceive of applying the same discipline where it comes to our sexual health. We don't all need to become marathon runners, but it would seem that in matters of pleasure, many of us can barely hobble around the block.

From early learning onward, we are taught that sex is bad, pleasure is wrong, your body is a point of shame, nudity is humiliating, and your urges are dirty. Danger and threat lurk all around. And the result, Kramer claims, is a physical shutting down of the body, a literal inability to feel. We are in the throes of a "plague of disembodiment," he tells me. "We have actually forgotten how to feel in certain ways and forgotten our sexual functioning." Interoception—again, awareness of what is taking place inside your own body, what it's feeling—appears to be something of a lost art. And it's no wonder: we work when we're exhausted, deprive ourselves of nourishment when we're starving, gorge in the absence of hunger, and pass our days scrunched in front of a glowing screen that doesn't engage the physical self at all. On a sexual level, add in the morass of "our virulently anti-body culture," as Kramer calls it, and we perhaps start to apprehend how it could be that parts of our bodies—though they may be positively electrified with nerves—become insensate.

But as with other skills, sensation and pleasure can be learned, and indeed, strengthened with time. Kramer likens his field to Tibetan Buddhism, wherein the "practice is the practice." Here, science is beginning to bear him out. Work in neurology has now repeatedly found that practices like meditation can alter the structure of the brain. Our minds are plastic, and energy flows where attention goes, to quote the adage. What this means with regard to sex is that repeated experiences of pleasure can alter neural pathways. We can educate ourselves to feel more.

"In doing somatic work, openings happen, epiphanies perhaps, great insights," Kramer tells me. They're physical epiphanies, realizations that land in the body and alter the way we experience ourselves and the world. Sometimes these moments can be so powerful that they throw the person into a tizzy—"I have to change my life completely, toss out my lover, leave my job." Other times Kramer says, as in what Judith facilitated with Mona, people learn to "experience themselves as an erotic being for the first time."

▼▲▼▲▼

To Caffyn Jesse, the somatic practitioner in British Columbia, sexual bodywork is about far more than erotic recovery. It is healing at the level of the human soul. We talked by video conference between my home in Brooklyn and her home by the sea. At one point, she turns her computer so I can share in her view of conifer-strewn slopes over the sparkling strait. Jesse had originally trained to work as a counselor, but over the course of her own journey to address traumas occurring in childhood and as a young woman, she turned to bodywork. Eventually she studied sexological bodywork with Joseph Kramer in California.

To Jesse, a foundation of sexual somatic touch is helping clients empower their "choice and voice." She tells me that most people are "trained from early childhood to endure unwanted touch. We have very little opportunity to practice and create competency in actually knowing what we feel in our body, what a *yes* is for us, what's a *no* for us, what's a *maybe*, what does that feel like?" In response, Jesse says, she creates an environment where choice is not only welcome but becomes the basis for further inquiry. "Women in particular are trained to feel their pleasure through providing pleasure to someone else," she explains. In response to being asked what they want, women will often pivot to, "Well, what do you want to give me, how do you want to touch me?" The discovery process therefore helps women—and men—get in touch with what they actually want, and then learn to express it on a moment-by-moment basis. Jesse underscores the need to move at a client's own pace, establishing a sense of calm and safety. That might mean that sessions involve little to no genital touch at all for weeks or perhaps even years.

When I ask Jesse about what healing looks like in her sessions, she encourages me to look past the false tension between vulnerability and empowerment. She works with people across a wide spectrum of backgrounds. Some who come to her are deeply wounded and have shut down. ("Trauma," she says, "is the cultural norm where it comes to sex.") Others are looking to amplify their sexual potential. But she cautions against viewing this kind of bodywork as a means of linearly amplifying sensation: "Being very vulnerable and being very empowered aren't like opposite ends of a spectrum. Sometimes as we become more empowered we can feel our deeper vulnerabilities, and vice versa."

Even though her sessions can take a wide variety of forms, from simple bodily awareness exercises to ecstatic massage, what underpins all of her work is a belief in human sexual potential. When I ask her whether she thinks we are all capable of expansive erotic states, she appears to almost stumble over my question. Of course, she replies: "I totally know that. If I can do it, anybody can do it."

But, as she continues, I realize that perhaps it is my own understanding of eroticism that remains confined to thinking just about sensation. Jesse is talking about something else. To her, realizing this potential encompasses—but ultimately goes beyond—what is happening in our

bodies: "It is a conscious connection with our life and with other people. It is here and within us and it's within grasp for everyone." And
reaching it, she says, entails giving up the "models that we're all driven
by: of scarcity and not enoughness and having to do it right," and instead realizing that we are "held in the biosphere of belonging." Jesse
says that we cripple ourselves by seeking pleasure from without, in
wanting the next, biggest *thing*, because "what we find through these
practices is that it's already right here, it's right now. We can actually
choose it."

▼▲▼▲▼

Celeste Hirschman was one of Kramer's star pupils. After completing
her training at the Institute for Advanced Study of Human Sexuality,
she went on to run the bodywork course, and today she operates her
own erotic healing brand out of an airy space in the Haight-Ashbury
district of San Francisco where I met with her in 2016. She belongs to a
generation of women who believe that pleasure is a woman's right and
are keen to course-correct when reality does not match up to expectation. Hirschman and her colleagues often work with a young cohort of
women who, unlike Mona—who was in the position of surveying the
past with regret—are experiencing their sexual struggles in real time.

Hirschman likes using the phrase *Hottest Sexual Movie* to capture
the tastes of her clients and help them tease out their own erotic proclivities. Some may yearn for tenderness, others for brutality, and others still for romance, which she says is "as much of a fetish as anything
else." Many women, she says, are "hostages to the idea that romance
or sexuality or intimacy should look a certain way." What she wants
clients to see is that most desires deviate from the standard "recipe"
of climb-aboard penetration and pleasure, and almost all of them are
totally healthy. Allowing oneself to long for and participate in variations on bread-and-butter, male-orgasm-centered sex is nothing short
of a radical act. According to Hirschman, it has the power not only to
dismantle the centuries-long insistence that sex is a procreative performance, but also to foreground women's bodies and interests when it
comes to sexual choreography.

These declarations come relatively easily to Hirschman. Raised in
an intentional community called The Family in San Francisco, she

never really experienced shame around the naked body and its abilities. "I was a slut growing up," she tells me. "Plunging dresses, skirt up here," she gestures to her upper thigh. "There are not a lot of choices if you want to be a sexual woman—you can be a slut or you can pretend you're not really that sexual even if you are, and do it behind the scenes. I embraced the slut."

Hirschman initially set out to be a psychologist. "What else could you do around sex that has a socially approved route?" she asks rhetorically. She was admitted to a graduate program but soon left it: "I didn't like the DSM, I didn't like the medicalization." Eventually, she found her way to Joseph Kramer. "Sexological bodywork really focuses on your relationship with your own body. Joseph calls it facilitated erotic trance—you're taking someone through breathwork and erotic massage, so they can have a transformation that helps to remove shame and find new pleasure and reconnect with [their] body in a way [they] may never have been connected." However, the practice didn't feel complete to her. "How are people negotiating touch in their relationships? It's so hard for a woman to get one word out of her mouth—'a little to the left'—let alone to say, 'This is what turns me on,' or to say whatever she actually needs her partner to do." Wanting to integrate more psychological context into her work, she paired up with Danielle Harel to create Somatica, which she describes as "an interpersonal method to help people get the most out of erotic and emotional connection."

Hirschman draws heavily on the work of the late psychologist Jack Morin. Morin theorized that desire is the expression of conflict, typically an intense emotional experience from childhood, and that the ensuing process of self-soothing becomes sexual arousal.[5] There are two main pathways by which this process can play out. One is the path of repair. For instance, a girl who was ignored and denigrated may become a woman who wants very much to be worshiped and tended to. In the other, that early negative experience becomes the later erotic yearning. The girl who was abused becomes a woman who craves molestation, but by choice. This is hard for most therapists to cope with, says Hirschman. They may do work around healing the denigrated inner child, but stumble where it comes to denigration as a turn on. However, she says, "those challenging experiences shaped your erotic landscape and that's beautiful, there's nothing wrong with that. There is so much judgment around what is acceptable desire that a lot of people's arousal gets missed."

In this framework, biology takes a back seat to satisfying emotional needs. According to Hirschman, "desire is not about sex but about deeper core wounds getting healed through erotic experiences." As I understand Somatica, the relationship between client and practitioner becomes the site of healing. While touch is still a big part of the practice, unlike bodywork, it's a clothes-on method, "because not everyone is ready to get naked on a table," as Hirschman put it. The focus is on developing healthy attachment while also establishing individual autonomy. The latter is especially important for women, because so many grew up without boundaries, or were raised to believe they were bad. "Some people are so used to boundaries being walked all over that they won't even feel it when it's being crossed," she tells me. "I have to stick my finger up their nose for them to say, *there's* a boundary."

HEALING TRAUMA THROUGH TOUCH

Hirschman, like most of the somatic practitioners I spoke to, told me that trauma is rarely what brings women or a couple into treatment. Leveled desire, sexual boredom, mismatched libido, or communication breakdowns are what typically get people through the door. However, with crushing frequency, these expressions of sexual discontent are the ruinous carryovers of the past. "Traumas that we don't properly metabolize can show up in all kinds of ways," explains Judith. "And a lot of times the person who is suffering will not see the link. It affects us and we often don't even recognize it for what it is." For many women, exposure to trauma causes them to dismiss, sabotage, or misinterpret their desire: past violations chart their way into the present. The prevailing theory is that sexual trauma is psychologically upsetting, causing women to mentally associate sex with some past horror. But this is not the complete picture, as we saw in Chapter 4. Traumatic experiences also linger *physically*, in the nervous system, in the limbs, in elevated blood pressure, and in weakened immunity, often long after the person appears to be otherwise healed.

When Syd first showed up in Judith's office, resolving trauma was not the first thing on her mind. Syd, who is in her late twenties and identifies as half white and half black, came at the insistence of her longtime partner, Bruce, who is in his early forties. To say she was reluctant is an understatement: she was mortified. It was an all but established rule that they did not openly discuss their struggles in bed, and because they passed without comment, Syd had let herself believe that they weren't real, or at the very least, weren't significant.

Bruce was forever urging her to come. *I want you to come! Come on me! Are you gonna come?* It was the most horrible request. "He might as well be asking that I become a bird and fly out the window," Syd told me. She could give herself subdued—"meh"—orgasms, but she had rarely experienced one with a partner. She would tell herself, "Whatever, I'm just not that sexual, this isn't what my body is designed to do." But knowing this was disappointing to Bruce, she faked her pleasure—so routinely that sex had become a performance for his benefit. So part of her humiliation when Bruce booked a session with Judith was the sense of having given a poor show, without even knowing it.

Her horror only deepened at that first session, when Bruce admitted that he wanted her to be less passive in bed. As with orgasm, the request bordered on the impossible: How, in the absence of feeling good, could she simulate greater enthusiasm? Then began a series of what Syd described as "awful" afternoons of being asked to ask for what she wanted. Again, impossible requests. But rather than confess that this task was too much, she gritted her way through it, faking her enjoyment. She was terrified of actually expressing herself. "I didn't want to seem too needy, or too fussy and particular."

One day—it was a rainy, gloomy one, and Syd was fighting off a cold—she was sitting on one of Judith's plush chairs, trying to instruct Bruce as he passed his hands over her upper body. He was stroking her hair, her neck, caressing her shoulders. "Does that feel good?"

"Mhmm," Syd responded, struggling to find her customary assent. In fact, it felt awful. It made her skin crawl. She felt nauseous, anxious, like she wanted to run screaming from the room.

Judith noticed. "What's happening with you, Syd?" she asked.

Syd remained silent, the strokes continuing, until she burst out, "I want you to take your fucking hands off me!"

"I couldn't believe the words came from my mouth," she told me. "I was panting and sweating and all I could feel was that I needed him to stop touching me *that instant*."

Syd didn't get into the specifics of what had happened to her between the ages of fourteen and sixteen beyond saying that she was violated by someone she had been close to. Another humiliation. Not only because she believed she must have done something to bring on this attention, but worse—because she felt she hadn't been good enough to make it last. Perhaps the most painful comment she made over the course of our conversations was: "I knew it was obviously wrong. But it also made me feel special, like I had been chosen. I kind of wanted to be pleasing him."

Syd and Bruce had cautiously circumnavigated the subject before but had never addressed the heart of it: the facts, her feelings, how her body unconsciously continued to flare in defense. She had taken these omissions as part of their pact of silence. But her outburst, as frightening as it was to her at the time, opened the way to being able to speak frankly about her adolescence, and with that came a serious reassessment of boundaries. On the one hand, her integrity had been breached—repeatedly. She felt ashamed, disgusting, and deeply alone. And on the other, she felt that she had done something to turn off her trespasser. Suddenly, all of her subsequent relationships played out in a dizzying variation on these themes: having sex when someone wanted to have sex with her, and then trying wildly to retain their interest, even if she had no interest in him. It was a dance in which she had almost totally erased herself. "I had to become like a child again to know what I want," she said.

Syd's experiences highlight a crucial component of healing from trauma: finding safety—and even joy—in physical touch and sensation. Thoughtful practitioners, such as Wendy Maltz (from Chapter 4), have been vocal about the need for sexual healing in the aftermath of sexual violence. Wounds to women's most intimate selves need to be addressed through intimate care and rediscovery so that they can become whole again in their lives. Describing her own process of recovering from incest and child sexual abuse, somatic teacher Staci Haines wrote, "The abuse seemed to pour out of my body." But "through the healing," she added, "my sexuality emerged from a new place in me.

It became less and less about how sex was supposed to look and more about my own experience of sex and desire. . . . The more the trauma poured out of me, the more *I* filled *me* in."[6]

For Syd, giving voice to what had happened during her adolescence made it possible to begin disarming the past. It was slow going. "I needed to learn to stay in my body, rather than go back to this place of 'Oh, I'm built just for you.'" Judith introduced them to sensate focus, the practice first elaborated by Masters and Johnson as a way for couples to cultivate intimacy. Rather than viewing sex as a means to simply finish—an on-ramp to orgasm—sensate focus is about deliberate touch for its own sake, centered on awareness of sensation. In a sensate focus session, Syd might say, for example, "You can touch my arm," and for a set number of minutes, Bruce would just stroke her arm, attuned to texture, pressure, heat. Or "You can touch my knee." Or "Here, my foot." She might spend some minutes with her hands over his hands, or his calf, training her own fingers to receive feeling, as opposed to dispensing pleasure. Over the course of several weeks, they could take turns being the toucher and the touched. And sometimes Syd would still say, "I don't want to be touched anywhere." But the words were losing their horrible potency. There they were, loosed from her lips, and the world remained intact. Bruce had gone nowhere. Each time, she stated her boundaries, and she still waited for "the room to rip in half," but found instead a gathering steadiness. Gradually, she realized that drawing the parameters of what she did not want made her feel more connected to herself and closer to her partner. It was through saying no that she began to see places where she wanted to say yes. She asked Bruce to touch her breasts. "I waited for that sense of dread," she said, "but he was so reverential, and I experienced, like a flash of lightning, that sex could be something else."

CONCLUSION
BEYOND THE PHYSICAL

There are many paths to heaven, and sex is one of them.
—*Abraham Maslow, in* The Humanist, *September–October 1970*

IT'S SUNDAY IN Manhattan, one of those mornings suffused with the warmth of early spring, and I'm sitting cross-legged on a carpeted floor listening to a number of women crying. They're joyful tears, tears of relief and of release, tears that express their gratitude for human feeling and their sheer wonder at themselves. "I never knew this was possible," says a woman in her late fifties, wiping the wet from her face. She's been married for thirty-two years, and her partnership has covered a lot of terrain, good and bad. "I thought we'd already had the limit of all there is. But last night I realized there is no glass ceiling. I floated in the clouds of Mount Olympus."

The night before, with both male and female partners, the women had received what the master Tantra educator Charles Muir calls a "sacred spot massage," consisting of three intervals of progressively intimate touch intended to conclude with stimulating the region known as the G-spot. The givers, some of whom were routine intimates, others strangers until just the day before, were provided with detailed instructions. Each was to treat the woman partner as if she were the emissary for all of womanhood: she was to be adored for her inherent beauty, as well as her strife. Women carry so much violation and heartache in their bodies, Muir said. It's not surprising that "they shut down and stop wanting to have sex." The massage, he warned, was bound to elicit strong emotions. Hurts and sorrows tend to surface before women experience anything that might be described as good, and he urged their partners to resist the urge to comfort. Let the pain come, he said. Releasing hurt goes hand in hand with finding pleasure.

One queer woman who partnered with both a woman and a man, both of whom had previously been strangers, said, "I was afraid of being too intimate or too attached to someone I don't know. But I felt so safe. It was like walking with my sister. Being in love, expressing love, without having to fall in love."

Another described a "great cracking open" and said the experience "makes healing seem so reachable, attainable." She had previously consulted with a doctor about low libido, but now she observed, "There is no pathology. I've endured a lot of pain and I told myself stories about that—but they're old stories. Maybe it's time to let them go."

Muir, now in his early seventies, is one Tantra's main ambassadors to the West. Raised in the Bronx, these days he is an accessible and deliberately irreverent teacher. He motions graphically as he recounts his street-side education: "Fuck 'em hard and fuck 'em deep!" He references this time in his life to shed light on just how impoverished our intimate learning tends to be. Between pop culture, the locker room, and the "mixed-up messages from mom and dad," he said, sex is bound to be both confusing and deeply underestimated. Sex, he teaches, is far more than a means of getting off: it is a route to awakening.

Tantra is an esoteric practice originating in a number of ancient Hindu texts, most of which, contrary to popular belief, have nothing to do with sex. The word *Tantra*, from the Sanskrit, literally means "to weave" or "to loom," suggesting that the practice is one of bringing together disparate threads to end our separateness and divisions. The underlying idea is that of nonduality: it's not that pleasure counters pain, or that the ethereal is antonymous to the material; it's rather that all things, from the ordinary to the ecstatic, are equal means of liberation. Muir presents Tantra as being about the human arc to unity—to ourselves, to others, and to the infinitesimal miracle beyond. That said, he draws on humor to reach the more profane leanings of his students. By midmorning on the first day of the workshop, he was using a floppy purple dildo to "paint" the inner and outer lips of a felted vulva puppet. At other times he wielded a small electric rod that illuminated to a high-pitched drone, rather like the sound cue for a haunted house, alternately making fun of male self-marvel and urging us, his listeners, to understand the potential of the penis to be a healing wand of light. "Turn your orgasm into a prayer," he encouraged the men present, before making an ejaculatory gesture with the buzzing prop. "This one's for you, Jesus!"

In the West, Tantra (or Neo-Tantra, as it is often called) is all about running currents of energy—specifically, what the discipline regards as opposing and yet complementary qualities of the masculine and the feminine. A number of critics have questioned this normative view, advocating for more inclusive forms of Tantra that go beyond rigid male and female poles—and rightly so. Sex advocate and educator Barbara Carrellas has spoken to this issue, suggesting that everyone possesses male and female traits, whose proportions are in flux:

> The practice of Tantra, being the path of acceptance of everything, has always embraced opposites: good/evil, sacred/profane, higher/lower, earthly/spiritual, yin/yang, light/shadow. In embracing these opposites, Tantra is able to accept and contain "all that is," which means not only the opposing poles, but everything between the poles. In our Western society, however, most everything is regarded as either/or, and there's not much in between. Nothing is more polarized than gender. Therefore, the Western mind reasons, if Tantra unites opposites, it must require "opposite" genders. As if there were such a thing as opposing genders![1]

When pressed, Muir treads lightly around this subject, offering that we can think of Tantra as the meeting of different forms—giving versus receiving, soft versus hard, internal versus external. One of his driving messages is essentially that men are ejaculation-addicted cavemen, while women are pleasure-starved accommodators who tend to hurry things along. This pattern, he said, means that everyone misses out on the "limitless energy" of female sexuality.

While Muir's jokey demeanor might rub some the wrong way, it served, I think, as an effective ploy, making topics like "sacred sex" more palatable to his students than it might have been otherwise. Most of them were new to Tantra and secularly inclined; they spoke of craving something *more* from sex, but not quite knowing what that was. We might yearn for something greater—more feeling, more connection, something tantalizing but ineffable—yet we consistently find ourselves blocked. Like others, Muir underscores how modern couples are looking to one another for fulfillment that far surpasses the practical, everyday routines: they want deep meaning. Taking an optimistic view, he suggests that instead of wallowing in the isolated narcissism of the "Me generation," we can evolve into a "We generation," premised on mutual uplift.[2] Tantra, he said, is a way to expand beyond our customary barriers, dislodging those blocks through flashes of revelation, which can be achieved through sexuality. But doing so requires some major healing, especially for women. He told the class, "We need to send nerve messages to the brain and create some new files, to displace the old files of rape, and molestation and desecration of the temple."

SEX AND SPIRIT

Sexuality, as we know, links to almost every other aspect of our lives. It is self-perception and sensation; it's about how we desire, connect, and create. But it's also how we make meaning in the world, and as a result, it's attached to spirituality. I'm not writing here with reference to the world's religions, although all of them have weighed in on what is right and proper in the realm of human mating—at times celebrating our erotic mingling, at other times attempting to banish all but the perfunctory interactions. Rather, by spirituality, I mean that we can regard sexuality as something that surpasses everyday experience. The late sex therapist Gina Ogden, who devoted the latter part of her career to looking at female sexuality and spirituality, suggested that making this connection does not rest on doctrine or require faith in a divine authority. It is not a matter of privileging a particular gender, orientation, or relationship style. Instead, it is the conscious appreciation of the unfettered potential of sexuality, and along with it the understanding that desire is about a lot more than just desiring sex: it contains who we are, where we've been, and what we hope the future holds. She maintained that sexual energy pervades our lives from beginning to end. "It's not just about intercourse and orgasm," she once wrote. "It's about receptiveness and movement. It's about our most profound emotions and how we reach out to others. It's about how we think and feel and love."[3]

Ogden saw this connection as our innate inheritance and argued that it was only recently, in the human scheme of things, that we had lost touch with the sacred parts of sex—that is, the capacity for sex to bring about recovery and transformation and to reveal new facets of ourselves.[4] She maintained that for our ancient forebears, sex and spirit were not opposing forces, as we often think today. In much of modern Western culture, sex is aligned with sin, or at least viewed with skepticism. It is considered a wayward impulse, a base pursuit that runs counter to, or derails, loftier ambitions. Sex dwells in the physical, while spirit belongs to higher realms, uncontaminated by the body. The ways we have internalized these ideas show up all over the place, from treating our desires with guilt and shame to refusing to look at, touch, or even name parts of our bodies. We see it in the way we categorize the world according to right and wrong, good and bad, man and woman, and straight and queer. To each, we learn, belongs a moral rank.

This separation also shows up in the study of sex itself, which, as I've discussed, all too frequently focuses on physical function without attending to its emotional and existential significance. For all the possibility of resplendent relating, to both others and to ourselves, professionals and the general public alike struggle to appreciate all the ways in which sexuality begets something more than physical delight. We're often cynical about it. It's hard to approach Tinder from, say, a place of compassion. We struggle to see in the ordinary anything profound. Among professionals, the emphasis on eliminating dysfunction can ignore the qualities that make sex most nourishing. Such approaches might bring some relief, but rarely do they answer the deeper questions. What is it that we truly desire? Do we merely wish to get off, a la Masters and Johnson's stepwise model? Or is sex both the container and the vehicle for satisfying other longings, such as our yearning for healing, growth, and acceptance, or even for a taste of the sublime?

At the other end of the spectrum, typically outside the mainstream of medicine, are those who, like Muir, speak of sex as *sacred* or *divine*. Although this language readily appeals to some circles, for many—who perhaps just want to figure out how to enjoy themselves again—it can set off *woo woo* triggers, leaving them utterly nonplussed. The pendulum swings, in the words of sex educator and former therapist Rosalyn Dischiavo, between "plumbers" and "New Agers," leaving few options for the majority who travel in between. "Sexuality is not one thing," she told me. "It's the life force. And as such, it's biological, it's spiritual, it's emotional, it's psychological, it's relational. And if you leave any one of those out, you're going to miss something crucial."

And yet, apart from the New Age offerings, the central message for women, other than the drumbeat that they have naturally low libidos, is that good sex is about technique and communication. Have sex because it's good for you (like a brisk walk, it benefits your health). It will make your partnerships more stable. We rarely hear about sex as an opportunity for personal enhancement, or as a field in which we get to grow and play and discover ourselves throughout our entire lives. For younger women, especially, the message these days is that you should want sex because sex is fun and physically exciting. There is so much pressure to be nonchalant about it, to not appear needy or emotionally invested, and that leaves little room for considering *why* it is that we should want sex in the first place.

The outcry over the orgasm gap is a start. It at least makes plain that heterosexual women should be more than stewards of male pleasure. But it is only a start, and, as I've said, potentially a faulty one at that, because it runs the risk of prioritizing mechanics over meaning. Marci Graham, a facilitator at the sex-positive Human Awareness Institute, told me that many women believe they are "a receptacle for someone else's pleasure," but that they can learn to harness sexual energy for themselves. It might seem like a matter of simply shifting your mindset. However, Graham said, "the leap looks tiny, but it is actually giant. There are so many things to unravel inside and outside ourselves to get there."

Moving beyond sex as something to accomplish, or to cede, wherein orgasm is the ultimate arbiter of good or bad, is crucial for older women as well as younger ones. A number of women I spoke to talked about sex as though it were independent of the other aspects of their lives. Their schedules would be chock-full of responsibilities, from work to parenting; some also had to take care of aging family members. They scarcely had a moment to themselves, let alone the time to try to feel their own bodies, and yet they expected sex to just work in the narrow window they had allotted for it. Their shoulders would be up around their ears with stress, but they were still self-critical that they weren't in the mood. Although they often enjoyed the sex they had—it made them feel good, or energized, or happier—sex, and their sexuality with it, was mostly confined to the act, and afterward they would often go back to living "neck up," in the words of sex coach Patti Britton.

After speaking with some women who really enjoyed their sexuality, I saw more clearly how sexuality benefits from breathing room. It's not just how we comport ourselves in intimacy, it's how we relate to our own bodies—and hearts—on an ongoing basis. For Pam (from Chapter 8), it was allowing herself to "connect with [her] pussy" throughout the day as a way to tap back into her own body. For Syd (from Chapter 12), it was becoming more aware of boundaries, and consciously asking herself whether she craved closeness from her partner, as well as from others in her life—or not. One woman said, "My most memorable experiences have been when sex becomes something more than just doing it, more than just fucking. It's about healing. It's about self-forgiveness. It fills you up."

Another said, "When it's amazing, is when we really get naked. Not just taking our clothes off naked, but really revealed. And we get to discover each other. It's so exquisite to express and be told *I want to know what you are.*"

It begs the question, What should we be teaching girls, and how should we be encouraging women? The basics of anatomy and orgasm, or *cliteracy*, are absolutely a part of it. But the world of pleasure is not quantifiable; it is not just a matter of spasmic frequency. To become versed in the wide and changing tones of our eroticism, we need to understand more than bodily function; we must aim to achieve more than just the *normal* and go beyond the false pretense of parity. Peggy Kleinplatz says the answer is to go after "the stuff dreams are made of." Kleinplatz, a Canadian psychologist and sexologist, has criticized her field's focus on restoring merely physiological ability. Lousy therapy, like lousy sex, she points out, are both "predicated on participants who are willing to stop too soon and settle for too little."[5]

After her original assessments of the field revealed such a grim picture (as described in Chapter 8), Kleinplatz began researching what

makes for great sex. One might think that, with all our bedroom polling, this would be a crowded area of inquiry. But even though *mind-
blowing* is a frequent appendage to glossy headlines, studies on what
truly makes for pleasure are few and far between. Kleinplatz believes
therapists need to study "optimal" sexuality in order to understand
what lovers and professionals alike might "aspire toward." Accordingly,
we need to learn "from those who aim to get all that they can out of
their sexual encounters and refuse to settle for perfunctory sex."[6]

With her colleagues, Kleinplatz set about interviewing people
who have had magnificent and memorable experiences of intimacy
over their lifetimes. She reported that her interviewees were "dumb-
founded" when asked about sex acts, "as if they were incredulous at the
irrelevance of the question." Despite the heady promises of pop culture,
filled as it is with tips to make his thighs quiver or tricks to *get him to
commit*, the men and women she talked to said it wasn't about *what*
they did with their partners, it was all about their *way* of being with
them.[7]

I believe Kleinplatz's findings are significant for how women understand their desire. If women are having "dismal, disappointing, and
lackluster" sex, she said, "we will need to acknowledge that their low
desire may be evidence of good judgment."[8] In other words, perhaps
much of what is currently regarded as low desire is actually a healthy
response to bad sex. Kleinplatz argued that individuals should stop
beating themselves up for not wanting sex or feeling like they want sex
less than they should, and instead re-envision what kind of sex is worth
wanting in the first place.[9]

▼▲▼▲▼

The usual assumption is that women use sex to fulfill their emotional
needs, that it's not lust that motivates them, it's their desire for closeness. They'll hop in the sack to get the love and security they crave. So
physicality must not matter all that much to them: what they're mainly
after is its byproduct. But for the women here, there is something very
different going on. They are not hoping to dispense with the mechanics. Rather, they equate sex with spirit. It is through their physical enjoyment of sexuality that they are able to access even more reward.
Their delight in intimacy—in arousal and sensation—illuminates what

sex can be. It's not a hoop to jump through, something secondary, or at worst an ordeal. Instead, it's a way to reach a more profound part of themselves and their partners, a portal to the human interior.

For the women I spoke to, peak sexual experiences had little to do with interlocking body parts. When they described sex that was memorable or wonderful, it was in terms of feeling alert to their own senses and the magnitude of their own range. They spoke in terms of "waking up" to their own potential, of realizing limitlessness, and moreover, of the tender curiosity with which they might approach themselves on a given day. They felt they gained access to a deeper, often hidden part of themselves that, once touched, was cherished. Pleasure was not necessarily measured by the strength or count of orgasms, but was made possible by proceeding from a place of authentic and unabashed desire, a starting point which at times meant the desire to hold back or refrain. One woman, who told me that she loves sex, put it to me thusly: "When I am seen, when I am held, when I feel like we are voyagers traveling together inside unknown parts of ourselves, that loving journey is so much more powerful than any orgasm."

These experiences of eroticism and intimacy are worlds away from *ten tricks for amazing sex* or advice on how to *never miss an orgasm again*. Here, sex, reframed in terms of vulnerability, curiosity, acceptance, and compassion, becomes a state of creating meaning, rather than an act of creating arousal. As the above woman mentioned, sex was more important as a form of emotional unveiling than as a revelation of naked bodies. And embarking on that kind of journey of discovery—and self-discovery—can require us to relinquish our preconceived ideas about what sex is supposed to look like, feel like, or achieve. As one trauma survivor told me, "Sometimes when the sex is really beautiful I'll start sobbing, because I'm being touched in these places that had been violated and were closed off for so long. I feel profound gratitude that my partner and I can bring healing inside me and have sex to soothe away all that pain. I'm crossing this distance, I'm coming home."

The women who shared stories of loving sex or of having profound sexual experiences reminded me at times of careful cartographers. They were not inventing new lands so much as mapping the full extent of the existing territory. To revive desire and to discover pleasure are not one-off accomplishments. Part of why the mainstream discussions around sexuality are so misleading is that they allude to a false before and after, as though women and men can simply cross a threshold and everything will take care of itself from there on out. Instead, sexuality rewards our ongoing investigation. The shape of our desires changes as readily as any other aspect of our taste. By turn, our relationship to pleasure will evolve as we age, create, grieve, and connect with others and ourselves.

ACKNOWLEDGMENTS

My greatest debt of gratitude goes to the many women who cannot be named here, but whose candor made this book possible. They spoke bravely, thoughtfully, and movingly about their intimate lives, and I thank each of them for their generosity and for entrusting me with their stories. My deep appreciation also goes to the researchers, doctors, healers, and other experts who so patiently indulged my efforts to understand how they go about their work. Each made me see so much, and I want especially to thank Patti Britton, Lori Brotto, Meredith Chivers, Pam Costa, Marci Graham, Celeste Hirschman, Caffyn Jesse, Marty Klein, Nicole Prause, Leonore Tiefer, Kasia Urbaniak, Jason Weston, and Dimitry Yakoushkin, as well as Peggy Kleinplatz, whose writings and research I found myself drawing from repeatedly.

My thanks also go to those who read early chapters of this book, and whose input guided its final form: Meika Loe, Wendy Maltz, Stephen Snyder, and Alyson Spurgas, as well as Hillary Brenhouse and Ann Neumann (who both also deserve special recognition as cherished friends and vital sounding boards throughout this process).

I count myself as lucky indeed to have Rachel Vogel as an agent, who saw a book in a germ of an idea and patiently steered me toward its completion. Thanks, too, to Stephanie Knapp for the thoughtful edits and for believing in this project, to Laura Mazer for shepherding it along, and the rest of the team at Seal Press and Hachette Book Group, especially Lara Heimert, Sharon Kunz, and Kelly Lenkevich. Cosima Schreiber was a star fact-checker and I am grateful for her help in my hour of need. Katherine Streckfus is an extraordinary copyeditor, whose diligence and thoughtful suggestions improved every page of this book.

Though writing is considered a solitary endeavor, this project would not have been possible without my tribe of wonderful people, as well as my surrogate family at *Guernica*, who served as inspiration and ad hoc editors, pushed my thinking, and kept the swarms of doubt at bay. Michael Archer, Polly Auritt, May Coffin, Katie Flynn, Katherine Hallinan, Lauren LeBlanc, Abigail Martin, Nicole Miller, Rachel Riederer, Jessica Shaefer, and Tana Wojczuk have variously nurtured, housed, and encouraged me and kept me afloat through the tragedy that ran in parallel with this creation. Of invaluable support were my mother-in-law, JoAnne McShane, who deserves a reward for her help with toddler care, and my mother, Julia Rowland, who raised me to inquire and has been a constant source of inspiration.

Both my children were born alongside the research for and writing of this book, and I am endlessly grateful to their light, which keeps me aspiration-minded and ever filled with hope. And to my beloved, my favorite muse, and fellow traveler, Eddie McShane, thanks do not suffice. But I submit my gratitude all the same. Without him, none of this would have been possible.

NOTES

A NOTE ON HOW I WROTE THIS BOOK

1. See, e.g., Alison W. Henderson et al., "Ecological Models of Sexual Satisfaction Among Lesbian/Bisexual and Heterosexual Women," *Archives of Sexual Behavior* 38, no. 1 (2009): 50–65.

2. Eugenia Cherkasskaya and Margaret Rosario, "The Relational and Bodily Experiences Theory of Sexual Desire in Women," *Archives of Sexual Behavior* 48, no. 6 (2018): 1–23.

ONE: THE PLEASURE GAP

1. Gina Kolata, "The Sad Legacy of the Dalkon Shield," *The New York Times Magazine*, December 6, 1987, https://www.nytimes.com/1987/12/06/magazine/the-sad -legacy-of-the-dalkon-shield.html.

2. For complete testimony and discussion, see "Female Sexual Dysfunction Patient-Focused Drug Development Public Meeting," Center for Drug Evaluation and Research and US Food and Drug Administration, Silver Spring, Maryland, October 27, 2014, https://wayback.archive-it.org/7993/20170112081909/http://www .fda.gov/downloads/Drugs/NewsEvents/UCM423113.pdf. For an overview of major themes emerging from the meeting, see "The Voice of the Patient: Female Sexual Dysfunction," US Food and Drug Administration, June 2015, https://www.fda.gov /downloads/drugs/newsevents/ucm453718.pdf.

3. "Female Sexual Dysfunction Patient-Focused Drug Development Public Meeting."

4. Rates of female sexual concerns range considerably depending on the measure, end point, and population, as well as whether related distress is included as an assessment. McCool and colleagues in a review of 440 studies of premenopausal women found that 28 percent of women have hypoactive sexual desire disorder (HSDD) and 41 percent have female sexual dysfunction; in a cross-sectional study of American women, West et al. found that 27 percent of premenopausal women and 52 percent of naturally (as opposed to surgically) menopausal women had HSDD. Using data from more than 30,000 female respondents, Shifren and colleagues found the prevalence of any sexual problem was 43.1 percent, and 22.2 percent for sexually related personal distress. See Megan Elizabeth McCool, Andrea E. Zuelke, Melissa Ann Theurich, Helge Kneuttel, Christian Ricci, and Christian J. Apfelbacher, "Prevalence of Female Sexual Dysfunction Among Premenopausal Women: A Systematic Review and Meta-analysis of Observational Studies," *Sexual Medicine Reviews* 4, no. 3 (2016):

197–212; Suzanne L. West et al., "Prevalence of Low Sexual Desire and Hypoactive Sexual Desire Disorder in a Nationally Representative Sample of US Women," *Archives of Internal Medicine* 168, no. 13 (2008): 1441–1449; Jan L. Shifren et al., "Sexual Problems and Distress in United States Women: Prevalence and Correlates," *Obstetrics and Gynecology* 112, no. 5 (2008): 970–978.

5. Jeffrey Weeks, *The World We Have Won: The Remaking of Erotic and Intimate Life* (New York: Routledge, 2007).

6. Anthony Giddens, *The Transformation of Intimacy: Sexuality, Love and Eroticism in Modern Societies* (Stanford, CA: Stanford University Press, 1992).

7. Abraham Maslow proposed a five-part pyramid to describe human needs, starting with physiological requirements, such as food, shelter, and water, at the base, and self-actualization at the peak. Abraham Maslow, "A Theory of Human Motivation," *Psychological Review* 50, no. 4 (1943): 370–396. For the relationship comparison, see Eli Finkel, Chin Ming Hui, Kathleen Carswell, and Grace M. Larson, "The Suffocation of Marriage: Climbing Mount Maslow Without Enough Oxygen," *Psychological Inquiry* 25, no. 1 (2014): 1–41.

8. For comparative data by generation, see Jean Twenge et al., "Changes in American Adults' Sexual Behavior and Attitudes, 1972–2012," *Archives of Sexual Behavior* 44, no. 8 (2015): 2273–2285.

9. Debby Herbenick et al., "Sexual Behavior in the United States: Results from a National Probability Sample of Men and Women Ages 14–94," *Journal of Sexual Medicine* 7 (2010): 255–265. Also see Debby Herbenick et al., "Sexual Diversity in the United States: Results from a Nationally Representative Probability Sample of Adult Women and Men," *PloS One* 12, no. 7 (2017): e0181198.

10. These figures come from an industry-sponsored survey of more than three thousand people aged eighteen to thirty-four by Skyn Condoms. See "2017 SKYN® Condoms Millennial Sex Survey Reveals Nearly 50% of Respondents Sext at Least Once a Week," Cision PR Newswire, February 6, 2017, https://www.prnewswire.com /news-releases/2017-skyn-condoms-millennial-sex-survey-reveals-nearly-50-of -respondents-sext-at-least-once-a-week-300401985.html.

11. As one sociologist put it, "The modern western world has become cluttered with sexual stories." Kenneth Plummer, *Telling Sexual Stories: Power, Change and Social Worlds* (New York: Routledge, 2004), 3–4.

12. User data in 2017 from Pornhub found that amateur videos (amounting to 810,000 of the year's more than 4 million newly added videos) commanded viewers' attention more than other categories. "Pornhub Insights: 2017 Year in Review," Pornhub, January 9, 2018, https://www.pornhub.com/insights/2017-year-in-review.

13. Levy writes, "If Male Chauvinist Pigs were men who regarded women as pieces of meat, we would outdo them and be Female Chauvinist Pigs: women who make sex objects of other women and of ourselves." Ariel Levy, *Female Chauvinist Pigs: Women and the Rise of Raunch Culture* (New York: New Press, 2005), 5.

14. *Hollywood Reporter* announced, "It's clear that explicit jokes and boundary-pushing storylines are changing the definition of what sexual content is acceptable in primetime. Out are love triangles and awkward dates. In are jokes about anal sex, 'fisting' and teen masturbation." Lesley Goldberg, "Fisting, Anal Sex, Penis Pictures:

Broadcast TVs Ratings Grab Gets Raunchy," *Hollywood Reporter*, November 5, 2014, https://www.hollywoodreporter.com/news/fisting-anal-sex-penis-pictures -746403.

15. Despite the passage of the Equal Pay Act in 1963, when women earned an average of fifty-nine cents to the male earner's dollar, the gender pay gap has narrowed by less than half a cent per year, to about eighty cents to the dollar today. Some say this figure may underestimate the true extent of income inequality. See Janet Napolitano, "Women Earn More College Degrees and Men Still Earn More Money," *Forbes*, September 4, 2018. Rose and Hartmann found that "women today earn just 49 cents to the typical men's dollar, much less than the 80 cents usually reported. When measured by total earnings across the most recent 15 years for all workers who worked in at least one year, women workers' earnings were 49 percent—less than half—of men's earnings, a wage gap of 51 percent in 2015." Stephan J. Rose and Heidi Hartmann, "Still a Man's Labor Market: The Slowly Narrowing Gender Wage Gap," Institute for Women's Policy Research, November 2018, https://iwpr.org/publications /still-mans-labor-market.

16. Miranda Olff, "Sex and Gender Differences in Post-Traumatic Stress Disorder: An Update," *European Journal of Psychotraumatology* 8, suppl. 4 (2017): 1351204.

17. Janet Holland, Caroline Ramazanoglu, Sue Sharpe, and Rachel Thompson, *The Male in the Head: Young People, Heterosexuality and Power* (London: Tufnell Press, 1998).

18. Van Badham argued in *The Guardian* that in the decades following the women's movement, "sexual freedom has become another realm of women's experience for patriarchy to conquer. As soon as older feminists had won sexual liberation, patriarchy reframed it as sexual availability for men." See Van Badham, "That's Patriarchy: How Female Sexual Liberation Led to Male Sexual Entitlement," *The Guardian*, February 2, 2018, https://www.theguardian.com/commentisfree/2018/feb/02 /thats-patriarchy-how-female-sexual-liberation-led-to-male-sexual-entitlement.

19. Ashley M. Fox, Georgia Himmelstein, Hina Khalid, and Elizabeth A. Howell, "Funding for Abstinence-Only Education and Adolescent Pregnancy Prevention: Does State Ideology Affect Outcomes?" *American Journal of Public Health* 109, no. 3 (2019): 497–504.

20. In 2011, nearly half (45 percent, or 2.8 million) of the 6.1 million pregnancies in the United States were unintended. Specifically, 27 percent of all pregnancies were "wanted later," and 18 percent of pregnancies were "unwanted." See Guttmacher Institute, "Unintended Pregnancy in the United States," January 2019 Factsheet, https:// www.guttmacher.org/fact-sheet/unintended-pregnancy-united-states.

21. Raie Goodwach, "Fundamentals of Theory and Practice Revisited: Sex Therapy. Historical Evolution, Current Practice, Part I," *Australian and New Zealand Journal of Family Therapy* 26, no. 3 (2005): 155–164.

22. A survey of more than 52,000 American adults found:

Heterosexual men were most likely to say they usually-always orgasmed when sexually intimate (95%), followed by gay men (89%), bisexual men (88%), lesbian women (86%), bisexual women (66%), and heterosexual women (65%). Compared to women who orgasmed less frequently, women who orgasmed more frequently were more likely to: receive more oral sex, have longer duration of last sex, be more satisfied with their relationship, ask for what they want in bed, praise their partner for something they did in bed, call/email to tease about doing something sexual, wear sexy lingerie, try new sexual positions, anal stimulation, act out fantasies, incorporate sexy talk, and express love during sex. Women were more likely to orgasm if their last sexual encounter included deep kissing, manual genital stimulation, and/ or oral sex in addition to vaginal intercourse.

David A. Frederick et al., "Differences in Orgasm Frequency Among Gay, Lesbian, Bisexual, and Heterosexual Men and Women in a U.S. National Sample," *Archives of Sexual Behavior* 47, no. 1 (2017): 273–288.

23. "How to Give Her an Orgasm in 15 Minutes," *Men's Health*, March 14, 2016, https://www.menshealth.com/sex-women/a19517020/orgasm-in-15-minutes.

24. Two recent titles that I very much enjoyed are Julie Holland, *Moody Bitches: The Truth About the Drugs You're Taking, the Sleep You're Missing, the Sex You're Not Having, and What's Really Making You Crazy* (New York: Penguin, 2015); and Randi Hutter Epstein, *Aroused: The History of Hormones and How They Control Just About Everything* (New York: W. W. Norton, 2018).

25. Peggy J. Kleinplatz et al., "Beyond Sexual Stereotypes: Revealing Group Similarities and Differences in Optimal Sexuality," *Canadian Journal of Behavioral Science / Revue Canadienne Des Sciences Du Comportement* 45, no. 3 (2013): 250–258.

26. Ellen Huet, "The Dark Side of the Orgasmic Meditation Company," *Bloomberg Business Week*, June 18, 2018, https://www.bloomberg.com/news/features/2018-06-18 /the-dark-side-of-onetaste-the-orgasmic-meditation-company. The article's lengthy subtitle was "OneTaste is pushing its sexuality wellness education toward the mainstream. Some former members say it pushed them into sexual servitude and five-figure debts."

27. See, e.g., Emily Witt, *Future Sex: A New Kind of Free Love* (New York: Farrar, Straus and Giroux, 2016).

TWO: WHAT'S ALL THE FUSS ABOUT?

1. Center for Drug Evaluation and Research and US Food and Drug Administration, "The Voice of the Patient: A Series of Reports from the U.S. Food and Drug Administration's Patient-Focused Drug Development Initiative. Female Sexual Dysfunction. Public Meeting," October 27, 2014, https://www.fda.gov/media/92963 /download.

2. These truths are so self-evident that Baumeister added the following to a scholarly comment concerning the superior strength of the male drive: "Somewhat to my surprise, I learned that this conclusion is hotly disputed on political grounds, to the extent that most major sex textbooks either explicitly say it is wrong or at least present it as a quaint stereotype rather than an established fact. Popular wisdom is perhaps less questioning in this regard, and I recall the reaction of a female colleague when I mentioned that we had embarked on a literature review to see whether women desired sex less than men: 'Anyone who's ever had sex knows that!' she insisted. In any case, we did survey a great many findings, and essentially every measure and every study pointed to the same conclusion, namely that men are more sexually motivated than women." Roy F. Baumeister, "Gender and Erotic Plasticity: Sociocultural Influences on the Sex Drive," *Sexual and Relationship Therapy* 19, no. 2 (2004): 133–139.

3. Cindy M. Meston and David M. Buss, *Why Women Have Sex: Understanding Sexual Motivations from Adventure to Revenge (and Everything in Between)* (New York: Vintage, 2010).

4. Andrew Griffin, "Female Orgasm Mystery 'Solved': Scientists Finally Find Out Why Women Experience Sexual Pleasure: Women Have Monkeys to Thank, Researchers Say," *The Independent*, August 1, 2016, https://www.independent.co.uk /news/science/female-orgasm-mystery-solved-scientists-finally-find-out-why-women -experience-sexual-pleasure-a7165901.html.

5. Carl Zimmer, "Scientists Ponder an Evolutionary Mystery: The Female Orgasm," *New York Times*, August 1, 2016, https://www.nytimes.com/2016/08/02 /science/scientists-puzzle-over-a-biological-mystery-the-female-orgasm.html; Lucy Clarke-Billings, "Has the Mystery of the Female Orgasm Been Solved?" *Newsweek*, August 1, 2016, https://www.newsweek.com/has-mystery-female-orgasm-been-solved -485925.

6. Hillary Rosner, "Unravelling the Mystery of Female Desire: Scientists Finally Believe They've Discovered What Turns a Woman On," NBC News, September 29, 2009, www.nbcnews.com/id/32374911/ns/health-sexual_health/t /unraveling-mystery-female-desire; Rachel Nuwer, "The Enduring Enigma of Female Sexual Desire," BBC, July 1, 2016, www.bbc.com/future/story/20160630 -the-enduring-enigma-of-female-desire.

7. Jen Christensen, "Women's Desire for Sex Is Complicated, Not Strictly Hormonal, Study Finds," CNN, November 21, 2014, https://www.cnn.com/2014/11/21 /health/womens-sexual-appetite/index.html.

8. In their study of female pleasure, Kontula and Miettinen stated: "It is sometimes suggested that orgasms may not be important for female sexual pleasure. The argument has been that women can be fully satisfied sexually without experiencing an orgasm. However, based on previous sex surveys, the most important single predictor of sexual satisfaction for women is without a doubt the orgasm." Osmo Kontula and Anneli Miettinen, "Determinants of Female Sexual Orgasms," *Socioaffective Neuroscience and Psychology* 6, no. 1 (2016): 31624.

9. Peggy J. Kleinplatz et al., "Beyond Sexual Stereotypes: Revealing Group Similarities and Differences in Optimal Sexuality," *Canadian Journal of Behavioural Science / Revue Canadienne des Sciences du Comportement* 45, no. 3 (2013): 250–258; Peggy J. Kleinplatz et al., "The Components of Optimal Sexuality: A Portrait of 'Great Sex,'" *Canadian Journal of Human Sexuality* 18, nos. 1–2 (2009): 1–13.

10. Thomas Walter Laqueur, *Making Sex: Body and Gender from the Greeks to Freud* (Cambridge, MA: Harvard University Press, 2003), 3.

11. As quoted in Thomas Walter Laqueur, "Orgasm, Generation, and the Politics of Reproductive Biology," *Representations*, no. 14 (1986): 1.

12. "An instrument of venery," as referenced in Natalie Angier, *Woman: An Intimate Geography* (New York: Anchor, 2014), 67. A 1486 treatise on the persecution of witches identified the engorged clitoris as "the devil's teat." See Carina Kolodny and Amber Genuske, "The Cliteracy Project," *Huffington Post*, May 18, 2015, http:// projects.huffingtonpost.com/projects/cliteracy/intro.

13. Laqueur, *Making Sex*, 240.

14. Renaldus Columbus is also known as Realdo Colombo. This quotation and a wealth of historical information on the clitoris can be found on the website of French sociologist and researcher Odile Fillod, "Clit'Info," https://odilefillod.wixsite.com/clitoris.

15. Ibid.

16. Laqueur, *Making Sex*.

17. Acton claimed: "The majority of women (happily for them) are not very much troubled with sexual feeling of any kind." He also stated, "As a general rule, a modest woman seldom desires any sexual gratification for herself. She submits to her husband's embraces, but principally to gratify him; and, were it not for the desire of maternity, would far rather be relieved from his attentions." See Sheila Jeffreys, ed., "William Action," *Women's Source Library*, vol. 6, *The Sexuality Debates* (New York: Routledge, 2001), 42–74.

18. Laqueur, *Making Sex*, 11.

19. Freud at one point considered female masturbation, and with it clitoral stimulation, to be a masculine activity: "Elimination of clitoral sexuality is a necessary precondition for the development of femininity," he opined, "since it is immature and masculine in its nature." Peter Gay, ed., *The Freud Reader* (New York: W. W. Norton, 1995). Philosopher and author Elisabeth Lloyd told a journalist: "Very few women can climax through intercourse alone, but in Hollywood, that 8 percent [of women] is portrayed as 100 percent. . . . It's like, in some misguided bid for equality, we are trying to make women's orgasms serve the same function as men's." Sadie F. Dingfelder, "Understanding Orgasm," *APA Monitor* 42, no. 4 (April 2011), https://www.apa.org/monitor/2011/04/orgasm. For original research, see Kim Wallen and Elisabeth A. Lloyd, "Female Sexual Arousal: Genital Anatomy and Orgasm in Intercourse," *Hormones and Behavior* 59, no. 5 (2011): 780–792. Other research, however, suggests that vaginal intercourse may result in orgasm for 18 percent of women. See Debby Herbenick et al., "Women's Experiences with Genital Touching, Sexual Pleasure, and Orgasm: Results from a US Probability Sample of Women Ages 18 to 94," *Journal of Sex and Marital Therapy* 44, no. 2 (2018): 201–212.

20. Shere Hite wrote: "Masters and Johnson's theory that the thrusting penis pulls the woman's labia, which in turn pull the clitoral hood, thereby causing friction of the clitoral glans, and thereby causing orgasm, sound more like a Rube Goldberg scheme than a reliable way to orgasm." Shere Hite, *The Hite Report: A Nationwide Study of Female Sexuality* (New York: Seven Stories Press, 2004), 219.

21. Helen E. O'Connell et al., "Anatomy of the Clitoris," *Journal of Urology* 174, no. 4, Part 1 (2005): 1189–1195.

22. Barry R., Komisaruk et al., *The Science of Orgasm* (Baltimore: Johns Hopkins University Press, 2006), 3–4.

23. Osmo Kontula and Anneli Miettinen, "Determinants of Female Sexual Orgasms," *Socioaffective Neuroscience and Psychology* 6, no. 1 (2016): 31624; Juliet Richters et al., "Sexual Practices at Last Heterosexual Encounter and Occurrence of Orgasm in a National Survey," *Journal of Sex Research* 43, no. 3 (2006): 217–226.

24. Lisa Wade, "Are Women Bad at Orgasms? Understanding the Gender Gap," in *Gender, Sex, and Politics: In the Streets and Between the Sheets in the 21st Century*, ed. Shira Tarrant (New York: Routledge, 2015): 227–237.

25. Ibid.

26. Elizabeth A. Armstrong et al., "Accounting for Women's Orgasm and Sexual Enjoyment in College Hookups and Relationships," *American Sociological Review* 77, no. 3 (2012): 435–462.

27. Eric W. Corty and Jenay M. Guardiani, "Canadian and American Sex Therapists' Perceptions of Normal and Abnormal Ejaculatory Latencies: How Long Should Intercourse Last?" *Journal of Sexual Medicine* 5, no. 5 (2008): 1251–1256.

28. James G. Pfaus et al., "The Whole Versus the Sum of Some of the Parts: Toward Resolving the Apparent Controversy of Clitoral Versus Vaginal Orgasms," *Socioaffective Neuroscience and Psychology* 6, no. 1 (2016): 32578.

29. Cindy M. Meston et al., "Women's Orgasm," *Annual Review of Sex Research* 15, no. 1 (2004): 173–257.

30. Roy F. Baumeister, "Gender Differences in Erotic Plasticity: The Female Sex Drive as Socially Flexible and Responsive," *Psychological Bulletin* 126, no. 3 (2000): 347.

31. David M. Buss, *The Evolution of Desire: Strategies of Human Mating* (New York: Basic Books, 2016), 224.

32. Ibid., 225.

33. These theories are summed up in Elisabeth Lloyd, *The Case of the Female Orgasm: Bias in the Science of Evolution* (Cambridge, MA: Harvard University Press, 2006), and Meston et al., "Women's Orgasm." Psychologist David Barash also has a lively series of online posts. See "The Evolutionary Mystery of Female Orgasm," *Chronicle of Higher Education*, 2012, https://www.chronicle.com/blogs/brainstorm/a-valentine%E2%80%99s-present-the-evolutionary-mystery-of-female-orgasm-part-1/43957.

34. Lloyd, *The Case of the Female Orgasm.*

35. Steven Jay Gould, "Male Nipples and Clitoral Ripples," *Columbia: A Journal of Literature and Art*, no. 20 (1993): 80–96.

36. David Barash, "The Evolutionary Mystery of Female Orgasm, Part 3: A Nonadaptive By-Product?" *Chronicle of Higher Education*, February 23, 2012, https://www.chronicle.com/blogs/brainstorm/the-evolutionary-mystery-of-female-orgasm-part-iii-a-nonadaptive-by-product/44039.

37. In a review of Symons's book *The Evolution of Human Sexuality*, Hrdy wrote, "A gentlemanly breeze from the 19th century drifts from the pages." Sarah Blaffer Hrdy, "The Evolution of Human Sexuality: The Latest Word and the Last," *Quarterly Review of Biology* 54, no. 3 (1979): 309–314.

38. As quoted in Dinitia Smith, "A Critic Takes on the Logic of Female Orgasm," *New York Times*, May 17, 2005, https://www.nytimes.com/2005/05/17/science/a-critic-takes-on-the-logic-of-female-orgasm.html.

39. Sarah Blaffer Hrdy, *The Woman That Never Evolved* (Cambridge, MA: Harvard University Press, 1999).

40. Hrdy writes, "No function other than sexual stimulation of the female has ever been assigned to the clitoris, and this is very likely the reason that it has been a subject either tabooed or ignored in the textbooks. . . . Are we to assume, then, that this organ is irrelevant—a pudendal equivalent of the intestinal appendix? It would be safer to suspect that, like most organs—including even the underrated appendix—it

serves a purpose, or once did. But the purpose . . . appears to be transmitting the pleasurable sexual stimulations that sometimes culminate in orgasm." Ibid., 167.

41. Ibid., 174.

42. Angier, *Woman: An Intimate Geography*, 78.

43. See Morton Hunt, *The New Know-Nothings: The Political Foes of the Scientific
Study of Human Nature* (New York: Routledge, 2017).

44. Meston et al., "Women's Orgasm."

45. Daniel Bergner, *What Do Women Want?: Adventures in the Science of Female
Desire* (New York: Canongate Books, 2013).

46. Carole S. Vance, "Pleasure and Danger: Toward a Politics of Sexuality," in
Pleasure and Danger: Exploring Female Sexuality, ed. Carole Vance (New York: Routledge, 1984), 4.

THREE: LEARNING (NOT) TO LUST

1. When used correctly, condoms are about 98 percent effective at preventing
pregnancy and sexually transmitted infections; however, when fitted or stored im-
properly their efficacy drops to 85 percent.

2. Jesseca Boyer, "New Name, Same Harm: Rebranding of Federal Abstinence-
Only Programs," Guttmacher Institute, February 28, 2018, https://www.gutt
macher.org/gpr/2018/02/new-name-same-harm-rebranding-federal-abstinence
-only-programs.

3. John S. Santelli, Leslie M. Kantor, Stephanie A. Grilo, Ilene S. Speizer, Laura D.
Lindberg, Jennifer Heitel, Amy T. Schalet, et al., "Abstinence-Only-Until-Marriage:
An Updated Review of US Policies and Programs and Their Impact," *Journal of Ado-
lescent Health* 61, no. 3 (2017): 273–280.

4. Boyer, "New Name, Same Harm."

5. Naomi Wolf, *The Beauty Myth: How Images of Beauty Are Used Against Women*
(New York: Random House, 1991); Ariel Levy, *Female Chauvinist Pigs: Women and the
Rise of Raunch Culture* (New York: Free Press, 2005).

6. American Psychological Association, Task Force on the Sexualization of Girls,
"Report of the APA Task Force on the Sexualization of Girls," 2007, https://www.apa
.org/pi/women/programs/girls/report-full.pdf.

7. Tracy Moore, "Why She's Faking an Orgasm," *MEL*, January 12, 2018, https://
melmagazine.com/en-us/story/why-shes-faking-an-orgasm.

8. Michelle Fine, "Sexuality, Schooling, and Adolescent Females: The Missing
Discourse of Desire," *Harvard Educational Review* 58, no. 1 (1988): 29–54.

9. Deborah L. Tolman, *Dilemmas of Desire: Teenage Girls Talk About Sexuality*
(Cambridge, MA: Harvard University Press, 2002).

10. Ibid., 188. The dilemma of desire, according to Tolman "pits girls' embodied
knowledge and feelings, their sexual pleasure and connection to their bodies and to
others through their desire, against physical, social, material and psychological dangers associated with their sexuality."

11. Peggy Orenstein, *Girls and Sex: Navigating the Complicated New Landscape*
(New York: Harper, 2016).

12. Ibid., 13. Orenstein wrote, "Hypersexualization is ubiquitous, so visible as to
be nearly invisible: it is the water in which girls swim, the air they breathe. Whatever

else they might be—athletes, artists, scientists, musicians, newscasters, politicians—they learn that they must, as a female, first and foremost project sex appeal."

13. Ibid., 72.

14. Meg-John Barker et al., *Mediated Intimacy: Sex Advice in Media Culture* (Cambridge: Polity Press, 2018).

15. A study of 810 men found that "men felt more masculine and reported higher sexual esteem when they imagined that a woman orgasmed during sexual encounters with them, and that this effect was exacerbated for men with high masculine gender role stress." Furthermore, "these results suggest that women's orgasms do function—at least in part—as a masculinity achievement for men." Sara B. Chadwick and Sari M. van Anders, "Do Women's Orgasms Function as a Masculinity Achievement for Men?" *Journal of Sex Research* 54, no. 9 (2017): 1141–1152.

16. Sara I. McClelland, "'What Do You Mean When You Say That You Are Sexually Satisfied?' A Mixed Methods Study," *Feminism and Psychology* 24, no. 1 (2013): 74–96.

17. Sara I. McClelland, "Intimate Justice: A Critical Analysis of Sexual Satisfaction," *Social and Personality Psychology Compass* 4, no. 9 (2010): 663–680.

18. Sarah N. Bell and Sara I. McClelland, "When, If, and How: Young Women Contend with Orgasmic Absence," *Journal of Sex Research* 55, no. 6 (2018): 679–691.

19. See Chadwick and van Anders, "Do Women's Orgasms Function as a Masculinity Achievement for Men?"; Claire M. A. Salisbury and William A. Fisher, "'Did You Come?' A Qualitative Exploration of Gender Differences in Beliefs, Experiences, and Concerns Regarding Female Orgasm Occurrence During Heterosexual Sexual Interactions," *Journal of Sex Research* 51, no. 6 (2014): 616–631.

20. Gayle Brewer and Colin A. Hendrie, "Evidence to Suggest That Copulatory Vocalizations in Women Are Not a Reflexive Consequence of Orgasm," *Archives of Sexual Behavior* 40, no. 3 (2011): 559–564.

21. Aina Hunter, "Ouch: 80 Percent of Women Faking Orgasms, Says Study," CBS News, November 2, 2010, https://www.cbsnews.com/news/ouch-80-percent-of-women-faking-orgasms-says-study.

22. Mina Azodi, "The Crazy Way I Faked It," *Cosmopolitan*, October 26, 2010, https://www.cosmopolitan.com/sex-love/advice/a3349/the-craziest-way-i-faked-it.

23. Jessamyn Neuhaus, "The Importance of Being Orgasmic: Sexuality, Gender, and Marital Sex Manuals in the United States, 1920–1963," *Journal of the History of Sexuality* 9, no. 4 (2000): 447–473.

24. Stopes wrote, "In modern times, the old traditions, the profound primitive knowledge of the needs of both sexes have been lost, and nothing but a muffled confusion of individual gossip disturbs a silence, shamefaced or foul." Marie Carmichael Stopes, *Married Love: A New Contribution to the Solution of Sex Difficulties* (London: Pelican Press, 2015).

25. As quoted in Anne Koedt, "The Myth of the Vaginal Orgasm," in *Radical Feminism: A Documentary Reader* , Barbara Crow, ed. (New York: New York University Press, 1970), 371–377.

26. Each interview consisted of 350 questions, and some participants provided diaries recording daily sexual activity. Alfred C. Kinsey et al., *Sexual Behavior in the Human Female* (Bloomington: Indiana University Press, 1998).

27. Koedt, "Myth of the Vaginal Orgasm."

28. Annamarie Jagose, a researcher at the University of Sydney, has argued that the orgasm gap has deep historical roots stemming from the nineteenth-century view that heterosexuality was not just a way to reproduce, but *the* expression of coupled eroticism. According to this view, the ideal of mutual satisfaction *stalled out* in the mid-twentieth century. As many researchers from the past seventy-odd years have noted, penetrative intercourse is remarkably unsuited for female pleasure. And yet, Jagose said, we've been unable to move past this apparent contradiction. The revelation arrives anew, sparking crisis and commentary, but we remain largely fixed in the idea that male and female orgasm work best as a simultaneous combustion. Jagose wrote, "However cannily got up as a sound bite, the fate of such information—35% of women don't orgasm during sex because they don't get the right kind of clitoral stimulation from their partner; 39% of women mostly orgasm via masturbation—is to be repeated again and again without ever loosening the cultural imagination's allegiance to heterosexual intercourse and its figuration of the sexual reciprocity that is the ethical model for modern heterosexuality." Annamarie Jagose, "Some Notes on the Female Orgasm in 2015," *The Conversation*, December 15, 2015, http://theconversation.com/some-notes-on-the-female-orgasm-in-2015 -52212.

29. See, e.g., Maggie Jones, "What Teenagers Are Learning from Online Porn," *The New York Times Magazine*, February 7, 2018; Gail Dines, *Pornland: How Porn Has Hijacked Our Sexuality* (Boston: Beacon Press, 2010); Pamela Paul, *Pornified: How Pornography Is Damaging Our Lives, Our Relationships, and Our Families* (New York: Henry Holt, 2005).

30. Meg-John Barker, "Five Problematic Sex Messages Perpetuated by Advice Manuals," *The Conversation*, May 8, 2018, https://theconversation.com /five-problematic-sex-messages-perpetuated-by-advice-manuals-93674.

31. Gill, Rosalind, "Postfeminist Media Culture: Elements of a Sensibility," *European Journal of Cultural Studies* 10, no. 2 (2007): 147–166.

32. A. Dana Ménard and Peggy J. Kleinplatz, "Twenty-One Moves Guaranteed to Make His Thighs Go Up in Flames: Depictions of 'Great Sex' in Popular Magazines," *Sexuality and Culture* 12, no. 1 (2008): 1–20.

FOUR: WHAT THE BODY REMEMBERS

1. Some maintain that this figure is too low and that the true prevalence of rape and attempted rape is closer to one in four women. National figures further gloss over the violence that is concentrated in some parts of the country as well as among certain demographic and identity groups, including LGBTQ women, African American women, and Native American women.

2. See Rape, Abuse & Incest National Network, "Victims of Sexual Violence: Statistics," accessed December 2018, https://www.rainn.org/statistics/victims-sexual -violence; National Coalition Against Domestic Violence, "National Statistics," accessed December 2018, https://ncadv.org/statistics; National Sexual Violence Resource Center, "Statistics," accessed December 2018, https://www.nsvrc.org/statistics.

3. Barbara Bradley Hagerty, "An Epidemic of Disbelief: What New Research Reveals About Sexual Predators, and Why Police Fail to Catch Them," *The*

Atlantic, August 2019, https://www.theatlantic.com/magazine/archive/2019/08
/an-epidemic-of-disbelief/592807/?.

4. Judith L. Herman, *Trauma and Recovery: The Aftermath of Violence—From
Domestic Abuse to Political Terror* (New York: Basic Books, 2015), 7.

5. The researchers found that the lifetime economic burden of childhood sexual
abuse (CSA) "is approximately $9.3 billion, the lifetime cost for victims of fatal CSA
per female and male victim is on average $1,128,334 and $1,482,933, respectively, and
the average lifetime cost for victims of nonfatal CSA is . . . $282,734 per female vic-
tim." Elizabeth J. Letourneau, Derek S. Brown, Xiangming Fang, Ahmed Hassan, and
James A. Mercy, "The Economic Burden of Child Sexual Abuse in the United States,"
Child Abuse and Neglect 79 (2018): 413–422.

6. Edward O. Laumann et al., "Sexual Dysfunction in the United States: Prevalence and Predictors," *Journal of the American Medical Association* 281, no. 6 (1999):
537–544.

7. Ibid.

8. Ruth Rosen, *The World Split Open: How the Modern Women's Movement
Changed America* (New York: Penguin, 2000), 143.

9. Ann Wolbert Burgess and Lynda Lytle Holmstrom, "Recovery from Rape and
Prior Life Stress," *Research in Nursing and Health* 1, no. 4 (1978): 165–174; Judith L.
Herman, *Trauma and Recovery: The Aftermath of Violence—From Domestic Abuse to
Political Terror* (New York: Basic Books, 2015), 28.

10. Bessel A. van der Kolk, *The Body Keeps the Score: Brain, Mind, and Body in the
Healing of Trauma* (New York: Penguin, 2014), 20.

11. Ibid., 88.

12. As quoted in Stephen Porges, "Why the Vagal System Holds the Key to the
Treatment of Trauma," National Institute for the Clinical Application of Behavioral
Medicine, May 15, 2018.

13. Terrence McCoy, "CNN's Don Lemon Tells Bill Cosby Rape Accuser She
Should Have Bitten Comedian's Genitals," *Washington Post*, November 19, 2014,
https://www.washingtonpost.com/news/morning-mix/wp/2014/11/19/cnns-don
-lemon-tells-bill-cosby-rape-accuser-she-should-have-bitten-comedians-genitals.

14. Van der Kolk, *The Body Keeps the Score*, 91.

15. Ibid., 94.

16. James C. McKinley Jr., "Vicious Assault Shakes Texas Town," *New York Times*,
March 9, 2011, https://www.nytimes.com/2011/03/09/us/09assault.html.

17. Conor Friedersdorf, "Is Porn Culture to Be Feared?," *The Atlantic*, April 7,
2016, https://www.theatlantic.com/politics/archive/2016/04/porn-culture/477099.

18. Amanda Cawston, "The Feminist Case Against Pornography: A Review and Re-evaluation," *Inquiry* 62, no. 6 (2019); Julia Long, "Pornography Is
More Than Just Sexual Fantasy: It's Cultural Violence," *Washington Post*, May
27, 2016, https://www.washingtonpost.com/news/in-theory/wp/2016/05/27
/pornography-is-more-than-just-sexual-fantasy-its-cultural-violence.

19. PornHub Insights, "2018 Year in Review," December 11, 2018, https://www
.pornhub.com/insights/2018-year-in-review#searches.

20. Julia Long, "Pornography Is More Than Just Sexual Fantasy: It's Cultural Violence," *Washington Post*, May 27, 2016, https://www.washingtonpost.com

/news/in-theory/wp/2016/05/27/pornography-is-more-than-just-sexual-fantasy-its
-cultural-violence.

21. Rachel Yehuda and Linda M. Bierer, "Transgenerational Transmission of Cortisol and PTSD Risk," *Progress in Brain Research* 167 (2007): 121–135.

FIVE: TRADITION AND ITS DISCONTENTS

1. Carol Botwin, "Is There Sex After Marriage?" *New York Times*, September 16, 1979, https://www.nytimes.com/1979/09/16/archives/is-there-sex-after-marriage .html.

2. Though prevalence varies depending on how the condition is measured, in general rates are thought to be lower among younger women and higher among menopausal (and surgically menopausal) women, though lower among women over sixty-five.

3. Helen Singer Kaplan, *The Sexual Desire Disorders: Dysfunctional Regulation of Sexual Motivation* (New York: Brunner-Routledge, 1995).

4. Ibid., 12.

5. MarketResearch.com, "Wedding Services in the US—Industry Market Research Report," last modified 2019, https://www.marketresearch.com/IBIS World-v2487/Wedding-Services-Research-12402785; Maggie Seaver, "The National Average Cost of a Wedding Is $33,931," The Knot, last modified 2018, https://www .theknot.com/content/average-wedding-cost.

6. D'Vera Cohn, Wendy Wang, and Gretchen Livingston, "Barely Half of US Adults Are Married—A Record Low," Pew Research Social and Demographic Trends, December 14, 2011, https://www.pewsocialtrends.org/2011/12/14/barely-half-of -u-s-adults-are-married-a-record-low; Andrew J. Cherlin, *Marriage, Divorce, Remarriage: Social Trends in the United States* (Cambridge, MA: Harvard University Press, 1992).

7. Christopher Ryan, "An Inconvenient Truth: Sexual Monogamy Kills Male Libido," *Psychology Today*, May 2, 2008, https://www.psychologytoday.com/us/blog /sex-dawn/200805/inconvenient-truth-sexual-monogamy-kills-male-libido.

8. Jen Gunter, "When the Cause of a Sexless Relationship Is—Surprise!—the Man," *New York Times*, March 10, 2018, https://www.nytimes.com/2018/03/10/style /sexless-relationships-men-low-libido.html.

9. Lea Winerman, "By the Numbers: Antidepressant Use on the Rise," *American Psychological Association Monitor*, November 2017, https://www.apa.org /monitor/2017/11/numbers.

10. See cartoon at "Jack Ziegler: New Yorker Cartoonist," *New Yorker*, published April 2, 2001, https://jackziegler.com/product/i-was-on-hormone-replacement-for -two-years-before-i-realized-that-what-i-really-needed-was-steve-replacement.

11. Sarah H. Murray and Robin R. Milhausen, "Sexual Desire and Relationship Duration in Young Men and Women," *Journal of Sex and Marital Therapy* 38, no. 1 (2012): 28–40.

12. Aaron E. Carroll and Rachel Vreeman, *Don't Put That in There: And 69 Other Sex Myths Debunked* (New York: St. Martin's Press, 2014), 59.

13. Markham Heid, "Here's How Much Sex You Should Have Every Week," *Time*, March 7, 2017, http://time.com/4692326/how-much-sex-is-healthy-in-a-relationship.

14. Jean M. Twenge et al., "Declines in Sexual Frequency Among American Adults, 1989–2014," *Archives of Sexual Behavior* 46, no. 8 (2017): 2389–2401.

15. Matthew Haag, "It's Not Just You: Americans Are Having Less Sex," *New York Times*, March 8, 2017, https://www.nytimes.com/2017/03/08/us/americans-less-sex -study.html.

16. Dr. Phil, "Sexless Marriage," September 12, 2002, https://www.drphil.com /advice/sexless-marriages.

17. Amy Muise et al., "Sexual Frequency Predicts Greater Well-Being, but More Is Not Always Better," *Social Psychological and Personality Science* 7, no. 4 (2015): 295–302.

18. Shervin Assari, "Reasons for Avoiding Sex Are Often Treatable," CNN, March 13, 2018, https://www.cnn.com/2017/08/01/health/avoiding-sex-partner/index .html.

19. Christa D'Souza, "Life After Lust—The Appeal of Sexless Marriage," *The Guardian*, June 1, 2012, https://www.theguardian.com/lifeandstyle/2012/jun/01 /life-lust-appeal-sexless-marriage.

20. Nathan D. Leonhardt et al. "The Significance of the Female Orgasm: A Nationally Representative, Dyadic Study of Newlyweds' Orgasm Experience," *Journal of Sexual Medicine* 15, no. 8 (2018): 1140–1148.

21. Peggy Kleinplatz, "Desire Disorders or Opportunities for Optimal Erotic Intimacy," in *Treating Sexual Desire Disorders: A Clinical Casebook*, ed. Sandra R. Leiblum (New York: Guilford Press, 2010).

22. See, e.g., Tracy Clark Flory, "The Truth About Female Desire: It's Base, Animalistic and Ravenous," Salon, June 2, 2013, https://www.salon.com/2013/06/02 /the_truth_about_female_desire_its_base_animalistic_and_ravenous.

23. Amelia Hill, "Is Sex the Answer to Your Relationship Woes?" *The Guardian*, January 21, 2018, https://www.theguardian.com/lifeandstyle/2018/jan/21 /is-sex-the-answer-to-your-relationship-problems-michele-weiner-davis-guidance.

24. Lori A. Brotto and Kelly B. Smith, "Sexual Desire and Pleasure," *APA Handbook of Sexuality and Psychology* 1 (2014): 205–244.

25. See, e.g., Rosemary Basson, "Rethinking Low Sexual Desire in Women," *BJOG: An International Journal of Obstetrics and Gynaecology* 109, no. 4 (2002): 357–363.

26. Cindy M. Meston and David M. Buss, *Why Women Have Sex: Understanding Sexual Motivations from Adventure to Revenge (and Everything in Between)* (New York: Vintage, 2010).

27. Rosemary Basson, "The Female Sexual Response: A Different Model," *Journal of Sex and Marital Therapy* 26, no. 1 (2000): 51–65.

28. Louann Brizendine, "Love, Sex and the Male Brain," CNN, March 25, 2010, www.cnn.com/2010/OPINION/03/23/brizendine.male.brain/index.html.

29. Wendy Wang, "Who Cheats More? The Demographics of Infidelity in America," Institute for Family Studies, January 10, 2018, https://ifstudies.org/blog /who-cheats-more-the-demographics-of-cheating-in-america.

30. Kristen P. Mark, Erick Janssen, and Robin R. Milhausen, "Infidelity in Heterosexual Couples: Demographic, Interpersonal, and Personality-Related Predictors of Extradyadic Sex," *Archives of Sexual Behavior* 40, no. 5 (2011): 971–982.

31. As quoted in Frank Bass, "Cheating Wives Narrowed Infidelity Gap over Two Decades," *Bloomberg*, July 1, 2013, https://www.bloomberg.com/news/articles/2013-07 -02/cheating-wives-narrowed-infidelity-gap-over-two-decades.

32. Joris Lammers, Janka I. Stoker, Jennifer Jordan, Monique Pollmann, and Diederik A. Stapel, "Power Increases Infidelity Among Men and Women," *Psychological Science* 22, no. 9 (2011): 1191–1197.

33. Wednesday Martin, *Untrue: Why Nearly Everything We Believe About Women, Lust, and Infidelity Is Wrong and How the New Science Can Set Us Free* (New York: Little, Brown, 2018).

34. Daniel Bergner, *What Do Women Want?: Adventures in the Science of Female Desire* (New York: Canongate Books, 2013).

35. Michael J. Rosenfeld, "Who Wants the Breakup? Gender and Breakup in Heterosexual Couples," in *Social Networks and the Life Course* (New York: Springer, 2016), 221–243.

36. As quoted in Yanan Wang, "Women Are More Likely to Initiate Divorce," *Washington Post*, August 27, 2015, https://www.washingtonpost.com/news/soloish /wp/2015/08/27/why-women-are-more-likely-to-initiate-divorce.

37. William J. Scarborough et al., "Attitudes and the Stalled Gender Revolution: Egalitarianism, Traditionalism, and Ambivalence from 1977 Through 2016," *Gender and Society* 33, no. 2 (2018): 173–200, https://doi.org/10.1177/0891243218809604.

38. Arlie R. Hochschild, with A. Machung, *The Second Shift: Working Parents and the Revolution at Home* (Berkeley: University of California Press, 1989); American Sociological Association, "Women More Likely Than Men to Initiate Divorces, but Not Non-marital Breakups," *Science Daily*, August 22, 2015, https://www.sciencedaily .com/releases/2015/08/150822154900.htm.

39. Jessie Bernard, *The Future of Marriage* (New Haven, CT: Yale University Press, 1972).

40. See Walter R. Gove, "Sex, Marital Status, and Mortality," *American Journal of Sociology* 79, no. 1 (1973): 45–67.

41. Hochschild, *Second Shift*.

42. Kathleen Deveny, "We're Not in the Mood," *Newsweek*, June 29, 2003, https:// www.newsweek.com/were-not-mood-138387.

43. See Heidi Stevens, "'Choreplay' vs. Foreplay," *Chicago Tribune*, January 20, 2008, https://www.chicagotribune.com/news/ct-xpm-2008-01-20-0801170448-story .html.

44. Bobby Box, "How Sharing Housework Can Save Your Sex Life," *Playboy*, May 9, 2018, https://www.playboy.com/read/how-sharing-housework-can-save-your -sex-life-1.

45. Lloyd Garver, "Men: Want More Sex? Do the Laundry!" CBS News, September 12, 2007, https://www.cbsnews.com/news/men-want-more-sex-do-the-laundry -12-09-2007.

46. Sabino Kornrich et al., "Egalitarianism, Housework, and Sexual Frequency in Marriage," *American Sociological Review* 78, no. 1 (2013): 26–50.

47. Lori Gottlieb, "Does a More Equal Marriage Mean Less Sex?" *The New York Times Magazine*, February 9, 2014, https://www.nytimes.com/2014/02/09/magazine /does-a-more-equal-marriage-mean-less-sex.html.

48. Karen Sims and Marta Meana, "Why Did Passion Wane? A Qualitative Study of Married Women's Attributions for Declines in Sexual Desire," *Journal of Sex and Marital Therapy* 36 (2010): 360–380.

49. Ibid.

50. Catherine Elton, "Learning to Lust: For Many Women Troubled by Low Sexual Desire, Too Much of the World Around Them Can Derail Sensuality. That Turns Out to Be Very Fixable—But Not by a Pill," *Psychology Today*, May 1, 2010, https://www.psychologytoday.com/us/articles/201005/learning-lust.

51. As quoted in Evan Fertel, "Who Is This About? An Exploratory Study of Erotic Self-Focus" (MA thesis, University of Nevada Masters, 2015).

52. Esther Perel, *Mating in Captivity: Unlocking Erotic Intelligence* (New York: Harper, 2007).

SIX: IT'S ALL IN YOUR HEAD

1. Dwight Furrow, *American Foodie: Taste, Art, and the Cultural Revolution* (London: Rowman and Littlefield, 2016).

2. Paola Sandroni, "Aphrodisiacs Past and Present: A Historical Review," *Clinical Autonomic Research* 11, no. 5 (2001): 303–307.

3. Furrow, *American Foodie*.

4. See, e.g., Meika Loe, *The Rise of Viagra: How the Little Blue Pill Changed Sex in America* (New York: New York University Press, 2004); Leonore Tiefer, *Sex Is Not a Natural Act and Other Essays* (Boulder: Westview Press, 2004).

5. Laurence Klotz, "How (Not) to Communicate New Scientific Information: A Memoir of the Famous Brindley Lecture," *British Journal of Urology* 96, no. 7 (2012): 956–957.

6. Ibid.

7. Irwin Goldstein, "The Hour Lecture That Changed Sexual Medicine—The Giles Brindley Injection Story," *Journal of Sexual Medicine* 9, no. 2 (2012): 337–342.

8. Klotz, "How (Not) to Communicate," 956–957.

9. Goldstein, "The Hour Lecture."

10. Charles Bankhead, "Exposing the Truth About ED: An Hour 'Changed the World,'" MedPage Today, July 26, 2013, https://www.medpagetoday.com/urology/erectiledysfunction/40623.

11. David M. Friedman, *A Mind of Its Own: A Cultural History of the Penis* (New York: Simon and Schuster, 2008).

12. John Tozzi and Jared S. Hopkins, "The Little Blue Pill: An Oral History of Viagra. The Story of the Drug That Changed Sex and Made Billions," *Bloomberg*, December 11, 2017, https://www.bloomberg.com/news/features/2017-12-11/the-little-blue-pill-an-oral-history-of-viagra.

13. Irwin Goldstein, Tom F. Lue, Harin Padma-Nathan, Raymond C. Rosen, William D. Steers, and Pierre A. Wicker, for the Sildenafil Study Group, "Oral Sildenafil in the Treatment of Erectile Dysfunction," *New England Journal of Medicine* 338, no. 20 (1998): 1397–1404.

14. Robert D. Utiger, "A Pill for Impotence," *New England Journal of Medicine* 338 (1998): 1458–1459; Elizabeth Landua, "Sex Is Doctor's Life's Work," CNN, June 3, 2013, https://www.cnn.com/2013/05/31/health/lifeswork-sex-medicine/index.html.

15. Tozzi and Hopkins, "The Little Blue Pill."

16. Joby Warrick, "Little Blue Pills Among the Ways CIA Wins Friends in Afghanistan," *Washington Post*, December 26, 2008, www.washingtonpost.com/wp-dyn/content/article/2008/12/25/AR2008122500931.html.

17. Tozzi and Hopkins, "The Little Blue Pill."

18. Gina Kolata, "Doctors Debate Use of Drug to Help Women's Sex Lives," *New York Times*, April 25, 1998, https://www.nytimes.com/1998/04/25/us/doctors-debate-use-of-drug-to-help-women-s-sex-lives.html.

19. See, e.g., Sandra M. Foote and Lynn Etheredge, "Increasing Use of New Prescription Drugs: A Case Study. Recent Experience with New Antidepressants Suggests That Without More Efforts to Identify and Promote Effective Use, Biomedical Innovation May Fall Short of Its Promise," *Health Affairs* 19, no. 4 (2000): 165–170.

20. C. Lee Ventola, "Direct-to-Consumer Pharmaceutical Advertising: Therapeutic or Toxic?" *Pharmacy and Therapeutics* 36, no. 10 (2011): 669.

21. Ibid.

22. Mark Peyrot, N. M. Alperstein, D. V. Doren, and L. G. Poli, "Direct-to-Consumer Ads Can Influence Behavior," *Marketing Health Services* 18, no. 2 (1998): 26.

23. Gina Kolata, "Impotence Pill: Would It Also Help Women?" *New York Times*, April 4, 1998, https://www.nytimes.com/1998/04/04/us/impotence-pill-would-it-also-help-women.html.

24. Brian Deer, "Sex Drugs and Rock 'n' Roll: Viagra Is the Sex Sensation of the Century," *Sunday Times*, September 6, 1998, accessed at https://briandeer.com/pfizer-viagra.htm.

25. As quoted in Molly Redden, "The Controversial Doctor Behind the New 'Viagra for Women': Is Irwin Goldstein Advancing the Frontiers of Medicine, or the Bottom Line of the Pharmaceutical Industry?" *Mother Jones*, September 2, 2015, https://www.motherjones.com/politics/2015/09/irwin-goldstein-controversial-doctor-behind-new-viagra-women.

26. Gardiner Harris, "Pfizer Gives Up Testing Viagra on Women," *New York Times*, February 28, 2004, https://www.nytimes.com/2004/02/28/business/pfizer-gives-up-testing-viagra-on-women.html.

27. Arthur L. Burnett, Ajay Nehra, Rodney H. Breau, Daniel J. Culkin, Martha M. Faraday, Lawrence S. Hakim, Joel Heidelbaugh, et al., "Erectile Dysfunction: AUA Guideline," *Journal of Urology* 200, no. 3 (2018): 633–641.

28. US Department of Health and Human Services, Food and Drug Administration, Center for Drug Evaluation and Research, "Low Sexual Interest, Desire, and/or Arousal in Women: Developing Drugs for Treatment, Guidance for Industry," October 2016, https://www.fda.gov/media/100833/download.

29. Stephen H. King, Alexander V. Mayorov, Preeti Balse-Srinivasan, Victor J. Hruby, Todd W. Vanderah, and Hunter Wessells, "Melanocortin Receptors, Melanotropic Peptides and Penile Erection," *Current Topics in Medicinal Chemistry* 7, no. 11 (2007): 1111–1119.

30. Rachel Ratner, "How Does New Libido-Boosting Drug for Women Work?" *Live Science*, June 25, 2019, https://www.livescience.com/65784-how-womens-libido-drug-works.html.

31. Anita H. Clayton, Stanley E. Altof, Sheryl Kingsberg, Leonard R. Derogatis, Robin Kroll, Irwin Goldstein, Jed Kaminetsy, et al., "Bremelanotide for Female Sexual Dysfunctions in Premenopausal Women: A Randomized, Placebo-Controlled Dose-Finding Trial," *Women's Health* 12, no. 3 (2016): 325–337.

32. Mohammad Reza Safarinejad and Seyyed Yousof Hosseini, "Salvage of Sildenafil Failures with Bremelanotide: A Randomized, Double-Blind, Placebo Controlled Study," *Journal of Urology* 179, no. 3 (2008): 1066–1071.

33. Fox 5 San Diego, "Doctor Highlights New Drug for Sexual Desire," June 5, 2013, https://www.youtube.com/watch?v=qjsl-kMvTxk.

34. Tiefer was sufficiently concerned about the medicalization of women's sexual health that in 2000 she launched a highly visible campaign, "The New View," which drew support from a number of prominent social scientists. According to campaign materials, "The goal of the New View Campaign is to expose biased research and promotional methods that serve corporate profit rather than people's pleasure and satisfaction. The Campaign challenges all views that reduce sexual experience to genital biology and thereby ignore the many dimensions of real life." The campaign ended in 2016. See www.newviewcampaign.org.

35. Roy Moynihan and Barbara Mintzes, *Sex, Lies and Pharmaceuticals: How Drug Companies Plan to Profit from Female Sexual Dysfunction* (Berkeley, CA: Greystone Books, 2010), 3.

36. Ibid.

37. See Stephen M. Stahl, "Mechanism of Action of Flibanserin, a Multifunctional Serotonin Agonist and Antagonist (MSAA), in Hypoactive Sexual Desire Disorder," *CNS Spectrums* 20, no. 1 (2015): 1–6.

38. Antonie Meixel et al., "Hypoactive Sexual Desire Disorder: Inventing a Disease to Sell Low Libido," *Journal of Medical Ethics* 41, no. 10 (2015): 859–862.

39. Ellen Laan and Leonore Tiefer, "The Sham Drug Idea of the Year: 'Pink Viagra,'" *Los Angeles Times*, November 13, 2014, https://www.latimes.com/opinion/op-ed/la-oe-laan-tiefer-pink-viagra-20141114-story.html.

40. Cindy Whitehead subsequently launched a new endeavor called the Pink Ceiling, a hybrid venture capital consulting firm. One of its first investments was a company called Undercover Colors, which is developing nail polish that can detect exposure to date-rape drugs. The idea is that a woman could dip a manicured finger into her drink and it would change color in the presence of ketamine, ecstasy, Rohypnol, or GHB.

41. Jonathan Stempel, "Valeant Sued for Botching Marketing of Female Libido Pill," *Reuters*, November 2, 2016, https://www.reuters.com/article/us-valeant-sprout-lawsuit/valeant-sued-for-botching-marketing-of-female-libido-pill-idUSKBN12X22Q.

42. Loes Jaspers et al., "Efficacy and Safety of Flibanserin for the Treatment of Hypoactive Sexual Desire Disorder in Women: A Systematic Review and Meta-analysis," *JAMA Internal Medicine* 176, no. 4 (2016): 453–462.

43. Polina Marinova, "'Female Viagra' Founder Is Back as CEO After Valeant Gave the Billion-Dollar Drug Back for Free," *Fortune*, June 11, 2018, http://fortune.com/go/health/addyi-sprout-ceo-cindy-eckert.

44. Addyi is a prescription drug intended for women who qualify as having hypoactive sexual desire disorder. Doctors affiliated with the site diagnose women remotely before sending them the drug by mail.

45. Cynthia Koons, "The Women's Libido Pill Is Back, and So Is the Controversy," *Bloomberg Business Week*, June 13, 2018, https://www.bloomberg.com/news/features/2018-06-13/the-women-s-libido-pill-is-back-and-so-is-the-controversy.

46. Since Sprout relaunched the drug, Eckert has halved the monthly price to $400 and has promised that those without insurance coverage will pay no more than $99.

47. Eugenia Cherkasskaya and Margaret Rosario, "The Relational and Bodily Experiences Theory of Sexual Desire in Women," *Archives of Sexual Behavior* 48, no. 6 (2018): 1–23.

48. James Pfaus et al., "Who, What, Where, When (and Maybe Even Why)? How the Experience of Sexual Reward Connects Sexual Desire, Preference, and Performance," *Archives of Sexual Behavior* 41, no. 1 (2012): 31–62.

SEVEN: YOU CAN CHANGE YOUR MIND

1. John Bancroft, Cynthia Graham, Erik Janssen, and Stephanie Sanders, "The Dual Control Model: Current Status and Future Directions," *Journal of Sex Research* 46, nos. 2–3 (2009): 121–142; Emily Nagoski, *Come as You Are: The Surprising New Science That Will Transform Your Sex Life* (New York: Simon and Schuster, 2015).

2. Lucia O'Sullivan et al., "A Longitudinal Study of Problems in Sexual Functioning and Related Sexual Distress Among Middle to Late Adolescents," *Journal of Adolescent Health* 59, no. 3 (2016): 318–324.

3. Raymond C. Rosen, "Prevalence and Risk Factors of Sexual Dysfunction in Men and Women," *Current Psychiatry Reports* 2, no. 3 (2000): 189–195.

4. Jon Kabat-Zinn, *Full Catastrophe Living: Using the Wisdom of Your Body and Mind to Face Stress, Pain and Illness*, 15th anniv. ed. (New York: Bantam Dell, 2005).

5. Lori A. Brotto, *Better Sex Through Mindfulness: How Women Can Cultivate Desire* (Vancouver: Greystone Books, 2018).

6. Alfred C. Kinsey et al., *Sexual Behavior in the Human Female* (Bloomington: Indiana University Press, 1998).

7. Edward Shorter, *Written in the Flesh: A History of Desire* (Toronto: University of Toronto Press, 2005).

8. Helen Singer Kaplan, "Hypoactive Sexual Desire," *Journal of Sex and Marital Therapy* 3, no. 1 (1977): 3–9; Helen Singer Kaplan, *Disorders of Sexual Desire and Other New Concepts and Techniques in Sex Therapy* (New York: Simon and Schuster, 1979).

9. Leonore Tiefer, *Sex Is Not a Natural Act and Other Essays* (Boulder: Westview Press, 2004); Leonore Tiefer et al., "Beyond Dysfunction: A New View of Women's Sexual Problems," *Journal of Sex and Marital Therapy* 28, suppl. 1 (2002): 225–232.

10. See Roy Baumeister, "Gender Differences in Erotic Plasticity: The Female Sex Drive as Socially Flexible and Responsive," *Psychological Bulletin* 126, no. 3 (1999): 347–374.

11. Rosemary Basson, "The Female Sexual Response: A Different Model," *Journal of Sex and Marital Therapy* 26, no. 1 (2000): 51–65.

12. Rosemary Basson, "Rethinking Low Sexual Desire in Women," *BJOG: An International Journal of Obstetrics and Gynaecology* 109, no. 4 (2002): 357–363.

13. Stephen B. Levine, "Reexploring the Concept of Sexual Desire," *Journal of Sex and Marital Therapy* 28, no. 1 (2002): 39–51.

14. Michael Sand and William A. Fisher, "Women's Endorsement of Models of Female Sexual Response: The Nurses' Sexuality Study," *Journal of Sexual Medicine* 4, no. 3 (2007): 708–719.

15. Karen E. Sims, "Why Does Passion Wane? A Qualitative Study of Hypoactive Sexual Desire Disorder in Married Women" (PhD diss., University of Nevada, Las Vegas, 2007).

16. Lori A. Brotto, "The DSM Diagnostic Criteria for Hypoactive Sexual Desire Disorder in Women," *Archives of Sexual Behavior* 39, no. 2 (2010): 221–239.

17. In response, the sexual medicine community, under the direction of Irwin Goldstein, created an expert panel to validate an autonomous definition of hypoactive sexual desire disorder, thus paving the way for pharma to continue developing compounds to address the condition. Irwin Goldstein et al., "Hypoactive Sexual Desire Disorder: International Society for the Study of Women's Sexual Health (ISSWSH) Expert Consensus Panel Review," *Mayo Clinic Proceedings* 92, no. 1 (2017): 114–128.

18. See Katherine Angel, "The History of 'Female Sexual Dysfunction' as a Mental Disorder in the 20th Century," *Current Opinion in Psychiatry* 23, no. 6 (2010): 536; Katherine Angel, "Contested Psychiatric Ontology and Feminist Critique: 'Female Sexual Dysfunction' and the Diagnostic and Statistical Manual," *History of the Human Sciences* 25, no. 4 (2012): 3–24; Alyson K. Spurgas, "Interest, Arousal, and Shifting Diagnoses of Female Sexual Dysfunction, or: How Women Learn About Desire," *Studies in Gender and Sexuality* 14, no. 3 (2013): 187–205.

19. As quoted in Brotto, *Better Sex Through Mindfulness*.

20. Meredith L. Chivers and Lori A. Brotto, "Controversies of Women's Sexual Arousal and Desire," *European Psychologist* 22, no. 1 (2017): 5–26.

21. Meredith L. Chivers et al. "Agreement of Self-Reported and Genital Measures of Sexual Arousal in Men and Women: A Meta-analysis," *Archives of Sexual Behavior* 39, no. 1 (2010): 5–56.

22. Ibid.

23. James W. Pennebaker and Tomi-Ann Roberts, "Toward a His and Hers Theory of Emotion: Gender Differences in Visceral Perception," *Journal of Social and Clinical Psychology* 11, no. 3 (1992): 199–212.

24. Gina R. Silverstein et al., "Effects of Mindfulness Training on Body Awareness to Sexual Stimuli: Implications for Female Sexual Dysfunction," *Psychosomatic Medicine* 73, no. 9 (2011): 817–825.

EIGHT: THE LANGUAGE OF LANGUAGE AND THE LANGUAGE OF TOUCH

1. Yitzchak M. Binik and Marta Meana, "The Future of Sex Therapy: Specialization or Marginalization?" *Archives of Sexual Behavior* 38, no. 6 (2009): 1016–1027.

2. As quoted in Janice M. Irvine, *Disorders of Desire: Sexuality and Gender in Modern American Sexology* (Philadelphia: Temple University Press, 2005).

3. As quoted in Raie Goodwach, "Fundamentals of Theory and Practice Revisited: Sex Therapy. Historical Evolution, Current Practice, Part I," *Australian and New Zealand Journal of Family Therapy* 26, no. 3 (2005): 155–164.

4. John D'Emilio and Estelle B. Freedman, *Intimate Matters: A History of Sexuality in America* (Chicago: University of Chicago Press, 1997).

5. Leonore Tiefer, "Historical, Scientific, Clinical and Feminist Criticisms of 'The Human Sexual Response Cycle' Model," *Annual Review of Sex Research* 2, no. 1 (1991): 1–23.

6. Leonore Tiefer, *Sex Is Not a Natural Act and Other Essays* (Boulder: Westview Press, 2004).

7. William H. Masters and Virginia E. Johnson, *Human Sexual Inadequacy* (Boston: Little, Brown, 1970), 219–220.

8. Michael W. Wiederman, "The State of Theory in Sex Therapy," *Journal of Sex Research* 35, no. 1 (1998): 88–99.

9. In their 1970 text, Masters and Johnson described the practice: "The partner who is pleasuring is committed first to do just that: give pleasure. At a second level in the experience, the giver is to explore his or her own component of personal pleasure in doing the touching—to experience and appreciate the sensuous dimensions of hard and soft, smooth and rough, warm and cool, qualities of texture and, finally, the somewhat indescribable aura of physical receptivity expressed by the partner being pleasured. After a reasonable time . . . the marital partners are to exchange roles of pleasuring (giving) and being pleasured (getting)." Masters and Johnson, *Human Sexual Inadequacy*, 68.

10. Michael W. Wiederman, "The State of Theory in Sex Therapy," *Journal of Sex Research* 35, no. 1 (1998): 88–99.

11. Helen Singer Kaplan, *The Sexual Desire Disorders: Dysfunctional Regulation of Sexual Motivation* (New York: Routledge, 1995), 5.

12. Ibid., 4.

13. Helen Singer Kaplan, *The New Sex Therapy: Active Treatment of Sexual Dysfunctions* (New York: Brunner-Routledge, 1974).

14. Joseph LoPiccolo and Julia Heiman, "Cultural Values and the Therapeutic Definition of Sexual Function and Dysfunction," *Journal of Social Issues* 33, no. 2 (1977): 166–183.

15. Lauren M. Walker, "Back to the Basics: Origins of Sex Therapy, Sexual Disorder and Therapeutic Techniques," *Reproductive System and Sexual Disorders* 1, no. 2 (2012).

16. Peggy Kleinplatz, "Is That All There Is? A New Critique of the Goals of Sex Therapy," in *New Directions in Sex Therapy: Innovations and Alternatives*, ed. P. Kleinplatz (New York: Routledge, 2013), 116.

17. Gina Ogden, "Introduction: Are We Asking Questions That Help Our Patients," in *Extraordinary Sex Therapy: Creative Approaches for Clinicians*, ed. Gina Ogden (New York: Routledge, 2017), 1.

18. Michael E. Metz and Barry W. McCarthy, "The 'Good-Enough Sex' Model for Couple Sexual Satisfaction," *Sexual and Relationship Therapy* 22, no. 3 (2007): 351–362.

19. Leonore Tiefer, "Medicalizations and Demedicalizations of Sexuality Therapies," *Journal of Sex Research* 49, no. 4 (2012): 311–318.

20. Ibid.

21. Leonore Tiefer, "Sex Therapy as a Humanistic Enterprise," *Sexual and Relationship Therapy* 21, no. 3 (2006): 359–375. The shift away from the "humanistic enterprise" occurred in tandem with other changes in the field and society at large

that put a damper on previous experimentation. In 1978, the American Association of Sex Educators, Counselors and Therapists (AASECT) prohibited nudity and physical touch in the office. The years thereafter saw the election of Ronald Reagan and the rise of the Moral Majority.

22. As quoted in Irvine, *Disorders of Desire*.

23. Patti O. Britton, *The Art of Sex Coaching: Expanding Your Practice* (New York: W. W. Norton, 2011), 7.

24. Peggy Kleinplatz, "A Critical Evaluation of Sex Therapy," in *New Directions in Sex Therapy: Innovations and Alternatives*, ed. P. Kleinplatz (New York: Routledge, 2013), xviii.

25. Paula Leech, "Sexual Attitude Reassessment (SAR)," https://www.paulaleech .com/take-back-the-talk-workshop.

NINE: HUMAN POTENTIAL ON THE OPEN MARKET

1. Regena Thomashauer, *Pussy: A Reclamation* (Carlsbad, CA: Hay House, 2016).

2. "California Trying to Close Worthless-Diploma Schools," *New York Times*, August 31, 1994, https://www.nytimes.com/1994/08/31/us/california-trying -to-close-worthless-diploma-schools.html.

3. Patricia Leigh Brown and Carol Pogash, "The Pleasure Principle," *New York Times*, March 13, 2009, https://www.nytimes.com/2009/03/15/fashion/15commune .html.

4. David Felton, David Dalton, and Robin Green, *Mindfuckers: A Source Book on the Rise of Acid Fascism in America Including Material on Charles Manson, Mel Lyman, Victor Baranco and Their Followers* (San Francisco: Straight Arrow Books, 1972).

5. As quoted in Roc Morin, "Inside the Implosion of OneTaste, San Francisco's Orgasmic Meditation Cult," *Playboy*, October 9, 2018, https://www.playboy.com/read /one-taste-orgasmic-meditation.

6. As of 2019, Thomashauer has stopped running the Mastery and Creation courses. Her website states, "Regena is taking a brief pause to reimagine her offerings, with the aim of making her work more accessible to even more women."

7. Nora Krug, "How to Reclaim Trump's Slur, from the Author of the Best-seller 'P---y,'" *Washington Post*, October 10, 2016, https://www.washingtonpost.com /entertainment/books/the-only-woman-who-may-benefit-from-trumps-lewd -comments/2016/10/10/6e70a236-8e81-11e6-9c85-ac42097b8cc0_story.html.

8. Tom Wolfe, "The 'Me' Decade and the Third Great Awakening," *New York*, August 23, 1976, http://nymag.com/news/features/45938.

9. Catherine Rottenberg, *The Rise of Neoliberal Feminism* (New York: Oxford University Press, 2018).

10. Alex Witchel, "Counterintelligence: School for Goddesses," *New York Times*, January 23, 2000, https://www.nytimes.com/2000/01/23/style/counterintelligence -school-for-goddesses.html.

11. Rosalind Gill, "Postfeminist Media Culture: Elements of a Sensibility," *European Journal of Cultural Studies* 10, no. 2 (2007): 147–166.

12. Rachel Wood, "Look Good, Feel Good: Sexiness and Sexual Pleasure in Neoliberalism," in *Aesthetic Labour: Rethinking Beauty Politics in Neoliberalism*, ed. Ana Sofia Elias et al. (London: Palgrave Macmillan, 2017), 317–332.

13. Gill, "Postfeminist Media Culture."

TEN: OPENING TO CHOICE

1. Andrew J. Cherlin, *The Marriage-Go-Round: The State of Marriage and the Family in America Today* (New York: Vintage, 2009).

2. Anthony Giddens, *The Transformation of Intimacy: Sexuality, Love and Eroticism in Modern Societies* (Stanford, CA: Stanford University Press, 1992).

3. Eli J. Finkel et al., "The Suffocation Model: Why Marriage in America Is Becoming an All-or-Nothing Institution," *Current Directions in Psychological Science* 24, no. 3 (2015): 238–244.

4. Esther Perel, *The State of Affairs: Rethinking Infidelity* (New York: Harper, 2017).

5. Brenda H. Lee and Lucia F. O'Sullivan, "Ain't Misbehavin? Monogamy Maintenance Strategies in Heterosexual Romantic Relationships," *Personal Relationships* 25, no. 2 (2018): 205–232.

6. Ibid.

7. Ibid.

8. Anna Fitzpatrick, "'The Ethical Slut': Inside America's Growing Acceptance of Polyamory," *Rolling Stone*, September 16, 2017, https://www.rollingstone.com /culture/culture-features/the-ethical-slut-inside-americas-growing-acceptance-of -polyamory-112319; Susan Dominus, "Is an Open Marriage a Happier Marriage?" *The New York Times Magazine*, May 11, 2017, https://www.nytimes.com/2017/05/11 /magazine/is-an-open-marriage-a-happier-marriage.html.

9. Meg Barker and Darren Langdridge, "Whatever Happened to Non-monogamies? Critical Reflections on Recent Research and Theory," *Sexualities* 13, no. 6 (2010): 748–772.

10. Ethan C. Levine et al., "Open Relationships, Nonconsensual Nonmonogamy, and Monogamy Among U.S. Adults: Findings from the 2012 National Survey of Sexual Health and Behavior," *Archives of Sexual Behavior* 47, no. 5 (2018): 1–12.

11. Mara L. Haupert et al., "Prevalence of Experiences with Consensual Nonmonogamous Relationships: Findings from Two National Samples of Single Americans," *Journal of Sex and Marital Therapy* 43, no. 5 (2017): 424–440.

12. YouGov, "Relationships," September 23–25, 2016, https://d25d2506sfb94s .cloudfront.net/cumulus_uploads/document/cqmk3va41c/tabs_OP_Relationships _20160925.pdf.

13. Felim McGrath, "What to Know About Tinder in 5 Charts," GlobalWebIndex, April 24, 2015, https://blog.globalwebindex.com/trends/what-to-know-about-tinder.

14. Heath Schechinger, "Toward Inclusive Science and Practice—Here's What You Need to Know About Consensually Non-monogamous Relationships," *American Psychological Association Newsletter*, June 2017, https://www.apadivisions.org /division-44/publications/newsletters/division/2017/06/non-monogamy.

15. Amy C. Moors et al., "Unique and Shared Relationship Benefits of Consensually Non-monogamous and Monogamous Relationships: A Review and Insights for Moving Forward," *European Psychologist* 22, no.1 (2017): 55.

16. Elisabeth Sheff, *The Polyamorists Next Door: Inside Multiple Partner Relationships and Families* (Lanham, MD: Rowman and Littlefield, 2014).

17. See Terri Conley et al., "The Fewer the Merrier?: Assessing Stigma Surrounding Consensually Non-monogamous Romantic Relationships." *Analyses of Social*

Issues and Public Policy 13, no. 1 (2012): 1–30; Terri Conley et al., "Sexual Satisfaction Among Individuals in Monogamous and Consensually Non-monogamous Relationships," *Journal of Social and Personal Relationships* 35, no. 4 (2018): 509–531.

18. Conley et al., "Sexual Satisfaction."

19. Stevi Jackson and Sue Scott, "The Personal Is Still Political: Heterosexuality, Feminism and Monogamy," *Feminism and Psychology* 14, no. 1 (2004): 151–157.

20. Ibid.

21. Shulamith Firestone, *The Dialectic of Sex: The Case for Feminist Revolution* (New York: Verso, 2015).

22. Adrienne Rich, "Compulsory Heterosexuality and Lesbian Existence," *Signs: Journal of Women in Culture and Society* 5, no. 4 (1980): 631–660.

23. Georgia Dullea, "'Open Marriage' Isn't a Closed Book," *New York Times*, October 5, 1977, https://www.nytimes.com/1977/10/05/archives/open-marriage-isnt-a-closed-book-a-meaningful-relationship.html.

24. This anecdote appeared originally in Katherine Rowland, "The Honey Trap," *Guernica*, February 15, 2013, https://www.guernicamag.com/the-honey-trap.

25. Elisabeth Sheff, "Three Waves of Non-monogamy: A Select History of Polyamory in the United States," 2012, https://elisabethsheff.com/2012/09/09/three-waves-of-polyamory-a-select-history-of-non-monogamy.

26. Dossie Easton and Janet Hardy, *The Ethical Slut: A Practical Guide to Polyamory, Open Relationships and Other Adventures*, 2nd ed. (Berkeley, CA: Ten Speed Press, 2009), 270.

27. Terri D. Conley and Amy C. Moors, "More Oxygen Please!: How Polyamorous Relationship Strategies Might Oxygenate Marriage," *Psychological Inquiry* 25, no. 1 (2014): 56–63.

28. Esther Perel, *Mating in Captivity: Unlocking Erotic Intelligence* (New York: Harper, 2007), 46.

29. Perel, *State of Affairs*.

30. Tammy Nelson, *The New Monogamy: Redefining Your Relationship After Infidelity* (Oakland, CA: New Harbinger, 2012).

ELEVEN: PLAYING WITH POWER

1. Ijeoma Oluo, "Does This Year Make Me Look Angry?" *Elle*, January 11, 2018, https://www.elle.com/culture/career-politics/a15063942/ijeoma-oluo-women-and-rage-2018.

2. See Kay Hymowitz, "The Sexual Revolution's Angry Children," *City Journal*, Spring 2018, https://www.city-journal.org/html/sexual-revolutions-angry-children-15827.html.

3. Rebecca Traister, "Why Sex That's Consensual Can Still Be Bad. And Why We're Not Talking About It," *The Cut*, October 20, 2015, https://www.thecut.com/2015/10/why-consensual-sex-can-still-be-bad.html.

4. Rebecca Traister, *Good and Mad: The Revolutionary Power of Women's Anger* (New York: Simon and Schuster, 2018), 38.

5. Rape, Abuse & Incest National Network, "State Law Database," https://www.rainn.org/public-policy-action.

6. Peggy Kleinplatz, "Is That All There Is? A New Critique of the Goals of Sex Therapy," in *New Directions in Sex Therapy: Innovations and Alternatives*, ed. P. Kleinplatz (New York: Routledge, 2013), 104–105.

7. Meg Barker, Camelia Gupta, and Alessadra Iantaffi, "The Power of Play: The Potentials and Pitfalls in Healing Narratives of BDSM," in *Safe, Sane, and Consensual: Contemporary Perspectives on Sadomasochism*, ed. D. Langdridge and M. Barker (Basingstoke, UK: Palgrave Macmillan, 2007), 197–216.

8. Danielle Lindemann, "BDSM as Therapy?" *Sexualities* 14, no. 2 (2011): 151–172.

9. Esther Perel, "Why Egalitarian America Needs Dominant Sex," Psychotherapy Networker, n.d., https://www.psychotherapynetworker.org/blog/details/457/why-egalitarian-america-needs-dominant-sex.

10. Pat Ogden, with Janina Fisher, "Introduction," in *Sensorimotor Psychotherapy: Interventions for Trauma and Attachment* (New York: W. W. Norton, 2015).

11. Pat Ogden, "How to Use the Wisdom of the Body to Heal Trauma," National Institute for the Clinical Application of Behavioral Medicine, https://www.nicabm.com/tag/wisdom-of-the-body.

TWELVE: THE LIMITS OF TALK

1. Laqueuer offers, "The tale of the clitoris is a parable of culture, of how the body is forged into a shape valuable to civilization despite, not because of, itself." Thomas Walter Laqueur, *Making Sex: Body and Gender from the Greeks to Freud* (Cambridge, MA: Harvard University Press, 2003), 236.

2. Alex Comfort, *The New Joy of Sex: A Gourmet Guide to Lovemaking for the Nineties* (New York: Pocket Books, 1991), 49.

3. One observer went so far as to state, "There is a crisis in medical school education about sexual health in the United States." Eli Coleman, "Sexual Health Education in Medical School: A Comprehensive Curriculum," *AMA Journal of Ethics*, November 2014.

4. Joseph Kramer, as quoted in Suzanne Blackburn and Margaret Wade, *Reclaiming Eros: Sacred Whores and Healers* (Portland, ME: Suade Publishing, 2008).

5. Jack Morin, *The Erotic Mind: Unlocking the Inner Sources of Passion and Fulfillment* (New York: Harper Perennial, 1996).

6. Staci Haines, *Healing Sex: A Mind-Body Approach to Healing Sexual Trauma* (San Francisco: Cleis, 2007), xxx–xxxi.

CONCLUSION: BEYOND THE PHYSICAL

1. Barbara Carrellas, with Annie Sprinkle, *Urban Tantra: Sacred Sex for the Twenty-First Century* (New York: Ten Speed Press, 2017), 6.

2. Charles Muir and Caroline Muir, *Tantra: The Art of Conscious Loving*, 20th anniv. ed. (Kahului, HI: Source Tantra Publications, 2010).

3. Gina Ogden, *The Heart and Soul of Sex: Exploring the Sexual Mysteries* (Boston: Trumpeter, 2012).

4. Ibid. See also Gina Ogden, *The Return of Desire: A Guide to Rediscovering Your Sexual Passion* (Boston: Trumpeter, 2008).

5. Peggy Kleinplatz, "Is That All There Is? A New Critique of the Goals of Sex Therapy," in *New Directions in Sex Therapy: Innovations and Alternatives*, ed. P. Kleinplatz (New York: Routledge, 2013), 109.

6. Ibid.

7. Peggy Kleinplatz et al., "The Components of Optimal Sexuality: A Portrait of 'Great Sex,'" *Canadian Journal of Human Sexuality* 18, nos. 1–2 (2009): 1–14.

8. Kleinplatz, "Is That All There Is?," 115.

9. Peggy Kleinplatz, "Desire Disorders or Opportunities for Optimal Erotic Intimacy," in *Treating Sexual Desire Disorders: A Clinical Casebook*, ed. Sandra R. Leiblum (New York: Guilford Press, 2010).

SELECTED BIBLIOGRAPHY

American Psychological Association, Task Force on the Sexualization of Girls. "Report of the APA Task Force on the Sexualization of Girls." 2007. https://www.apa.org/pi/women/programs/girls/report-full.pdf.

Anand, Margot. *Love, Sex, and Awakening: An Erotic Journey from Tantra to Spiritual Ecstasy.* Woodbury, MN: Llewellyn Publications, 2017.

Angel, Katherine. "Contested Psychiatric Ontology and Feminist Critique." *History of the Human Sciences* 25, no. 4 (2012): 3–24. doi:10.1177/0952695112456949.

———. "The History of 'Female Sexual Dysfunction' as a Mental Disorder in the 20th Century." *Current Opinion in Psychiatry* 23, no. 6 (2010): 536–541. doi:10.1097/yco.0b013e32833db7a1.

Angier, Natalie. *Woman: An Intimate Geography.* New York: Mariner, 2014.

Armstrong, Elizabeth A., Paula England, and Alison C. K. Fogarty. "Accounting for Women's Orgasm and Sexual Enjoyment in College Hookups and Relationships." *American Sociological Review* 77, no. 3 (2012): 435–462. doi:10.1177/0003122412445802.

Barker, Meg-John, Rosalind Gill, and Laura Harvey. *Mediated Intimacy: Sex Advice in Media Culture.* Cambridge: Polity Press, 2018.

Barker, Meg, and Darren Langdridge. "Whatever Happened to Non-monogamies? Critical Reflections on Recent Research and Theory." *Sexualities* 13, no. 6 (2010): 748–772. doi:10.1177/1363460710384645.

Basson, Rosemary. "Female Sexual Response." *Obstetrics and Gynecology* 98, no. 2 (2001): 350–353. doi:10.1097/00006250-200108000-00029.

———. "The Female Sexual Response: A Different Model." *Journal of Sex and Marital Therapy* 26, no. 1 (2000): 51–65. doi:10.1080/009262300278641.

———. "Rethinking Low Sexual Desire in Women." *BJOG: An International Journal of Obstetrics and Gynaecology* 109, no. 4 (2002): 357–363. doi:10.1016/s1470-0328(02)91002-5.

Baumeister, Roy F. "Gender and Erotic Plasticity: Sociocultural Influences on the Sex Drive." *Sexual and Relationship Therapy* 19, no. 2 (2004): 133–139. doi.org/10.1080/14681990410001691343.

———. "Gender Differences in Erotic Plasticity: The Female Sex Drive as Socially Flexible and Responsive." *Psychological Bulletin* 126, no. 3 (2000): 347–374. doi:10.1037/0033-2909.126.3.347.

Bell, Sarah N., and Sara I. McClelland. "When, If, and How: Young Women Contend with Orgasmic Absence." *Journal of Sex Research* 55, no. 6 (2017): 679–691. doi:10.1080/00224499.2017.1384443.

Bergner, Daniel. *What Do Women Want?: Adventures in the Science of Female Desire.* New York: Canongate Books, 2013.

Bernard, Jessie. *The Future of Marriage.* New Haven, CT: Yale University Press, 1972.

Binik, Yitzchak M., and Marta Meana. "The Future of Sex Therapy: Specialization or Marginalization?" *Archives of Sexual Behavior* 38, no. 6 (2009): 1016–1027. doi:10.1007/s10508-009-9475-9.

Britton, Patti O. *The Art of Sex Coaching: Expanding Your Practice.* New York: W. W. Norton, 2011.

Brotto, Lori A. *Better Sex Through Mindfulness: How Women Can Cultivate Desire.* Vancouver: Greystone Books, 2018.

———. "The DSM Diagnostic Criteria for Hypoactive Sexual Desire Disorder in Women." *Archives of Sexual Behavior* 39, no. 2 (2010): 221–239.

———. "Evidence-Based Treatments for Low Sexual Desire in Women." *Frontiers in Neuroendocrinology* 45 (2017): 11–17. doi:10.1016/j.yfrne.2017.02.001.

Brotto, Lori A., Meredith L. Chivers, Roanne D. Millman, and Adrianne Albert. "Mindfulness-Based Sex Therapy Improves Genital-Subjective Arousal Concordance in Women with Sexual Desire/Arousal Difficulties." *Archives of Sexual Behavior* 45, no. 8 (2016): 1907–1921. doi:10.1007/s10508-015-0689-8.

Burgess, Ann Wolbert, and Lynda Lytle Holmstrom. "Rape Trauma Syndrome." *American Journal of Psychiatry* 131, no. 9 (1974): 981–986. doi:10.1176/ajp.131.9.981.

Buss, David M. *The Dangerous Passion: Why Jealousy Is as Necessary as Love and Sex.* New York: Free Press, 2011.

———. *The Evolution of Desire: Strategies of Human Mating.* New York: Basic Books, 2016.

Cacchioni, Thea. *Big Pharma, Women, and the Labour of Love.* Toronto: University of Toronto Press, 2015.

Carrellas, Barbara. *Urban Tantra: Sacred Sex for the Twenty-First Century.* New York: Ten Speed Press, 2017.

Chadwick, Sara B., and Sari M. van Anders. "Do Women's Orgasms Function as a Masculinity Achievement for Men?" *Journal of Sex Research* 54, no. 9 (2017): 1141–1152. doi:10.1080/00224499.2017.1283484.

Chemaly, Soraya L. *Rage Becomes Her: The Power of Women's Anger.* New York: Atria Books, 2018.

Cherkasskaya, Eugenia, and Margaret Rosario. "The Relational and Bodily Experiences Theory of Sexual Desire in Women." *Archives of Sexual Behavior* 48, no. 6 (2018): 1–23. doi:10.1007/s10508-018-1212-9.

Cherlin, Andrew J. *Marriage, Divorce, Remarriage: Social Trends in the United States.* Cambridge, MA: Harvard University Press, 1992.

———. *The Marriage-Go-Round: The State of Marriage and the Family in America Today.* New York: Vintage, 2010.

Chivers, Meredith L. "A Brief Review and Discussion of Sex Differences in the Specificity of Sexual Arousal." *Sexual and Relationship Therapy* 20, no. 4 (2005): 377–390. doi:10.1080/14681990500238802.

Chivers, Meredith L., Rosemary Basson, Lori A. Brotto, Cynthia A. Graham, and Kyle R. Stephenson. "Statistical and Epistemological Issues in the Evaluation of Treatment Efficacy of Pharmaceutical, Psychological, and Combination Treatments for Women's Sexual Desire Difficulties." *Journal of Sex and Marital Therapy* 43, no. 3 (2016): 210–217. doi:10.1080/0092623x.2016.1266538.

Chivers, Meredith L., and Lori A. Brotto. "Controversies of Women's Sexual Arousal and Desire." *European Psychologist* 22, no. 1 (2017): 5–26. doi:10.1027/1016-9040 /a000274.

Chivers, Meredith L., Michael C. Seto, Martin L. Lalumière, Ellen Laan, and Teresa Grimbos. "Agreement of Self-Reported and Genital Measures of Sexual Arousal in Men and Women: A Meta-analysis." *Archives of Sexual Behavior* 39, no. 1 (2010): 5–56. doi:10.1037/e512662013-034.

Conley, Terri D., and Amy C. Moors. "More Oxygen Please!: How Polyamorous Relationship Strategies Might Oxygenate Marriage." *Psychological Inquiry* 25, no. 1 (2014): 56–63. doi:10.1080/1047840x.2014.876908.

Conley, Terri D., Amy C. Moors, Jes L. Matsick, and Ali Ziegler. "The Fewer the Merrier?: Assessing Stigma Surrounding Consensually Non-monogamous Romantic Relationships." *Analyses of Social Issues and Public Policy* 13, no. 1 (2012): 1–30. doi:10.1111/j.1530-2415.2012.01286.x.

Conley, Terri D., Jennifer L. Piemonte, and Staci Gusakova. "Sexual Satisfaction Among Individuals in Monogamous and Consensually Non-monogamous Relationships." *Journal of Social and Personal Relationships* 35, no. 4 (2018): 509–531. doi:10.1177/0265407517743078.

Coontz, Stephanie. *Marriage, a History: From Obedience to Intimacy or How Love Conquered Marriage.* New York: Viking, 2005.

Davis, Rebecca Louise. *More Perfect Unions: The American Search for Marital Bliss.* Cambridge, MA: Harvard University Press, 2010.

D'Emilio, John, and Estelle B. Freedman. *Intimate Matters: A History of Sexuality in America.* Chicago: University of Chicago Press, 1997.

Dominus, Susan. "Is an Open Marriage a Happier Marriage?" *The New York Times Magazine*, May 11, 2017. www.nytimes.com/2017/05/11/magazine/is-an-open -marriage-a-happier-marriage.html.

Dooley, Erin M., Melanie K. Miller, and Anita Clayton. "Flibanserin: From Bench to Bedside." *Sexual Medicine Reviews* 5, no. 4 (October 2017): 461–469. doi:10.1016/j .sxmr.2017.06.003.

Easton, Dossie, and Janet W. Hardy. *The Ethical Slut: A Practical Guide to Polyamory, Open Relationships and Other Adventures*, 2nd ed. Berkeley, CA: Ten Speed Press, 2009.

Ehrenreich, Barbara. *Bright-Sided: How the Relentless Promotion of Positive Thinking Has Undermined America.* New York: Picador, 2010.

Fahs, Breanne. "Coming to Power: Women's Fake Orgasms and Best Orgasm Experiences Illuminate the Failures of (Hetero) Sex and the Pleasures of Connection." *Culture, Health and Sexuality* 16, no. 8 (2014): 974–988.

———. "'Freedom to' and 'Freedom from': A New Vision for Sex-Positive Politics." *Sexualities* 17, no. 3 (2014): 267–290.

Fahs, Breanne, Eric Swank, and Sara I. McClelland. "Sexuality, Pleasure, Power, and Danger: Points of Tension, Contradiction, and Conflict." In *APA Handbook of the Psychology of Women: History, Theory, and Battlegrounds*, edited by C. B. Travis and J. W. White, 229–247. Washington, DC: American Psychological Association, 2018.

Faludi, Susan. *Backlash: The Undeclared War Against American Women*. New York: Three Rivers Press, 2006.

Feuerstein, Georg. *Tantra: The Path of Ecstasy*. Boulder: Shambhala, 1998.

Fine, Cordelia. *Delusions of Gender: How Our Minds, Society, and Neurosexism Create Difference*. London: Icon Books, 2011.

———. *Testosterone Rex: Myths of Sex, Science, and Society*. New York: W. W. Norton, 2018.

Fine, Michelle. "Sexuality, Schooling, and Adolescent Females: The Missing Discourse of Desire." *Harvard Educational Review* 58, no. 1 (1988): 29–54.

Finkel, Eli J., Elaine O. Cheung, Lydia F. Emery, Kathleen L. Carswell, and Grace M. Larson. "The Suffocation Model: Why Marriage in America Is Becoming an All-or-Nothing Institution." *Current Directions in Psychological Science* 24, no. 3 (2015): 238–244. doi:10.1177/0963721415569274.

Firestone, Shulamith. *The Dialectic of Sex: The Case for Feminist Revolution*. New York: Verso, 2015.

Foucault, Michel, with Robert J. Hurley. *The History of Sexuality*, vol. 1, *An Introduction*. New York: Vintage, 1990.

Frederick, David A., H. Kate St. John, Justin R. Garcia, and Elisabeth A. Lloyd. "Differences in Orgasm Frequency Among Gay, Lesbian, Bisexual, and Heterosexual Men and Women in a U.S. National Sample." *Archives of Sexual Behavior* 47, no. 1 (2017): 273–288. doi:10.1007/s10508-017-0939-z.

Frith, Hannah. *Orgasmic Bodies: The Orgasm in Contemporary Western Culture*. Basingstoke, UK: Palgrave Macmillan, 2015.

Gagnon, John, and William Simon. *Sexual Conduct: The Social Sources of Human Sexuality*, 2nd ed. New Brunswick: Aldine Transaction, 2011.

Giddens, Anthony. *The Transformation of Intimacy: Sexuality, Love and Eroticism in Modern Societies*. Stanford, CA: Stanford University Press, 1992.

Gill, Rosalind. "Postfeminist Media Culture: Elements of a Sensibility." *European Journal of Cultural Studies* 10, no. 2 (2007): 147–166.

Goldstein, Irwin. "The Hour Lecture That Changed Sexual Medicine—The Giles Brindley Injection Story." *Journal of Sexual Medicine* 9, no. 2 (2012): 337–342. doi:10.1111/j.1743-6109.2011.02635.x.

Goldstein, Irwin, N. N. Kim, Anita H. Clayton, Leonard R. Derogatis, A. Giraldi, Sharon J. Parish, James Pfaus, J. A. Simon, Sheryl A. Kingsberg, Cindy Meston, Kim Wallen, and R. Worsley. "Hypoactive Sexual Desire Disorder: International Society for the Study of Women's Sexual Health (ISSWSH) Expert Consensus Panel Review." *Mayo Clinic Proceedings* 92, no. 1 (2017): 114–128.

Goodwach, Raie. "Fundamentals of Theory and Practice Revisited: Sex Therapy. Historical Evolution, Current Practice, Part I." *Australian and New Zealand Journal of Family Therapy* 26, no. 3 (2005): 155–164. doi:10.1002/j.1467-8438.2005.tb00663.x.

Gottlieb, Lori. "Does a More Equal Marriage Mean Less Sex?" *The New York Times Magazine*, February 6, 2014. www.nytimes.com/2014/02/09/magazine/does-a-more-equal-marriage-mean-less-sex.html.

Graham, Cynthia, Petra Boynton, and Kate Gould. "Women's Sexual Desire: Challenging Narratives of 'Dysfunction.'" *European Psychologist* 22, no. 1 (2017): 27–38. http://dx.doi.org/10.1027/1016-9040/a000282.

Grigoriadis, Vanessa. *Blurred Lines: Rethinking Sex, Power, and Consent on Campus.* New York: Eamon Dolan / Mariner Books, 2018.

Haines, Staci. *Healing Sex: A Mind-Body Approach to Healing Sexual Trauma.* San Francisco: Cleis, 2007.

Halperin, David, and Trevor Hoppe. *The War on Sex.* Durham, NC: Duke University Press, 2017.

Hayes, Richard D., Lorraine Dennersetin, C. M. Bennett, and C. K. Fairley. "What Is the 'True' Prevalence of Female Sexual Dysfunctions and Does the Way We Assess These Conditions Have an Impact?" *Journal of Sexual Medicine* 5, no. 4 (2008): 777–787. doi:10.1111/j.1743-6109.2007.00768.x.

Herbenick, Debby, Jessamyn Bowling, Tsung-Chieh (Jane) Fu, Brian Dodge, Lucia Guerra-Reyes, and Stephanie Sanders. "Sexual Diversity in the United States: Results from a Nationally Representative Probability Sample of Adult Women and Men." *PloS One* 12, no. 7 (2017): e0181198.

Herbenick, Debby, Tsung-Chieh (Jane) Fu, Jennifer Arter, Stephanie Sanders, and Brian Dodge. "Women's Experiences with Genital Touching, Sexual Pleasure, and Orgasm: Results from a US Probability Sample of Women Ages 18 to 94." *Journal of Sex and Marital Therapy* 44, no. 2 (2018): 201–212.

Herbenick, Debby, Michael D. Reece, Vanessa R. Schick, Stephanie A. Sanders, Brian S. Dodge, and J. Dennis Fortenberry. "Sexual Behavior in the United States: Results from a National Probability Sample of Men and Women Ages 14–94." *Journal of Sexual Medicine* 7 (2010): 255–265.

Henderson, Alison W., Keren Lehavot, and Jane M. Simoni. "Ecological Models of Sexual Satisfaction Among Lesbian/Bisexual and Heterosexual Women." *Archives of Sexual Behavior* 38, no. 1 (2009): 50–65. doi:10.1007/s10508-008-9384-3.

Herman, Judith Lewis. *Trauma and Recovery: Aftermath of Violence—From Domestic Abuse to Political Terror.* New York: Basic Books, 2015.

Hochschild, Arlie Russell, with Anne Machung. *The Second Shift: Working Parents and the Revolution at Home.* Berkeley: University of California Press, 1989.

Holland, Julie. *Moody Bitches: The Truth About the Drugs You're Taking, the Sleep You're Missing, the Sex You're Not Having, and What's Really Making You Crazy.* New York: Penguin, 2015.

Hrdy, Sarah Blaffer. *The Woman That Never Evolved.* Cambridge, MA: Harvard University Press, 1999.

Irvine, Janice M. *Disorders of Desire: Sexuality and Gender in Modern American Sexology.* Philadelphia: Temple University Press, 2005.

Jackson, Stevi, and Sue Scott. "The Personal Is Still Political: Heterosexuality, Feminism and Monogamy." *Feminism and Psychology* 14, no. 1 (2004): 151–157. doi:10.1177/0959353504040317.

Jesse, Caffyn. *Healers on the Edge: Somatic Sex Education.* Salt Spring Island, Canada: Erospirit, 2017.

Kalman, Hildur. "Faking Orgasms and the Idea of Successful Sexuality." *Janus Head* 13, no. 1 (2013): 97–118.

Kaplan, Helen Singer. *Disorders of Sexual Desire and Other New Concepts and Techniques in Sex Therapy.* New York: Simon and Schuster, 1979.

———. "Hypoactive Sexual Desire." *Journal of Sex and Marital Therapy* 3, no. 1 (1977): 3–9.

————. *The New Sex Therapy: Active Treatment of Sexual Dysfunctions*. New York: Brunner-Routledge, 1974.

————. *The Sexual Desire Disorders: Dysfunctional Regulation of Sexual Motivation*. New York: Brunner-Routledge, 1995.

Kingsberg, Sheryl. "Hypoactive Sexual Desire Disorder: When Is Low Sexual Desire a Sexual Dysfunction?" *Journal of Sexual Medicine* 7, no. 8 (2010): 2907–2908. doi:10.1111/j.1743-6109.2010.01948.x.

Kinsey, Alfred C., Wardell B. Pomeroy, Clyde E. Martin, and Paul H. Gerhard. *Sexual Behavior in the Human Female*. Bloomington: Indiana University Press, 1998.

Kipnis, Laura. *Unwanted Advances: Sexual Paranoia Comes to Campus*. New York: Harper, 2017.

Klein, Marty. *America's War on Sex: The Continuing Attack on Law, Lust, and Liberty*. Westport, CT: Praeger, 2012.

Kleinplatz, Peggy J. "A Critical Evaluation of Sex Therapy." In *New Directions in Sex Therapy: Innovations and Alternatives*, edited by P. Kleinplatz. New York: Routledge, 2013.

————. "Is That All There Is? A New Critique of the Goals of Sex Therapy." In *New Directions in Sex Therapy: Innovations and Alternatives*, edited by P. Kleinplatz. New York: Routledge, 2013.

————. "What's New in Sex Therapy? From Stagnation to Fragmentation." *Sexual and Relationship Therapy* 18, no. 1 (2003): 95–106. doi:10.1080/14681990310000 61290.

Kleinplatz, Peggy J., A. Dana Ménard, Marie-Pierre Paquet, Nicolas Paradis, Meghan Campbell, Dino Zuccarino, and Lisa Mehak. "The Components of Optimal Sexuality: A Portrait of 'Great Sex.'" *Canadian Journal of Human Sexuality* 18, nos. 1–2 (2009): 1–14.

Kleinplatz, Peggy J., A. Dana Ménard, Nicolas Paradis, Meghan Campbell, and Tracy L. Dalgleish. "Beyond Sexual Stereotypes: Revealing Group Similarities and Differences in Optimal Sexuality." *Canadian Journal of Behavioural Science/ Revue Canadienne Des Sciences Du Comportement* 45, no. 3 (2013): 250–258. doi:10.1037/a0031776.

Klotz, Laurence. "How (Not) to Communicate New Scientific Information: A Memoir of the Famous Brindley Lecture." *British Journal of Urology* 96, no. 7 (2005): 956–957. doi:10.1111/j.1464-410x.2005.05797.x.

Kolk, Bessel A. van der. *The Body Keeps the Score: Brain, Mind, and Body in the Healing of Trauma*. New York: Penguin, 2014.

Komisaruk, Barry R., Carlos Beyer-Flores, and Beverly Whipple. *The Science of Orgasm*. Baltimore: Johns Hopkins University Press, 2006.

Kontula, Osmo, and Anneli Miettinen. "Determinants of Female Sexual Orgasms." *Socioaffective Neuroscience and Psychology* 6, no. 1 (2016): 31624. doi:10.3402/snp .v6.31624.

Kornrich, Sabino, Julie Brines, and Katrina Leupp. "Egalitarianism, Housework, and Sexual Frequency in Marriage." *American Sociological Review* 78, no. 1 (2013): 26–50. doi:10.1177/0003122412472340.

Laan, Ellen, and Alessandra H. Rellini. "Can We Treat Anorgasmia in Women? The Challenge to Experiencing Pleasure." *Sexual and Relationship Therapy* 26, no. 4 (2011): 329–341.

Laqueur, Thomas Walter. *Making Sex: Body and Gender from the Greeks to Freud.* Cambridge, MA: Harvard University Press, 2003.

———. "Orgasm, Generation, and the Politics of Reproductive Biology." *Representations*, no. 14 (1986): 1–41. doi:10.2307/2928434.

Laumann, Edward O., Anthony Paik, and Raymond C. Rosen. "Sexual Dysfunction in the United States: Prevalence and Predictors." *Journal of the American Medical Association* 281, no. 6 (1999): 537. doi:10.1001/jama.281.6.537.

Lee, Brenda H., and Lucia F. O'Sullivan. "Ain't Misbehavin? Monogamy Maintenance Strategies in Heterosexual Romantic Relationships." *Personal Relationships* 25, no. 2 (2018): 205–232. doi:10.1111/pere.12235.

Leiblum, Sandra R. "Pharmacotherapy for Women: Will We, Won't We, Should We?" *Sexual and Relationship Therapy* 20, no. 4 (2005): 375–376. doi:10.1080/146819 90500297022.

Leonhardt, Nathan D., Brian J. Willoughby, Dean M. Busby, and Erin K. Holmes. "The Significance of the Female Orgasm: A Nationally Representative, Dyadic Study of Newlyweds' Orgasm Experience." *Journal of Sexual Medicine* 15, no. 8 (2018): 1140–1148. doi:10.1016/j.jsxm.2018.05.018.

Levine, Ethan C., Debby Herbenik, Omar Martinez, and Tsung-Chieh Fu. "Open Relationships, Nonconsensual Nonmonogamy, and Monogamy Among U.S. Adults: Findings from the 2012 National Survey of Sexual Health and Behavior." *Archives of Sexual Behavior* 47, no. 5 (2018): 1439–1450. doi:10.1007/s10508-018-1178-7.

Levy, Ariel. *Female Chauvinist Pigs: Women and the Rise of Raunch Culture.* New York: Free Press, 2005.

Lindemann, Danielle. "BDSM as Therapy?" *Sexualities* 14, no. 2 (2011): 151–172. doi:10.1177/1363460711399038.

Lloyd, Elisabeth Anne. *The Case of the Female Orgasm: Bias in the Science of Evolution.* Cambridge, MA: Harvard University Press, 2006.

Loe, Meika. *The Rise of Viagra: How the Little Blue Pill Changed Sex in America.* New York: New York University Press, 2004.

Lorde, Audre. "Uses of the Erotic: The Erotic as Power." *Sister Outsider: Essays and Speeches.* Berkeley, CA: Crossing Press, 2012.

Maltz, Wendy. *The Sexual Healing Journey: A Guide for Survivors of Sexual Abuse.* New York: William Morrow, 2012.

Martin, Wednesday. *Untrue: Why Nearly Everything We Believe About Women, Lust, and Infidelity Is Wrong and How the New Science Can Set Us Free.* New York: Little, Brown, 2018.

Masters, William H., and Virginia E. Johnson. *Human Sexual Response.* Boston: Little Brown, 1966.

McClelland, Sara I. "Intimate Justice: A Critical Analysis of Sexual Satisfaction." *Social and Personality Psychology Compass* 4, no. 9 (2010): 663–680. doi:10.1111/j.1751-9004.2010.00293.x.

———. "'What Do You Mean When You Say That You Are Sexually Satisfied?' A Mixed Methods Study." *Feminism and Psychology* 24, no. 1 (2013): 74–96. doi:10.1177/0959353513508392.

Meixel, Antonie, Elena Yanchar, and Adriane Fugh-Berman. "Hypoactive Sexual Desire Disorder: Inventing a Disease to Sell Low Libido." *Journal of Medical Ethics* 41, no. 10 (2015): 859–862. doi:10.1136/medethics-2014-102596.

Ménard, A. Dana, and Peggy J. Kleinplatz. "Twenty-One Moves Guaranteed to Make His Thighs Go Up in Flames: Depictions of 'Great Sex' in Popular Magazines." *Sexuality and Culture* 12, no. 1 (2008): 1–20. doi:10.1007/s12119-007 -9013-7.

Meston, Cindy M., and David M. Buss. *Why Women Have Sex: Understanding Sexual Motivation, from Adventure to Revenge (and Everything in Between)*. New York: Vintage, 2010.

Meston, Cindy M., Roy J. Levin, Marca L. Sipski, Elaine M. Hull, and Julia R. Heiman. "Women's Orgasm." *Annual Review of Sex Research* 15, no. 1 (2004): 173–257.

Moors, Amy C., Jes L. Matsick, and Heath A. Schechinger. "Unique and Shared Relationship Benefits of Consensually Non-monogamous and Monogamous Relationships: A Review and Insights for Moving Forward." *European Psychologist* 22, no. 1 (2017): 55. doi:10.1027/1016-9040/a000278.

Morin, Jack. *The Erotic Mind: Unlocking the Inner Sources of Sexual Passion and Fulfillment*. New York: Harper Perennial, 1996.

Moynihan, Ray, and Barbara Mintzes. *Sex, Lies and Pharmaceuticals: How Drug Companies Plan to Profit from Female Sexual Dysfunction*. Berkeley, CA: Greystone Books, 2010.

Muir, Charles, and Caroline Muir. *Tantra: The Art of Conscious Loving*, 20th anniv. ed. Kahului, HI: Source Tantra Publications, 2010.

Muise, Amy, Ulrich Schimmack, and Emily A. Impett. "Sexual Frequency Predicts Greater Well-Being, But More Is Not Always Better." *Social Psychological and Personality Science* 7, no. 4 (2015): 295–302. doi:10.1177/1948550615616462.

Murray, Sarah H., and Robin R. Milhausen. "Sexual Desire and Relationship Duration in Young Men and Women." *Journal of Sex and Marital Therapy* 38, no. 1 (2012): 28–40. doi:10.1080/0092623x.2011.569637.

Nagoski, Emily. *Come As You Are: The Surprising New Science That Will Transform Your Sex Life*. New York: Simon and Schuster, 2015.

O'Connell, Helen E., Kalavampara V. Sanjeevan, and John M. Hutson. "Anatomy of the Clitoris. Part 1." *Journal of Urology* 174, no. 4 (2005): 1189–1195. doi:10.1097/01 .ju.0000173639.38898.cd1189.

Ogden, Gina. *The Heart and Soul of Sex: Exploring the Sexual Mysteries*. Boston: Trumpeter, 2012.

———. *The Return of Desire: A Guide to Rediscovering Your Sexual Passion*. Boston: Trumpeter, 2008.

Orenstein, Peggy. *Girls and Sex: Navigating the Complicated New Landscape*. New York: Harper, 2016.

O'Sullivan, Lucia F., E. Sandra Byers, Lori Brotto, and Jason Fletcher. "A Longitudinal Study of Problems in Sexual Functioning and Related Sexual Distress Among Middle to Late Adolescents." *Journal of Adolescent Health* 59, no. 3 (2016): 318–324. doi:10.1016/j.jadohealth.2016.05.001.

Perel, Esther. *Mating in Captivity: Unlocking Erotic Intelligence*. New York: Harper, 2007.

———. *The State of Affairs: Rethinking Infidelity*. New York: Harper, 2017.

Pfaus, James G. "Reviews: Pathways of Sexual Desire." *Journal of Sexual Medicine* 6, no. 6 (2009): 1506–1533.

Pfaus, James G., Tod E. Kippin, and Genaro Coria-Avila. "What Can Animal Models Tell Us About Human Sexual Response?" *Annual Review of Sex Research* 14, no. 1 (2003): 1–63.

Pfaus, James G., Gonzalo R. Quintana, Conall Mac Cionnaith, and Mayte Parada. "The Whole Versus the Sum of Some of the Parts: Toward Resolving the Apparent Controversy of Clitoral Versus Vaginal Orgasms." *Socioaffective Neuroscience and Psychology* 6, no. 1 (2016): 32578. doi:10.3402/snp.v6.32578.

Plummer, Kenneth. *Telling Sexual Stories: Power, Change and Social Worlds.* New York: Routledge, 2004.

Richters, Juliet, Richard de Visser, Chris Riseel, and Anthony Smith. "Sexual Practices at Last Heterosexual Encounter and Occurrence of Orgasm in a National Survey." *Journal of Sex Research* 43, no. 3 (2006): 217–226. doi:10.1080/00224490609552320.

Rosen, Raymond C. "Prevalence and Risk Factors of Sexual Dysfunction in Men and Women." *Current Psychiatry Reports* 2, no. 3 (2000): 189–195. doi:10.1007/s11920-996-0006-2.

Rosen, Ruth. *The World Split Open: How the Modern Women's Movement Changed America.* New York: Penguin, 2000.

Rosenfeld, Michael J. "Who Wants the Breakup? Gender and Breakup in Heterosexual Couples." In *Social Networks and the Life Course*, 221–243. New York: Springer: 2018.

Rottenberg, Catherine. *The Rise of Neoliberal Feminism.* New York: Oxford University Press, 2018.

Ryan, Christopher, and Cacilda Jethá. *Sex at Dawn: How We Mate, Why We Stray, and What It Means for Modern Relationships.* New York: HarperPerennial, 2012.

Salisbury, Claire M. A., and William A. Fisher. "'Did You Come?' A Qualitative Exploration of Gender Differences in Beliefs, Experiences, and Concerns Regarding Female Orgasm Occurrence During Heterosexual Sexual Interactions." *Journal of Sex Research* 51, no. 6 (2014): 616–631. doi:10.1080/00224499.2013.838934.

Sand, Michael, and William A. Fisher. "Women's Endorsement of Models of Female Sexual Response: The Nurses' Sexuality Study." *Journal of Sexual Medicine* 4, no. 3 (2007): 708–719. doi:10.1111/j.1743-6109.2007.00496.x.

Scarborough, William J., Ray Sin, and Barbara Risman. "Attitudes and the Stalled Gender Revolution: Egalitarianism, Traditionalism, and Ambivalence from 1977 Through 2016." *Gender and Society* 33, no. 2 (2018). doi:10.1177/0891243218809604.

Sela, Yael, and Gayle Brewer. "Women Pretending Orgasm." In *Encyclopedia of Evolutionary Psychological Science*, edited by Todd K. Shackelford and Viviana A. Weekes-Shackelford, 1–6. New York: Springer, 2018. doi:10.1007/978-3-319-16999-6_2006-1.

Shifren, Jan L., Brigitta Monz, Patricia A. Russo, Anthony Segreti, and Catherine B. Johannes. "Sexual Problems and Distress in United States Women: Prevalence and Correlates." *Obstetrics and Gynecology* 112, no. 5 (2008): 970–978. doi:10.1097/AOG.0b013e3181898cdb.

Sims, Karen E., and Marta Meana. "Why Did Passion Wane? A Qualitative Study of Married Women's Attributions for Declines in Sexual Desire." *Journal of Sex and Marital Therapy* 36, no. 4 (2010): 360–380. doi:10.1080/0092623x.2010.498727.

Snyder, Stephen. *Love Worth Making: How to Have Ridiculously Great Sex in a Long-Lasting Relationship*. New York: St. Martin's, 2018.

Spurgas, Alyson K. "Interest, Arousal, and Shifting Diagnoses of Female Sexual Dysfunction, or: How Women Learn About Desire." *Studies in Gender and Sexuality* 14, no. 3 (2013): 187–205. doi:10.1080/15240657.2013.818854.

———. "Low Desire, Trauma and Femininity in the DSM-5: A Case for Sequelae." *Psychology and Sexuality* 7, no. 1 (2016): 48–67. doi:10.1080/19419899.2015.1024471.

Stopes, Marie Carmichael. *Married Love: A New Contribution to the Solution of Sex Difficulties*. London: Pelican Press, 2015.

Talese, Gay. *Thy Neighbor's Wife*. New York: HarperCollins, 2009.

Thomashauer, Regena. *Pussy: A Reclamation*. Carlsbad, CA: Hay House, 2016.

Tiefer, Leonore. "Beyond the Medical Model of Women's Sexual Problems: A Campaign to Resist the Promotion of Female Sexual Dysfunction." *Sexual and Relationship Therapy* 17, no. 2 (2002): 127–135. doi:10.1080/14681990220121248.

———. "Historical, Scientific, Clinical and Feminist Criticisms of 'The Human Sexual Response Cycle' Model." *Annual Review of Sex Research* 2, no. 1 (1991): 1–23.

———. *Sex Is Not a Natural Act and Other Essays*. Boulder: Westview Press, 2004.

———. "Sex Therapy as a Humanistic Enterprise." *Sexual and Relationship Therapy* 21, no. 3 (2006): 359–375. doi:10.1080/14681990600740723.

Tolman, Deborah L. *Dilemmas of Desire: Teenage Girls Talk About Sexuality*. Cambridge, MA: Harvard University Press, 2002.

Tozzi, John, and Jared Hopkins. "The Little Blue Pill: An Oral History of Viagra. The Story of the Drug That Changed Sex and Made Billions." *Bloomberg*, December 11, 2017. www.bloomberg.com/news/features/2017-12-11/the-little-blue-pill-an-oral-history-of-viagra.

Traister, Rebecca. *Good and Mad: The Revolutionary Power of Women's Anger*. New York: Simon and Schuster, 2018.

Twenge, Jean M., Ryne A. Sherman, and Brooke E. Wells. "Changes in American Adults' Sexual Behavior and Attitudes, 1972–2012." *Archives of Sexual Behavior* 44, no. 8 (2015): 2273–2285.

——— "Declines in Sexual Frequency Among American Adults, 1989–2014." *Archives of Sexual Behavior* 46, no. 8 (2017): 2389–2401. doi:10.1007/s10508-017-0953-1.

Vance, Carole S. "Pleasure and Danger: Toward a Politics of Sexuality." In *Pleasure and Danger: Exploring Female Sexuality*, edited by Carole Vance, 1–27. New York: Routledge, 1984.

Velten, Julia, and Lori A. Brotto. "Interoception and Sexual Response in Women with Low Sexual Desire." *PloS One* 12, no. 10 (2017). doi:10.1371/journal.pone.0185979.

Wade, Lisa. "Are Women Bad at Orgasms? Understanding the Gender Gap." In *Gender, Sex, and Politics: In the Streets and Between the Sheets in the 21st Century*, edited by Shira Tarrant, 227–237. New York: Routledge, 2015.

Wade, Lisa D., Emily C. Kremer, and Jessica Brown. "The Incidental Orgasm: The Presence of Clitoral Knowledge and the Absence of Orgasm for Women." *Women and Health* 42, no. 1 (2005): 117–138. doi:10.1300/j013v42n01_07.

Walker, Lauren M. "Back to the Basics: Origins of Sex Therapy, Sexual Disorder and Therapeutic Techniques." *Reproductive System and Sexual Disorders* 1, no. 2 (2012). doi:10.4172/2161-038x.1000109.

Wallen, Kim, and Elisabeth A. Lloyd. "Female Sexual Arousal: Genital Anatomy and Orgasm in Intercourse." *Hormones and Behavior* 59, no. 5 (2011): 780–792. doi:10.1016/j.yhbeh.2010.12.004.

Weeks, Jeffrey. *The World We Have Won: The Remaking of Erotic and Intimate Life.* New York: Routledge, 2007.

Wiederman, Michael W. "The State of Theory in Sex Therapy." *Journal of Sex Research* 35, no. 1 (1998): 88–99. doi.org/10.1080/00224499809551919.

West, Suzanne L., Aimee A. D'Aloisio, and Robert O. Agans. "Prevalence of Low Sexual Desire and Hypoactive Sexual Desire Disorder in a Nationally Representative Sample of US Women." *Archives of Internal Medicine* 168, no. 13 (2008): 1441–1449. doi:10.1001/archinte.168.13.1441.

Witt, Emily. *Future Sex: A New Kind of Free Love.* New York: Farrar, Straus and Giroux, 2016.

Wood, Rachel. "Look Good, Feel Good: Sexiness and Sexual Pleasure in Neoliberalism." In *Aesthetic Labour: Rethinking Beauty Politics in Neoliberalism,* edited by Ana Sofia Elias, Rosalind Gill, and Christina Scharff, 317–332. London: Palgrave Macmillan, 2017.

INDEX

Eddie McShane

Katherine Rowland was previously the publisher and executive director of *Guernica*. An independent writer and researcher, she holds a master's degree in sociomedical sciences from Columbia University, where she was a National Science Foundation Graduate Research Fellow in medical anthropology. She has contributed to *Nature*, the *Financial Times*, *Green Futures*, *The Guardian*, *The Independent*, *Aeon*, *Psychology Today*, and other publications. She lives in Brooklyn with her family.